BONDS OF LOYALTY

German-Americans and World War I

Minorities in American History

BONDS OF LOYALTY

German-Americans and World War I

Frederick C. Luebke

Northern Illinois University Press

DE KALB

Frederick C. Luebke is professor of History at University of Nebraska, Lincoln, Nebraska.

The illustrations used in this book were obtained through the courtesy of The Newberry Library, Chicago, Northern Illinois University, DeKalb, and the University of Nebraska, Lincoln.

Library of Congress Cataloging in Publication Data

Luebke, Frederick C   1927–
    Bonds of loyalty; German-Americans and World War I.

    Bibliography: p.
    1. Germans in the United States.   2. European War,
1914–1918—United States.   I. Title.
D620.L83   301.45'31'073   73–15097
ISBN 0–87580–045–9
ISBN 0–87580–514–0 (pbk.)

For Norma

Contents

Foreword

Minority History, once a euphemism disguising unpleasant or intractable social realities, has come in our time to be viewed as a source of American vitality and self-illumination. In an era when American society has been undergoing a vast realignment of its human resources, institutions, and habits of mind, Americans are more prone than ever to see that the experiences of ethnic, regional, social, economic, occupational, political, religious, intellectual and other well-defined groups have spotlighted and personalized strategic problems in the American past.

The Minorities in American History series will encompass a whole range of such group experiences. Each is intended to illuminate brightly a critical event, movement, tradition, or dilemma. By so doing, these books will individualize the problems of a complex society, giving them both broad pertinence and sharp definition. In addition, the special insights afforded by the increasingly sophisticated methodology of the "new history" will be reflected in an expanding list of ethnohistory studies where sociological theory and quantitative analysis will further inform, document, and shape the dramatic narrative.

BONDS OF LOYALTY is a model account and analysis of German-America during World War I. Combining a traditional narrative with the most refined social science methods, it is the first fully-realized original synthesis to appear since 1940 depicting this imperfectly understood major ethnic group. Unlike earlier historians who concentrated on the political story, Frederick Luebke sees the war as the traumatic climax of an ethno-cultural struggle that long had festered just below the headlines. This is the story of the most numerous, the most diverse, and the most influential non-English speaking ethnic group in nineteenth-century America in an era of supreme tragedy for all Americans, but especially for Americans of German origin. Lutheran, Catholic, Jew and sectarian, church German and club German, these immigrants, so authoritatively portrayed by Luebke, came from every province and principality in central Europe where the continent's religio-political crises had registered with unusual force and intensity. With deftness and economy, Luebke makes vivid the predicament of the only large nineteenth-century immigrant group in the United States with a cultural legacy that matched the dominant English heritage. Ironically, the very acceptability of German-Americans as Americans, their high rating as fellow Teutons, and the flattering stereotypes Anglo-Americans had of them encouraged an assertive ethnic counter culture that actively challenged American folkways even as a whole series of issues symbolically dramatized the clash of cultures. Contests over Sabbatarianism, prohibition, woman suffrage, compulsory education, and immigration restriction seemed to cast doubt on the worthiness of German-Americans and repeatedly jeopardized what appeared to be the most successful achievement in everyday cultural pluralism that the nation had ever experienced. When their very "Americanness" drove German-Americans to embark on political action to defend their life style, they could not quite avoid being identified in the popular mind with the power politics of Wilhelmine Germany. With the outbreak of war, the new distinction between the hyphenated Teuton and the unhyphenated Anglo-Saxon would strain relations between the racial Teutonic cousins to the breaking point as mounting fear and distrust played havoc with a multi-ethnic America that divided its sympathies among the warring nations of Europe.

In this book, Professor Luebke brings to bear an unequaled understanding of German-America as well as a seasoned command of the most refined research methods in ethno-political and demographic history. Blending a discriminating, rich factuality with a masterful knowledge of the relations between cultural patterns and social attitudes, this outstanding scholar of German-America meticulously explores the ultimate as well as the immediate impact of World War I on every phase of German-American life. Clearly this important study in its analytic sweep and suggestiveness, in its sober separation of stereotype from reality raises key questions about the dynamics of a multi-ethnic nation and of the relationship between individual freedom and pluralism in a world in constant flux that are only beginning to be charted and understood with depth and sensitivity.

MOSES RISCHIN, Series Editor
San Francisco State University

Preface

This book is an effort to explain why American society lashed out at its German element during World War I. Ever since colonial times, Americans had received German immigrants gladly and regarded them highly. Yet when the United States entered the war against Germany in 1917, people were swept into a strong wave of anti-German hysteria. Citizens of German origin were individually harassed and persecuted, German ethnic organizations were attacked, and serious efforts were made to eliminate German language and culture in the United States.

The crisis of war did not by itself create conflicts between the native-born and the German-Americans. Rather, war was the occasion that converted latent tensions into manifest hostility. For this reason little understanding is gained by identifying scapegoats, either German-American extremists, who allegedly provoked the government to repressive measures, or superpatriots, who by their immoderate rhetoric may have incited Americans to riot. Instead, one must search for the roots of the conflict in the varied social and cultural characteristics of the German immigrants and in their interaction over several decades with dominant elements of American society. In my attempt to penetrate the bewildering diversity of the German ethnic group in

America I have pursued distinctions in attitude toward German language and culture, believing that differences in behavior during the World War I period may best be understood in such terms.

These variations, in turn, are basic to an understanding of the stereotypes through which the native-born perceived the Germans in their midst. They help to explain why the early twentieth-century view, with its emphasis on "hyphenism" (implying divided political loyalties), fits only a fraction of the German-American population. They also illuminate the diversity of German ethnic response to the European war during the neutrality period and show why the American war with Germany was so much more difficult for some German-Americans than for others. Finally, these distinctions are related to the impact of the war on ethnic institutions and explain why some, notably the churches and their auxiliary agencies, were able to weather the storm and transform themselves into acceptably American institutions and why others, chiefly those dedicated to the maintenance of German language and culture, atrophied in the postwar period.

There has been a tendency in the past for immigration historians to interpret the experience of a given ethnic group on the basis of evidence drawn from leadership sources. They have assumed, for example, that the editorial stance of German-language publications reflected commonly held attitudes and that persons capable of gaining attention in the newspapers were somehow typical of the group. Thus, the pro-German pronouncements of officials of the National German-American Alliance during the neutrality period were always sure-fire copy, while citizens of German origin whose opinions were consonant with those of the majority were unable to attract journalistic attention. By relying excessively on elite-type sources, some historians were led to assume a uniformity of attitude and behavior among the Germans that had little basis in fact.

Other historians have sought to resolve the difficulty by using the term "German-American" in a limited sense, applying it only to those members of the group who actively promoted German culture in the United States or who openly sympathized with Germany. Such a narrowed usage, however, presents other problems. When superpatriots reacted against German-American chauvinists during the war, they heeded no such distinctions. To illustrate, even though German Mennonites were the antithesis of the "professional German-Americans," to use Theodore Roosevelt's term, they were the most grievously abused of any German culture group in the United States. Moreover, the limited definition suggests that to be German-American was to be un-American, that immigrants could be American only when they conformed to established patterns or accepted Anglo-American norms as their own. This usage thus denies implicitly the pluralist character of American society and culture. For these reasons I employ the term "German-American" in its typical nineteenth-century sense to include all persons who by reason of their place of birth, name, speech, or other behavior were identified by Americans as being German in some way.

Finally, I must note my disagreement with those historians who have concluded that periods of rampant nativism (including the era of World War I) hindered the assimilation of the Germans by frightening them into a withdrawal from the main currents of American life, thereby extending the vitality of their immigrant institutions and crystalizing their cultural isolation. I believe that nativism generally had the opposite effect. Hostility and intolerance caused most Germans to perceive their ethnicity as a source of social deprivation or discomfort. A few reacted by asserting their Germanness with new vigor; naturally they captured the attention of contemporary observers and historians. But many others sought to slough off their ethnicity and accommodate themselves to the new standards as painlessly as possible. Still others were apathetic and sought to avoid tension-producing situations. Much evidence demonstrates that Germans generally assimilated rapidly even though their enormous numbers encouraged them to create strong ethnic institutions and to sustain them beyond the period of their utility as agencies to ease the movement of individuals into American society. In my view, the Germans had a rich ethnic life in America in spite of, rather than because of, recurring waves of nativist intolerance.

The intellectual debts I have incurred in writing this book are beyond reckoning. They arise from many conversations and much correspondence, not only with historians but also with persons whose memories remain seared by events of the First World War. But I am especially obligated to those scholars whose books and articles have led me to understand the history of Germans in America as social process. They have fundamentally conditioned my point of view and hence my interpretation. I have also learned much from several graduate students at the University of Nebraska who joined me in studying the historical problem treated in this book. Sarah Rosenberg, Laurence Pizer, and James Potter produced thoughtful seminar papers; Clifford L. Nelson and Burton W. Folsom II wrote excellent theses. My colleagues at the University of Nebraska have also been generous in their willingness to discuss and criticize ideas and interpretations. I am grateful to Professor Lloyd Ambrosius of my department and Professor Robert Swierenga of Kent State University, who read portions of the manuscript, and to Professor Paul Kleppner of Northern Illinois University, who read the entire manuscript. Each offered valuable criticisms. I acknowledge a special debt to Professor Moses Rischin of San Francisco State University, who has patiently counseled and encouraged me since May 1969, when he responded to a letter outlining the idea for the book. In no sense, of course, are these scholars responsible for any errors of fact or interpretation that remain in these pages.

My foremost obligation is to my wife, Norma Wukasch Luebke, who has made this book possible in many ways. Most directly, however, I benefited from her keen editorial skills, including her ability to grace criticism with charming wit. This volume is affectionately dedicated to her.

Lincoln, Nebraska   F.C.L.

BONDS OF LOYALTY

German-Americans and World War I

CHAPTER ONE

Death in Collinsville

APRIL AND MAY 1918

Americans of German ethnic origin were trapped in a crisis of loyalty in 1917 when the United States joined Britain and France in the war against the German Empire. A great majority of these German-Americans had developed a firm allegiance to the United States. At the same time, however, bonds of affection for their German culture remained strong and led them to define American interests in international affairs in ways deemed disloyal by many leaders in government. Suppression of assumed disloyalty was the natural result and instances of action taken against German-Americans are innumerable. Most were petty; some were serious. Among the most tragic was the lynching of Robert Prager in Collinsville, Illinois, in the early morning hours of 5 April 1918.[1]

Prager had left his native Dresden, Germany, for the United States in 1905 when he was nineteen years old. Limited in intelligence and in education, he drifted from place to place, working at a variety of jobs. In 1912, while living in or near Gary, Indiana, he was arrested for theft. Subsequently convicted, he spent the next year in an Indiana reformatory. Following his release on parole in 1914, Prager settled in Saint Louis, Missouri, where he remained until 1917. There he established a number of friendships and became active in an Odd Fellows lodge.

When the United States declared war against Germany in April 1917, Prager felt a strong sense of loyalty to his adopted country. He took out his first citizenship papers and tried unsuccessfully to enlist in the United States Navy. He complied with the law that required him to register for the draft, and he registered as an enemy alien at the office of the United States marshal in Saint Louis, listing his occupation as a baker. After brief stays in Columbia, Missouri, and Gillespie, Illinois, he drifted to Collinsville, a rural market center and coal mining community of about 4,000 persons, located ten miles northeast of Saint Louis across the Mississippi River in Illinois. Prager was employed there as a baker by Lorenzo Bruno, who dismissed him several months later because of Prager's stubborn, uncompromising personality.

Prager thereupon sought employment in the coal mines. Although he was not a member of the United Mine Workers, officials of the local union permitted him to work in a mine at Maryville, a hamlet four miles north of Collinsville, until his application for membership could be acted upon. Maryville, like many other communities in southern Illinois and across the nation at that time, was experiencing a climax of hysteria, rooted in superpatriotism, in which German spies and sympathizers were believed to be everywhere threatening the very foundations of society. It was rumored that dynamite had been stolen from the Maryville mine and that an agent of the German Kaiser planned to hamper the war effort by blowing up the mine—miners and all. Several persons came under suspicion and were forced publicly to declare their loyalty and kiss the American flag.

As a German alien, Prager was also suspect. A stranger, unmarried, stubbornly argumentative, given to Socialist doctrines, blind in one eye, he looked like a spy to the miners of Maryville. Actually, a less likely candidate for espionage could hardly be found, but these miners were not inclined to rational analysis. The superintendent of the mine believed that allegations made against Prager were unfounded, but the union officials were not so sure. After all, they thought, he was a subject of the Kaiser, and some of his remarks had a disloyal ring. One report even claimed that Prager had asked a mine examiner about the effects an explosion would have on the Maryville mine. It was clear that this man was a bad risk and that he should be denied union membership.

After work on Wednesday evening, 3 April 1918, a group of miners seized Prager, paraded him in the streets of Maryville, denounced him as a German spy, and warned him to take permanent leave of the place. That same evening the union leaders, Moses Johnson and James Fornero, met with Prager to speak with him regarding his status. According to their account of the meeting, Prager had previously expressed sympathy for the German cause so intemperately that they feared for his safety. Hence they personally escorted Prager from Maryville to Collinsville, where they sought to place him in the protective custody of the police. Since no charges were being filed against Prager, the Collinsville police refused to cooperate. Johnson and Fornero thereupon took Prager to his home and arranged to meet him the next day at the sheriff's office in Edwardsville, the county seat.

The next day was Prager's last. To his mind there was little to distinguish protective custody from arrest. Why go to Edwardsville and the county jail? Fevered by the injustice of his plight, Prager resolved to return instead to Maryville and appeal directly to the miners for his rights. He prepared a document which stated his case (he thought) and which asserted his loyalty for the United States. But more than anything else, his statement exposed his deep resentment over having been denied union membership and a means of making a living. His emotions swept reason aside as he attacked Fornero as the chief author of his distress. Prager then had his proclamation typewritten and a dozen carbon copies made. These he posted in various places around Maryville. Anticipating the miners' ire, he went into hiding for several hours and then returned to Collinsville under the cover of darkness.

That evening, after they had read Prager's statement, a group of the Maryville miners, perhaps as many as seventy-five nurtured their animosities in their favorite Collinsville saloon. Deciding that the time had come for patriotic action, they began to hunt for their "German." They found him at his home at about 9:30 P.M.

Prager was thoroughly frightened by the mob at his door. He offered little resistance. At first he tried to identify himself with the miners. "Brothers," he assured them, "I am a loyal U.S.A. workingman." It was useless; he was informed that he had ten minutes to get out of town. Recognizing the hopelessness of his situation, Prager agreed to leave, and the crowd began to disperse.

For some persons the fun was much too brief. They urged that a flag-kissing ceremony be staged. One of their number had brought along an American flag. Prager was asked to further demonstrate his loyalty by coming along with them. Terrified, he agreed. "All right," Prager said, "I will go if you will not hurt me."

Thus began the patriotic exercises that chilly April night in Collinsville, Illinois. Prager was dragged into the street. His shoes were yanked off his feet, and he was stripped of his outer clothing. "Old Glory" was draped about him and tied around his waist. Bareheaded, barefooted, and half-blind, the pathetic figure stumbled along, leading the mob down the main street toward the center of town. His tormentors demanded that he sing the "Star-Spangled Banner." He could not. But he gallantly substituted "We'll Fight for the Red, White, and Blue" to the tune of "Columbia the Gem of the Ocean."

Someone had the good sense to call the police. As the parade approached the business district, an officer named Fred Frost charged into the crowd, seized Prager away from his captors, and with the aid of two other policemen, ran with him to the police station in the city hall, three blocks away. There he was placed in the protective custody of a jail cell. The mob gathered outside the building, indecisive and leaderless.

At that moment, the mayor of Collinsville, Dr. John H. Siegel, arrived at the scene. He had been meeting with several other leaders of the community, planning a Liberty Loan drive. Attracted by the noise of the assembly, the mayor hurried to the police station, where he was apprised of the situation. After some effort, Siegel succeeded in calming the crowd. He urged them to disperse and assured them that appropriate charges against Prager would be referred to the federal authorities.

Meanwhile the police resorted to two extraordinary courses of action, with ironic results. First, Officer Frost slipped out of the building, got into a police car, and drove down a poorly lighted side street toward the main thoroughfare where the mob was gathered. As he approached the crowd Frost began accelerating rather than slowing down. Seeing him coming, the people gave way. They gathered the impression that Frost had escaped with Prager. Incredibly, however, Frost returned almost immediately, before the crowd could break up, and the subterfuge was exposed. Later, he explained that he had the only key to Prager's cell in his pocket. The other officers, he reasoned, would be unable to get the man out of his cell to a hiding place unless he returned.

The second unusual move was a decision to quell the mob spirit by closing all the drinking establishments in town. An officer was dispatched with the order. As he made his rounds of the saloons, he brought the exhilarating news that a German spy was in jail and that a large crowd had gathered there. Fortified with the courage that comes in bottles, patrons ventured into the night air to join the super-patriots, who, by this time, were demanding admittance into the jail. Among the new recruits was Joseph Riegel, an ex-soldier whose wife had left him because of his excessive drinking.

Riegel elbowed his way through the mob to the steps of the city hall where he confronted Mayor Siegel. The mayor himself believing that someone had indeed spirited Prager away, insisted that the prisoner was gone. Incredulous, the crowd demanded proof. Riegel stepped forward, flashed his discharge papers, and asked the mayor if he would trust an army veteran to inspect the premises. Siegel thought that by admitting one representative of the mob he could satisfy their curiosity and still maintain a semblance of order. The door was opened to admit Riegel, and the mob swarmed in.

A preliminary search of the building proved fruitless, and it appeared that the police had removed the prisoner while the mayor spoke. Some disappointed persons began to abuse the mayor and the police as pro-Germans. Others suggested the names of several other Collinsville residents who might substitute for Prager. At one time during the search, Riegel and the others went back outside and sur-rounded the structure. They decided on one more look, how-ever, and this time they discovered their quarry hiding in the basement amidst a pile of sewer tiles. Prager was seized by the arms and was taken triumphantly outside to the milling mob, which by this time numbered several hun-dred persons.

The parade was resumed. This time the procession headed toward the outskirts of the city on the road to Saint Louis. Wesley Beaver, who had found Prager in the tiles, proudly carried an American flag while Riegel and another man escorted Prager down the main street. Approaching automobiles and street cars were stopped by the mob. Prager was shown to the occupants and again forced to kiss the flag and sing patriotic songs.

The police meanwhile made no effort to disperse the mob or to rescue its victim, as they had earlier in the evening. Indeed, as Prager was being dragged from the city hall, one officer of the law excused himself because he heard the telephone ringing. The four policemen, with a few other allegedly respectable, responsible citizens, followed the procession at a safe distance. They said later that they in-tended to dash into the crowd and save Prager if the mob attempted to hang him. But when the parade reached the city limits, the police stopped. Their authority did not extend beyond that point. Meanwhile, Mayor Siegel stayed in town. Afterward he asserted that if the police had fired one shot, the mob would have hanged him and the four officers as well.

Some of the leaders of the mob clearly intended that the march should climax in a tar-and-feather ceremony. Shortly after Prager had been recaptured at the city hall, a young man named Harry Lindemann, an auto mechanic, appeared on the scene driving an automobile. Several men jumped aboard his vehicle and ordered him to drive several miles down the highway to a farm at Monk's Mound where, they believed, they could get some tar and feathers. Unsuccessful in this venture, Lindemann and his passengers returned to Collinsville and met the mob just outside the city limits on the bluffs overlooking the flood plain of the Mississippi River. The headlights of three automobiles illuminated the scene as the crowd clustered near a tree at the edge of the road. Prager was being questioned once more. "Are you a German spy?" "Did you steal powder from the Maryville mine?" "Why didn't you keep your date with Moses Johnson?" "Who else is mixed up with you in this business?" Utterly worn by his ordeal, Prager's protests and appeals became much less frequent than before.

There was confusion regarding the punishment that should be administered to the suspect. It soon became clear that the more vicious in the crowd would have their way. Someone found a half-inch towing rope in Lindemann's car. A boy was directed to climb the tree and to put the rope over a sturdy limb. A noose was formed and adjusted about Prager's neck. According to one account, Riegel pulled on the rope but could not raise his victim off the ground. "Come on fellows, we're all in on this, let's not have any slackers here," he called out. Several others, perhaps as many as fifteen, grabbed the rope, as someone else advised that everyone in the crowd ought to touch the rope. The German was pulled into the air.

But these were amateur assassins; they had neglected to tie their victim's hands. Prager grabbed the rope at his throat as a voice demanded, "Let him down! Let him say something if he wants to." The ropemen responded, and the writhing figure was lowered to the ground. Prager was able to stand without help. One man shouted, "Now are you going to tell us whether anybody is mixed up with you?" Another asked if he had any relatives.

Prager spoke: "Brothers, I would write a letter." Permission was granted. Paper and pen were produced. Prager stumbled over to the fender of an automobile, and there scribbled a brief note to his parents in Dresden. "Dear parents," he wrote in German, "I must on this fourth day of April, 1918, die. Please pray for me, my dear parents. This is my last letter and testament. Your dear son and brother, Robert Paul Prager."

As he handed the note to Riegel, Prager asked for permission to pray. He knelt and, according to one witness, prayed aloud in German, asking forgiveness for his sins and asserting his innocence of disloyalty. Then he walked unassisted back to the tree and the rope.

The crowd became more agitated. Questions and demands were again flung at Prager. One shouted, "Well, if he won't come in with anything, string him up." A boy produced a handkerchief which was used to bind the victim's hands. Joseph Riegel was later asked who it was that had tied him up. "It might have been me," he confessed, "I was drunk. I might have done it. I had a lot of liquor in me when I started, and because I had been in the army the crowd kind of made me the big man and I was kind of swelled up about that."

More than 200 persons were present, and most were onlookers too fearful or too fascinated by the grisly proceedings to interfere. "All right, boys," Prager moaned, "go ahead and kill me, but wrap me in the flag when you bury me." With the unity and mindlessness that pervades a mob, Prager was yanked a full ten feet into the air.

The time was 12:30 A.M.; the date, Friday, 5 April 1918. Three hours had elapsed since the mob of Maryville miners had left the saloon to instruct Robert Paul Prager in the lessons of patriotism. How many men pulled on the rope, and who they were has never been determined.

By nightfall millions of Americans had heard of Collinsville, Illinois, and what had happened there. Reporters from the *Saint Louis Post-Dispatch* arrived early on the scene. Their detailed stories were immediately filed with the wire services and reprinted in all the major newspapers of the land. National press reaction to Prager's lynching overwhelmingly denounced the mob and demanded that the persons guilty of the despicable deed be punished. The *New York Times* called for justice in order "to vindicate the name of America" and "to stamp out lynching as a demonstration of patriotism." Closer to the scene, the *Edwardsville Intelligencer* was equivocal. Prager's hanging was indeed "an unlawful and unjustifiable act." At the same time, this newspaper clucked, "it is a fact that we are at war with Germany and that no one in Germany could say or do things that are said and done here every day and live. A traitor over there is dealt with summarily."[2] Distant observers did not hesitate to condemn the violence of the mob, but newspapermen who lived in close association with the people involved, and with the behavior they perceived as disloyal, found it more difficult to criticize their neighbors.

Local civil authorities were also reluctant to accuse or condemn. The chief of police in Collinsville (a man who got no closer than a telephone to the events of that evening) saw some virtue in the lynching. "In one way I believe it is a good thing they got Prager," he announced in a masterpiece of indiscretion. "If he had been spirited away by the police I believe the mob would have vented its rage by hanging two or three Collinsville persons who have been suspected of disloyalty."[3]

Mayor Siegel gave conflicting accounts of his part in the affair, as he tried to put his attempts to forestall violence in the best possible light. Both the mayor and the chief insisted that since the murder had been committed outside the city limits it was not within their authority to arrest anyone or to conduct an investigation. Siegel diverted attention from himself and the Collinsville police by dispatching a telegram to United States Senator Lee S.

Overman, chairman of the Senate Judiciary Committee, in which he urged the passage of a stringent sedition law, one that would impose a severe penalty on disloyalty. Prager's death, the mayor asserted, "was the direct result of a widespread feeling in this community that the Government will not punish disloyalty." He insisted that he had repeatedly reported instances of disloyalty to the federal authorities, but nothing happened because of the inadequacies of the law. The mob, according to Siegel, was frustrated in its desire to curb disloyalty and had taken matters into its own hands. Thus, in the mayor's logic, Prager's death was due, not to the failure of the police to maintain order, but to the negligence of Congress. This idea was not original with Siegel. Rather, it was a commonly held point of view, repeated endlessly in the newspapers, but labeled preposterous by a few journals. The *New Republic* rejected it as "a species of sickening cant."[4]

While local officials made their excuses, state authorities were outraged by the behavior of the Collinsville mob. Illinois' popular, able Governor Frank O. Lowden was furious. He immediately declared his intention to use the force of his office to bring the persons guilty of the lynching to justice. He sent an assistant attorney general to investigate the incident and threatened Collinsville with martial law if local officials failed to maintain order.[5]

There was also concern in the national capital. Senator Overman's committee heard much testimony in support of repressive legislation. Several witnesses echoed the argument used by Mayor Siegel and offered the recent regrettable incident in Illinois as evidence. Senator William Borah, a noted progressive leader, lectured his colleagues on the Prager case citing it as an example of what happens when the law is too lax. The distinguished senator from Massachusetts, Henry Cabot Lodge, announced that he favored consigning disloyalists to the tender mercies of a military tribunal—"try them by court martial and shoot them." Senator Overman agreed that "we have got to catch those [disloyal] scoundrels and spies all over the country."[6] The judiciary committee subsequently reported out a bill in the form of amendments to the existing Espionage Act of 15 June 1917. Severely circumscribing traditional civil liberties in a way designed to slake the thirst of superpatriots, Congress enacted the bill on 16 May 1918, shortly before the trial of Prager's murderers got under way.

The response of the executive branch was less forthright. President Woodrow Wilson and his cabinet discussed the affair at length on Saturday, 6 April. Like Mayor Siegel, these eminent persons let it be known that their government had no warrant for interference and that the deplorable lynching reflected the failure of Congress to act upon pending legislation. Attorney General Thomas Gregory privately rejected this line of reasoning and identified irrational hysteria as the problem. He sent special representatives to Illinois to advise and assist in the effort to check the increasing instances of mob violence against alleged disloyalists. Alarmed by the public mood, Gregory and several others in the federal government publicly condemned vigilante justice. Moreover, they urged President Wilson to use the immense prestige of his office to calm the nation's nerves.[7]

But the President, whose renowned idealism was often more apparent than real, chose to remain silent. In a private letter dated 12 April 1918 to a German-American in Chicago, Wilson promised to "cooperate with every effort to see to it that the loyal residents of the United States of German birth or descent are given genuine proof of the sincerity of our constitutions." He bemoaned the fact that "acts of injustice and even violence should be based upon suspicion" attached "to those who do not deserve it."[8]

It was not until 26 July 1918, nearly two months after the Prager case had disappeared from the pages of American newspapers and after the hysteria in its most virulent form had subsided, that President Wilson issued a public proclamation deploring mob spirit in the United States. Wilson's sentiment was noble and his rhetoric lofty, but his effort was too little, too late. His statement, released as a printed address to his fellow countrymen, was inevitably buried in the back pages of the nation's great dailies.[9] Had the President spoken out as emphatically and clearly as had Governor Lowden, he might have mitigated, though certainly not removed, the misery of many Americans of German origin.

The Prager murder was by no means an isolated example of the hysteria that was sweeping across the nation in the spring of 1918. The number of German-Americans abused by superpatriots increased sharply during the next several weeks. While these incidents were symptomatic of a deeper malaise, it is likely that the behavior of the Collinsville mob encouraged intolerance in neighboring communities.

On Saturday night, 6 April 1918, Morris Gotler, a merchant of nearby East Alton, was forced to kiss the American flag and was threatened with hanging. A band of young men sought Gotler at his home. He ran out the back door and fled to a saloon, but was captured and taken to a school yard near by. There the mob held "patriotic" exercises. Gotler's offense was that he ignored a merchants' agreement to close their doors during a demonstration promoting the sale of Liberty bonds.[10]

On the same day, William Heiserman, a farmer of Kenney, Illinois, near Springfield, was severely beaten by several men on the main street of town for having made allegedly pro-German remarks. Two United States flags were then nailed on the exterior of his residence. Heiserman was threatened with tar and feathers if he removed them. Meanwhile in Athens, Illinois, a "loyalist committee" forced John Rynders, a grocer, to swear allegiance and to kiss the flag. The banner was then tied about his neck and, thus attired, the man was required to lead a Liberty Day parade the next day. Rynders' offense was a refusal to contribute groceries for a dinner associated with the bond selling efforts of the community.[11]

On that same weekend four drunken patriots of Pocahontas, Illinois, compelled John Paulaites at the point of a revolver to kiss a flag which they had ripped from the wall of their victim's home. Thirty miles west of Collinsville, in

Saint Charles, Missouri, John Schmidt was fired from his job in a factory in order to prevent a strike of 175 other employees. Schmidt's offense was the refusal to purchase Liberty bonds. Following his release, Schmidt fled the city.[12]

Pastors of German-immigrant churches were frequently victimized by the advocates of coercive patriotism. On 8 April the Reverend A. F. Meyer, pastor of a rural German Lutheran congregation near Pinckneyville, Illinois, was admitted into a Saint Louis hospital for treatment of injuries suffered at the hands of five men who objected to allegedly unpatriotic remarks he had made in a sermon. Seventy-five years of age, Meyer had been tarred (though not feathered) and subjected to other physical abuse. The Reverend Henry von Gemmigen, a pastor of a congregation near Maryville, was harassed from April until early May, when he fled with his family to Kansas.[13]

A more celebrated case concerned the pastor of Saint Boniface Catholic Church in Edwardsville, the Reverend J. D. Metzler. A one-time officer in the German army, Metzler was an American citizen and had served the Edwardsville parish for more than two decades. The sixty-three-year-old clergyman had antagonized some of his parishioners by indulging in allegedly pro-German comments and by refusing to permit the Angelus to be rung by daylight-saving time. An "Americanization committee" visited Father Metzler on the evening following Prager's murder. From that time on, the Angelus was rung at 6:00 rather than 7:00 P.M. On the following Sunday morning, Metzler failed to appear at mass. He had vanished without a word. Informed of a complex plot to tar and feather him, the priest had gone into hiding. Three weeks later he reappeared at Sunday services to announce that he had been granted a leave of absence. In his farewell sermon he urged his parishioners (many of whom were German-Americans) to purchase all the Liberty bonds they possibly could.[14]

Intolerance was manifested in many other ways. A federation of German Catholic societies in Illinois postponed in-

definitely its annual convention, scheduled for Peoria in
May 1918, when the host city "withdrew its hospitality." In
Staunton, Illinois, the local Vigilance Corps posted signs
throughout its strongly German community that the use of
a foreign language had become "exceedingly distasteful to
Americans" and that English should be spoken in public.
Persons unable to speak English were advised to be silent.
The city fathers of Steeleville, Illinois, passed an ordinance
simply forbidding the German language to be spoken in
their community, any time, anywhere. Offenders were
made liable to fine and imprisonment. The Steeleville vigilance committee made a special point of informing the local German Lutheran pastor of the ordinance.[15]

German-language instruction in public schools was
halted or curtailed in Saint Louis, Edwardsville, East Saint
Louis, and several other communities in the Saint Louis
vicinity during April and May 1918. Similarly, the Saint
Louis Board of Aldermen were subjected to intense pressure to repeal the city ordinance which required the publication of official notices in the German-language press of
the city. In the course of that fight, Mayor Kiel, himself of
German descent, threatened a libel suit against the *Saint
Louis Republic* because it charged him with having made
"pro-German efforts" to confuse the language issue. During
the same weeks, the Saint Louis aldermen proposed ordinances to change the names of streets having German
names.[16]

An extraordinary climate of fear had been created. German-Americans responded in a variety of ways to demonstrate their loyalty to America. Some shifted suspicion from
themselves by reporting the disloyal remarks of their fellows. Indeed, one perverse woman in Saint Louis sued her
husband for divorce on the grounds of his allegedly pro-
German conversation and conduct.[17] But the most significant adjustments were made by German-American
institutions and organizations. Of these, the churches were
especially eager to conform to the standards demanded by
superpatriots.

WE WOULD HAVE LESS OF THIS

IF WE HAD MORE OF THIS

Life, 4 April 1918

This cartoon appeared in an influential periodical on the same day that Robert Prager was lynched in Collinsville, Illinois.

On the day following Prager's death, a conference of Lutheran pastors was held in Staunton, Illinois. Returning
from that meeting, the pastor of Trinity Lutheran Church
in Edwardsville announced that services in his church the
next day would be of a patriotic nature. In East Saint Louis,
members of Saint Peter's German Lutheran Church met
after services on 7 April. They voted to drop the word "German" from the official name of their congregation and resolved to invest $2,000 of the church's funds in war bonds.
A week later, the mother church of German Lutheranism
in Saint Louis resolved to translate its name from Dreiei-
nigkeitskirche to Trinity Church and to specify English as
its official language. At the same time, the congregation
agreed unanimously to buy $1,000 worth of bonds. The Ger-
man Methodist congregation in Belleville, Illinois, agreed
to change its name to the Jackson Street Methodist Church.
A German Evangelical congregation in Alton, Illinois, took
similar action.[18]

German-language services were dropped throughout the
area during April. In Collinsville, Holy Cross Lutheran
Church considered dropping all German services, although
its pastor favored retaining some German services for those
members unable to speak English. A spokesman for the
Lutheran Church—Missouri Synod announced that all
twenty-eight congregations of his denomination in Saint
Louis had discontinued German-language services and
that all instruction in the German language in the twenty-
two Lutheran parochial schools of the city had ceased.
Meanwhile, Archbishop Glennon of Saint Louis announced
that he was considering a request that the use of German
be discontinued in the seventeen predominantly German
Catholic parishes of the city. He hastened to add that Latin
was the main language used and that only the sermon and
the routine announcements were given in the German language.[19]

Some churches in the area publicized their participation
in and donations to Red Cross activities to prove their loyalty. Liberty bond purchases became standard. In Saint

Louis, students at the German Lutheran Concordia Seminary raised $4,000 for this purpose. At a campus meeting supporting bond sales, one professor, Dr. Theodore Graebner, endeavored to dissociate the German Kaiser from American Lutheran belief. He struck two blows in one as he asserted that the emperor's real sympathies lay not with conservative Lutheranism but with "infidel German theologians," such as Friedrich Delitzsch and Adolf von Harnack. Graebner's theme was quickly picked up and used by other German Lutheran preachers in the area.[20]

German societies behaved much like the churches. The Vorwaerts Verein of New Athens, Illinois, changed its name to the New Athens Singing Society and announced that henceforth it would sing only English songs. In Saint Louis, the district convention of Turner societies resolved to conduct all its business in English. The proprietor of the *Westliche Post* in the same city announced that he was willing to abandon German-language publishing provided he could transfer his Associated Press franchise to an English-language newspaper. The month of April also saw the demise of the Saint Louis German-American Alliance, an organization that allegedly enrolled 12,000 members. In a questionable action by its executive committee, the society was disbanded quietly and unobtrusively.[21]

Such was the oppressive climate of coercive patriotism in Saint Louis and in the nearby sections of central and southern Illinois during the weeks following Prager's lynching in Collinsville. Similar catalogs of superpatriotic behavior and frightened responses by German-Americans could be compiled for many other areas of the nation. But the Prager affair was by no means over. His funeral and interment were reported nationally by the wire services and the efforts to bring his murderers to justice received widespread publicity.

On 10 April 1918 Prager was quietly buried in Saint Louis by his fraternal brothers of the Odd Fellows order. The German Imperial Government tried briefly to make propagandistic capital of the tragedy by offering to pay all of the burial expenses. A bill was submitted to the Swiss legation, which had offered to function as an intermediary. Before that transaction could be completed, however, Governor Lowden announced that the state of Illinois felt a moral obligation to pay the expenses of an appropriate funeral. A pastor of the Evangelical church conducted the services. In conformance with Prager's last request, a United States flag was draped across his coffin.[22]

Investigation into the crime began the same day it was committed. The governor met with several Illinois officials to plan their efforts. The state's attorney in Madison County, J. P. Streuber, was ordered to try to identify members of the mob. Assistants were subsequently sent from Springfield and Washington.

While Collinsville officials refused to conduct an investigation, the coroner of Madison County proceeded immediately with an inquest which lasted from Monday, 8 April 1918, until the following Thursday. Authority was vested in a coroner's jury consisting of six well-known Collinsville citizens. They heard much incriminating testimony from nearly three dozen witnesses, chief of whom was Joseph Riegel.[23]

Riegel was remarkably free with his testimony. Attorneys present at the inquest repeatedly informed him that he was not required to make any statements that could be used against him. But Riegel insisted he did not care. "When I got home that night," Riegel said, "I got to thinking about how I helped kill that fellow who never did anything to me and who [sic] I didn't even know, and I couldn't sleep. I want to tell it and get it off my mind. I am ready to take my medicine."[24] His attitude (and his testimony) was greatly changed later, after the coroner's jury recommended that Riegel and four other men be charged with murder, and after a defense attorney had been hired. Placed under arrest, the five men were held without bail pending the action of the grand jury.

The Madison County grand jury heard much of the same testimony given at the inquest. After two weeks of proceedings, indictments for murder were issued on 25 April against twelve persons, including the five already in custody. The grand jury also indicted the four Collinsville policemen for omission of duty and malfeasance in office, charging that they had "wilfully [sic] and corruptly failed to keep the peace."[25]

As the trial got underway on 13 May, suspicion and fear were common among the citizens of Madison County, many of whom were of German birth or descent. It was extraordinarily difficult to impanel a jury; few persons cared to become involved in the affair. Most prospective jurors insisted that they had formed an opinion on the case. By the time the fifth juryman had been selected, 335 prospective jurors had been excused or challenged. It was then that the state's attorney lodged a formal complaint against the work of the Madison County Sheriff Jenkin Jenkins in summoning prospective jurors. The most serious of the charges against the sheriff was that he and his deputies had summoned only those persons for jury duty whom they believed would be favorable to the defendants. The complaint also noted that one of the sheriff's deputies was an uncle of one of the defendants. The judge subsequently disqualified Jenkins and appointed a special bailiff to select prospective jurors. The sheriff, of course, was enraged by this turn of events. Several days later, on 27 May, he assaulted the state's attorney in an Edwardsville cafe, charging him with being pro-German. None of the jurors impaneled prior to Jenkins's dismissal bore obviously German names, but those added later included such names as Fiegenbaum, Dippold, Groshans, and Baumgartner. Perhaps Jenkins had observed that each of the prosecutors had German names: Assistant Attorney Generals Trautmann and Middlekauf and State's Attorney J. P. Streuber. Even the judge, Louis N. Bernreuter, was clearly of German descent.[26]

More than two weeks passed and over seven hundred persons were summoned before a full panel of twelve jurors was chosen. By comparison the trial itself was distressingly brief. The examination of witnesses began on 28 May;

three days later it was all over. Most of the time was taken by the prosecution. Some of the witnesses had testified earlier before the coroner's jury and the grand jury; others offered new testimony. Streuber summarized his case with a lengthy plea for law enforcement in which he pointed out the international implications of the affair.[27]

The defense presented its case in less than six hours. The attorneys emphasized the difficulty of determining individual actions on that dark April night. Hundreds of persons had been there. Half the defendants testified that they hadn't even been present at the hanging; the other defendants protested that they had been bystanders. Joseph Riegel repudiated virtually all of the testimony he had given earlier to newspaper reporters and to the coroner's jury. The defense had prepared much evidence to demonstrate that Prager was disloyal, but Judge Bernreuter properly ruled that such a patriotic plea was inadmissable and irrelevant to the proceedings.[28]

This ruling did not prevent the defense from concluding its case with the contention that Prager was a suspected German spy and that the lynching was justifiable under "unwritten law." Attorney Thomas Williamson asserted that when the law covering murder was written the country was not at war. Present conditions, he said, were different. He sought to buttress this extraordinary argument with the alleged rebuttal of former Ambassador to Germany James Gerard to the Kaiser's foreign minister. When the latter had alluded to German strength in America by observing that 500,000 reservists of the German army lived in the United States, Gerard had replied that there were also 500,000 lampposts on which to hang them. The act of the Collinsville mob was thus parallel to that of a householder who kills a burglar. In Williamson's view, the popular justice of this new unwritten law permitted citizens to protect themselves from disloyalty.[29]

After the conclusion of these arguments the judge declared a recess. At that moment the familiar strains of the "Star-Spangled Banner" filled the courthouse. The music was provided by a detachment of the Great Lakes Naval

Training Band, on duty in Edwardsville for recruiting purposes. The players stood in the rotunda of the building,
allegedly escaping a brief downpour of rain. Someone
urged the group to perform, assuring them that the court
was in recess and that no disturbance would be caused.[30]
Thus it happened that patriotic anthems and military marches served as a prelude to the judge's instructions to the
jury.

Judge Bernreuter was brief and concise. He pointed out
that it was not necessary for the state to prove that all or
any of the defendants had participated in the actual stran-
gulation of Prager. "Any defendant who aided, assisted,
or advised or encouraged the guilty persons by word,
act, or motions," the judge told the jurors, "was equally
guilty as an accessory." He also informed them that guilt
had to be proven beyond a reasonable doubt, that likelihood
or probability of guilt was insufficient grounds for conviction.[31]

Forty-five minutes later the jury returned a verdict of not
guilty. Two ballots had been taken. The first was eleven to
one for acquittal of all the defendants; the second was
unanimous. When the jury's verdict was announced, the
small courtroom rang with wild cheering and shouting as
the defendants' friends and relatives sprang to their feet in
celebration. The defendants, each of whom had worn a red,
white, and blue rosette throughout the trial, shook hands
with the members of the jury. Several members of the
panel later revealed that in their opinion the prosecution
had failed to prove guilt beyond a reasonable doubt.[32]

The next day State's Attorney Streuber appeared before
the court and requested that the charges of malfeasance
against the Collinsville police be dismissed. It would be
impossible, he said, to impanel a jury, given the publicity
the case had received. Since he was unable to get a conviction of the alleged murderers, Streuber felt that a trial of
the policemen would be equally futile.[33]

It is not surprising that Robert Prager was lynched in
Collinsville in April 1918, nor that his murderers escaped
all the penalties of law. Given the hundreds of instances in

which Americans of German origin or descent were abused during World War I, it is surprising rather that there were not more hangings. The state of war with Germany following a tension-ridden neutrality period of nearly three years, plus the war policies of the Wilson Administration, had created a climate of intolerance. Moreover, Prager as a person invited persecution. He was a German alien, unattractive and indiscreet. The incident occurred in a district where German-Americans constituted a major element of the population. Native Americans of Anglo-Saxon heritage had frequently experienced difficulties in their relations with this numerous and proud people. American Germans were often difficult to understand; they seemed separatistic or clannish. Their very success in the American environment made them appear as a threat. To understand why American society lashed out at its German element during World War I it is necessary to examine, among other dimensions of the problem, the history of German immigration to the United States during the decades preceding the war.

Notes

1. The narrative of Prager's ordeal and death, pp. 3–11, is based entirely upon newspaper sources, chiefly the *Saint Louis Post-Dispatch* and the *Edwardsville* [Illinois] *Intelligencer,* the latter a local paper published in the nearby county seat. As supplementary sources, I have used the *New York Times, Washington Post,* and *Chicago Tribune.* All are dated from 5 April to 3 June 1918. Another detailed account of the tragedy is by Donald R. Hickey, "The Prager Affair: A Study in Wartime Hysteria," *Journal of the Illinois State Historical Society,* 62 (Summer 1969): 117–34. Hickey relies heavily on the *Collinsville Advertiser* and *East Saint Louis Daily Journal.*
2. *Literary Digest,* 57 (20 April 1918): 16–17; *New York Times,* 6 April 1918; *Edwardsville Intelligencer,* 5 April 1918.
3. *Saint Louis Post-Dispatch,* 7 April 1918.
4. *Washington Post,* 6 April 1918; *Edwardsville Intelligencer,* 6 April 1918; *New Republic,* 14 (13 April 1918): 312.
5. *Chicago Tribune,* 6 April 1918; *New York Times,* 6 April 1918.
6. *New York Times,* 6 April 1918; *Saint Louis Post-Dispatch,* 6 April 1918.
7. *New York Times,* 6, 26 April 1918; Thomas Gregory to T. U. Taylor, 15 April 1918, quoted in Harry N. Scheiber, *The Wilson Administration and Civil Liberties, 1917–1921* (Ithaca: Cornell University Press, 1960), p. 51; *Washington Post,* 10 April 1918.
8. Woodrow Wilson to Otto C. Butz, Washington, D.C., 12 April 1918, Chicago Historical Society. Wilson sent the same letter to William E. Bohn of New York. It is quoted in the *Saint Louis Post-Dispatch,* 18 April 1918. Both Butz and Bohn were officers of the Friends of German Democracy.

9. [James D. Richardson, ed.], *Messages and Papers of the Presidents,* 22 vols. (New York: Bureau of National Literature, 1897–1929), 18: 8556f. Wilson's proclamation appeared, for example, on p. 7 of the *New York Times,* 27 July 1918, and on p. 6 of the *Chicago Tribune,* 27 July 1918.

10. *Edwardsville Intelligencer,* 10 April 1918.

11. Ibid.; *Saint Louis Post-Dispatch,* 7 April 1918.

12. *Edwardsville Intelligencer,* 10 April 1918; *Saint Louis Post-Dispatch,* 11 April 1918.

13. *Edwardsville Intelligencer,* 8 April 1918, 8 May 1918.

14. Ibid., 29 April 1918; *Saint Louis Post-Dispatch,* 16 April 1918, 20 May 1918.

15. *Saint Louis Post-Dispatch,* 21 April 1918, 17 May 1918; *Edwardsville Intelligencer,* 6 April 1918.

16. *Saint Louis Post-Dispatch,* 8–10 April 1918, 17–19 April 1918, 23–30 April 1918, 19 May 1918.

17. Ibid., 8 May 1918; *Edwardsville Intelligencer,* 6 April 1918.

18. *Saint Louis Post-Dispatch,* 11, 17 April 1918, 17 May 1918; *Edwardsville Intelligencer,* 6, 10 April 1918.

19. *Edwardsville Intelligencer,* 19 April 1918; *Saint Louis Post-Dispatch,* 17 April 1918.

20. *Edwardsville Intelligencer,* 26 April 1918, 3 May 1918, 13 June 1918; *Saint Louis Post-Dispatch,* 16, 19 April 1918.

21. *Saint Louis Post-Dispatch,* 12, 18, 26, 28 April 1918.

22. Ibid., 11 April 1918; *Edwardsville Intelligencer,* 8, 11 April 1918, 3 May 1918; *New York Times,* 3 June 1918.

23. *Edwardsville Intelligencer,* 6, 10, 12 April 1918; *Saint Louis Post-Dispatch,* 11 April 1918; *New York Times,* 12 April 1918.

24. *Saint Louis Post-Dispatch,* 11 April 1918.

25. *Edwardsville Intelligencer,* 18, 26, 27 April 1918.

26. Ibid., 14, 18, 21, 28 May 1918.

27. Ibid., 28, 29 May 1918, 1 June 1918; *Saint Louis Post-Dispatch,* 1, 2 June 1918.

28. Ibid.

29. *Edwardsville Intelligencer,* 1 June 1918; *Saint Louis Post-Dispatch,* 2 June 1918; *New York Times,* 2 June 1918.

30. *Saint Louis Post-Dispatch,* 2 June 1918.

31. Ibid.

32. Ibid.; *Edwardsville Intelligencer,* 3 June 1918.

33. *Saint Louis Post-Dispatch,* 3 June 1918.

CHAPTER TWO

Soul Germans and Stomach Germans

1870–1914

"We have two kinds of Germans in Milwaukee: soul Germans and stomach Germans, and the latter are in the vast majority," commented an observer at the turn of the century.[1] By this he meant that most Germans in Milwaukee, or in America for that matter, followed a way of life that was materialistic and emotional rather than ideological or rational, one that emphasized the warm embrace of ethnic life and its unquestioned customs and values. As he used the term, "stomach German" summarized all the habits of everyday life that were unconsciously related to German culture. It meant more than the convivial pleasures of a German beer garden or restaurant. It could include reading a German-language newspaper or magazine, enjoying a game of cards, or basking in the genial companionship of womenfolk gathered at church to quilt a blanket, chattering all the while in German.

The "soul German," by contrast, went beyond this to articulate, to idealize, to rationalize, consciously and deliberately, what he perceived to be his superior culture. Convinced that the German spirit and ideals were the noblest and loftiest in Western civilization, the "soul German" felt constrained to cultivate and perpetuate them among his fellow ethnics in America. Essential to this was the maintenance of the German language, which he believed to be the most beautiful in the world. As he saw it, his mission was to promote and defend German culture in the American setting, and to graft its ideals, if possible, onto American practicality and inventiveness to produce the finest civilization in the history of mankind.

Between these two extremes were many Germans in America whose livelihood depended, directly or indirectly, upon a constituency that retained the imported German language and culture. This grouping could include pastors of immigrant churches, editors of German-language newspapers, teachers in German-American schools, proprietors of German-American banks and insurance companies, employees of ethnic societies of all kinds, and indeed, restauranteurs, brewers, and saloonkeepers. Some of these were "soul Germans" of the purest type, but most found that their cultural ties to the German ethnic community could snap under economic, religious, or social pressure. They were only secondarily interested in the maintenance of German culture. In all of this, the Germans were not essentially different from other immigrant groups. Rather the difference lay in the number of Germans who came to American shores, the time of their arrival, and the quality of the cultural baggage they brought with them.

The Germans had always been the largest non-English-speaking immigrant group in America. In the colonial period, thousands of "Palatines" and other Germans swarmed into Pennsylvania, New York, and Maryland, filtering into the newly settled portions of those states, Virginia and the Carolinas. Following the American Revolution, immigration from Germany dropped off to a trickle, not more than a few hundred persons per year. A second great wave of German immigration began about 1830 in the Jacksonian era. It reached a climax in 1854 when 215,000 were counted entering the United States, which at that time had a total population of about 25,000,000. During the next decade, however, the numbers were greatly reduced by depression and the Civil War in the United States.[2]

The pattern of German immigration was closely related to economic and political conditions, especially in the second half of the nineteenth century. Germany had been deeply affected by the agricultural revolution. Technological improvements in transportation, together with the adoption of machinery to farm production, especially of wheat, permitted distant countries to compete for the German market. By 1875 Germany had become a wheat-importing country, a fact of devastating consequence for German farmers, and for the craftsmen, artisans, and shopkeepers who depended upon their patronage. At the same time, the growing industrial establishment of Germany, which was experiencing a depression during the 1880s, was as yet unable to absorb the economically distressed persons. The result was a flood of German emigration to America of unprecedented numbers. In the years from 1881 to 1892, approximately 1,700,000 persons from Germany arrived in America. Not all, of course, were escaping the constrictions of an economy in transition. Others fled from military service in the vaunted war machine of the new German Empire, which had been forged in 1870 by the Iron Chancellor, Otto von Bismarck.[3]

By the 1890s German industrial development had advanced to the point where a shortage of labor had actually developed. Emigration plummeted once more, averaging only about 30,000 per year until the outbreak of war in 1914. This meant that by the time of World War I the first generation of German immigrants in America was far outnumbered by the second, whose attitudes and behavior were much more deeply conditioned by the social process of assimilation.[4]

The size of the German ethnic group in the United States is revealed by the census of 1910. The total population of the country in that year fell just short of 92,000,000. Of this number, about 2,500,000 persons were born in Germany. The second generation (native-born persons with one or both parents born in Germany) swelled the number by an additional 5,780,000. Together, the first- and second-generation Germans, numbering well over eight million persons, were by far the most numerous immigrant group in the United States in 1910, representing 26 percent of the total foreign white stock in the country.[5] Of course, there were many second-generation German-Americans who assimilated rapidly and who did not identify in any meaningful way with the German culture and values. Some of them went out of their way to divest themselves of their ethnocultural inheritance. But their number was more than offset by persons of the third or later generations who continued to speak German and to cherish their heritage. This phenomenon was common in the large rural German settlements, most notably in Pennsylvania, where the German character of the population, established in colonial times, has persisted to the present time.

Like all immigrant groups, the Germans tended to settle among others of their kind. Thus, in 1910, more than 85 percent resided in the Middle Atlantic states and in the Midwest. Nonetheless, the Germans were the most numerous single immigrant group in all the geographic divisions of the country except New England and the mountain states of the West. Many of the later German immigrants, like their predecessors, settled on farms in the states of the upper Midwest and the Great Plains, but by 1910 two of every three newcomers from Germany lived in cities (defined as places of 2,500 or more inhabitants). This ratio was lower than the figure for all foreign-born (who were 72.1 percent urban) but considerably higher than the percent for the total population (46.3). The Germans were the most numerous single ethnic group in such major cities as Baltimore, Buffalo, Chicago, Cincinnati, Detroit, Los Angeles, Milwaukee, Pittsburgh, Saint Louis, and San Francisco. The census of 1910 showed 278,000 German-born in New York City and 182,000 in Chicago. Yet Milwaukee, Cincinnati, and Saint Louis were perhaps the most famous centers of German immigrant culture. Slightly more than half (53.5 percent) of the total population of Milwaukee was of German stock in 1910.[6]

This is not to suggest, however, that the Germans of the cities lived in sharply defined ghettos. Strongly German-American neighborhoods and wards could be identified, such as the "Over the Rhine" district in Cincinnati, but generally the Germans were well distributed throughout most cities in 1910. One demographic study has shown, for example, that on an index scale of 0 to 100 (with 0 indicating complete integration and 100 complete segregation) Saint Louis Germans registered an index of 29.9 in 1880. By 1910 the figure had dropped to 20.9. At the same time the index figure for Cincinnati Germans was 19.9 and Milwaukee's was 17.9.[7] Rural concentrations of German-Americans showed similar patterns. One rural county in Nebraska revealed an index as high as 49.4 in 1885, but figures close to thirty were more typical for concentrations of Germans in the Nebraska countryside.

A majority of German immigrants prospered in nineteenth-century America. Mobility studies demonstrate that they advanced themselves economically at a rapid rate, customarily exceeding most other ethnic groups and sometimes even surpassing the native-born. The census of 1890 offers the most complete information relating country of birth to occupation. The data show, for example, that the German-born were 1.6 times more likely to become dairy farmers than the total white male population. But among other kinds of farmers, except for the highly specialized, the Germans were underrepresented. Generally they tended to avoid employment in mining and lumbering, and were proportionately underrepresented in transportation. In manufacturing, they were very strong in food industries (bakers, butchers, meat packers, confectioners). Brewers were eight times as common among the German-born than among the white population at large; similarly, bartenders were twice as frequent. Large numbers were employed in domestic and personal services, especially barbering and hairdressing. Like other immigrants, the Germans found it difficult to secure employment in clerical work, banking, and other occupations that required a knowledge of English. Among merchants, however, the German-born were overrepresented and in the professions they were especially numerous among musicians, chemists, artists, and architects. Among physicians, lawyers, dentists, and teachers their proportion was low compared to the total population but higher than that of most other immigrant groups.[8]

Significant changes in occupation were also apparent between the first and second generations of Germans in America. In 1900, for example, laborers were slightly more common among the German-born than among the total population; among the second generation the figure was considerably less. Conversely, clerks and bookkeepers in trade and transportation were nearly three times as common in the second generation as compared to the first.[9]

Some German-American writers at the turn of the century were fond of pointing out the great successes of persons of German antecedents in American manufacturing and commerce. Names like Rockefeller, Wanamaker, Studebaker, Weyerhauser, Spreckels, Heinz, Frick, and Schwab were reverently intoned.[10] But most of these families had long since achieved total assimilation into American society. Their very success militated against German cultural chauvinism. Except for a few like Adolf Busch of the famous Saint Louis brewery, such persons did not often identify themselves as Germans and had few, if any, meaningful contacts with the German immigrant community.

The Germans who came to this country after the Civil War differed in several ways from their predecessors. Although most of the pre-Civil War immigrants were peasants, there were also significant numbers of well-educated, highly motivated political radicals and activists who had fled from Germany after the unsuccessful revolutions of 1848, the most famous of whom was Carl Schurz. But men of intellect or substance were less apparent in the later wave. While many immigrants were peasants who sought farms in the Midwest and the plains states, the proportion of urban workers increased during the 1870s and 1880s. They seemed to be of a lower cultural level, indifferent to the finer qualities of German culture, yet more obviously ethnocentric. Few were outspokenly dissatisfied with the motherland as many of the earlier emigrants had been. This was even true of the large numbers who had left to escape military service. The Germany from which they came had undergone vast changes. Essentially a "culture state" before 1870, Germany was now a dynamic empire, united under Bismarck's vigorous leadership, rapidly moving through a transitional phase to become an industrialized world power and a leader in state socialism and conservative reform. The Fatherland had thus become a source of nationalistic pride for many of its emigrants.[11]

While it is possible to generalize at length about the characteristics of the Germans as a group, such statements are always somewhat misleading because they obscure the individual person and the means he employed to cope with the problems of life in a new country. Even more seriously, they gloss over the extraordinary heterogeneity that was characteristic of the German immigrants.

Provincial differences, religious divisions, and social and political distinctions among the Germans were usually lost on native Americans, who tended to lump all Germans together on the basis of language usage. But even that had its limitations. The everyday language spoken by the German was usually quite different from the literary language of books and newspapers, of schools and churches. The dialect of the Bavarian, for example, was almost unintelligible to the Germans of East Friesland, whose *Plattdeutsch* was much closer to the language of his Dutch neighbors a few miles to the west. There were also significant cultural differences. A Pomeranian readily perceived that a Württemberger's life style, his habits and attitudes, were in marked contrast to his own. Moreover, several centuries of political autonomy for the petty German states had reinforced these linguistic and cultural differences. Not only were there Prussians, Saxons, and Hanoverians, but also Oldenburgers, Hesse-Darmstadters, Lippe-Detmolders, and dozens more. These identities, which meant nothing to most Americans, continued to have more relevance for many of their bearers than the all-inclusive label of German.

But the deepest divisions among Germans were religious. Attitudes, values, and behavior patterns were much more closely related to religious belief than they were to language, place of birth, or economic status. No other European people had been so divided historically between Catholics and Protestants; between Lutherans and Calvinists; between orthodox ritualists on one hand and pietists and mystical enthusiasts on the other. The Germans had a heritage of long, fierce religious wars between nations and petty states whose ecclesiastical identities were often determined, at least in part, by their ruling families. Thus, political boundaries tended to conform to religious lines. The Badenese, for example, were likely to be Catholic while Prussians historically were Lutheran. Suspicion, envy, persecution, and hatred of Germans for Germans was standard. Each European people, of course, had its provincial and regional differences and its internecine quarrels, but none was so deeply divided along religious lines as the German.

The German immigrant naturally brought his prejudices with him to America as part of his cultural baggage. He sought out others of his own kind in this country, often relatives or acquaintances, persons who shared his own culture, language, and religion and who were most likely to give him the advice and assistance he needed to make a start in America. In this way concentrations of like-minded Germans developed—Catholics here, Lutherans there, and Mennonites and other sectarians somewhere else. Each group had surprisingly little to do with the other. Each went its own way, developing its religiously oriented social, educational, and sometimes economic and political institutions. The only common bond these groups of Germans had, other than general culture and language, was a commitment to religious values. They identified themselves first of all as Catholics, Lutherans, Evangelicals, Mennonites, or

Methodists, and only secondarily (sometimes only incidentally) as Germans. Most, of course, were keenly conscious of
their German character and gave explicit expression to
their hopes and goals within that context. Yet when they
perceived that being German obstructed or prevented the
attainment of their goals as church people, the majority
were prepared to cast off their ethnicity to whatever extent
was possible or necessary. In short, they were *Kirchendeutschen*—"church Germans."[12]

German Catholics constituted the largest single subgroup
of church Germans. At the time of World War I, they numbered slightly less than the total membership of the several
German Protestant denominations. Because statistics of
churches have ordinarily lacked uniformity and reliability,
it is difficult to estimate with any precision the actual size
of the German Catholic group. Several estimates agree that
Germans made up about one-fifth of the Roman Catholic
constituency in the United States, which, according to the
religious census of 1916, numbered over eight million persons. Throughout much of the nineteenth century the German clergy within the Catholic church had fought to
achieve a separate, nongeographical administrative entity.
Although they never were granted ethnic-based dioceses,
hundreds of parishes were organized along these lines. Tolerated by the Americanizers within the church as necessary in a transitional period, ethnic parishes were
frequently established whenever any ethnic group was numerous enough to warrant them. In 1916 there were over
200 Catholic parishes that used German in their sermons
and songs. At the same time nearly 2,000 other parishes
conducted some services in English and some in German.[13]

Although significant concentrations of German Catholics
could be found in rural areas, a majority lived in cities by
the end of the nineteenth century. Most of the early immigrants had come from western and southern Germany,
which were predominantly Catholic regions. Since many of
them were also peasants, rural colonies of German Catholics were naturally established in Wisconsin, Indiana, Min-

nesota, and other states of the Old Northwest where land was still to be had cheaply. By contrast, after 1870 Catholics were more often workers headed for American cities. They put an unmistakably urban stamp upon German-American Catholicism. By 1906, for example, two-thirds of all persons indicating church membership in the very German city of Milwaukee were Roman Catholics.[14]

German Catholic churchmen were among the strongest advocates of parish schools. Intensely conservative, many of them were convinced that the preservation of the faith required the maintenance of the German language and culture and that this could best be accomplished through Catholic schools. Only in this way, they thought, could the youth of the church be kept within the fold. Despite this emphasis, by World War I English had become the common language of instruction in the schools of German Catholic parishes. German was frequently used in religion classes but otherwise it was more often a subject than a medium of instruction.

German Catholics had almost no formal contacts with other German-Americans. Besides their parish schools, they maintained hospitals, orphanages, and other institutions. Their press was especially active. Newspapers and periodicals serving exclusively German Catholics were published in all of the main centers of German population. Perhaps the most important German Catholic organization was the Central-Verein, a national federation of societies and clubs organized by German Catholic laymen.[15]

In spite of their impressive numbers, the German Catholics displayed fierce antagonisms against any group that seemed to infringe upon their rights. Their enemies could include fellow Catholics, chiefly Irish prelates, who had sharply criticized their efforts at language and culture maintenance and who had occasionally accused the Germans, albeit unjustly, of serving the goals of imperialistic elements in Germany. But Bismarck's Germany was often denounced in German Catholic publications with special loathing. The anti-Catholic dimension of the Iron Chancellor's Kulturkampf of the 1870s was a source of much bitterness.

Protestants also held high rank among the perceived enemies of Catholicism. Martin Luther and his latter-day followers were always the worst of heretics. In 1883, the four-hundredth anniversary of Luther's birth, the Catholic *Volkszeitung* of Baltimore, an archconservative paper with a national circulation, noted the occasion with a series of more than sixty articles ripping Luther, the Reformation, and Protestantism to shreds.[16] Nor were German Catholics permitted to forget the anti-Catholic heritage of Freemasonry. Other secret societies fared no better, especially when their members displayed the prejudices of nativism with its attendant espousal of prohibition, woman suffrage, and Sabbatarianism. Freethinkers were doubly damned because of their godlessness and their frequent embrace of socialism. Fearing that German Catholic workers would be captured by radical ideologies, the church waged a relentless war of words against socialism during the decade before World War I. The archbishop of Milwaukee even forbade his flock to hold membership in the locally strong Socialist party or to vote for its candidates.[17] Attacks from all quarters, real or imaginary, from Irish Catholics, German Lutherans, nativistic Protestants, Masons, freethinkers, and political radicals served to create a heightened sense of identity among German Catholics and to promote a conservative, defensive mentality.

German Lutherans were even more separatistic than the Catholics. This was due largely to their form of church government and organization. The Roman Catholic Church, with its all-embracing episcopal structure and multi-ethnic constituency, forced the Germans into a larger mold. Lutherans in America, by contrast, organized themselves into autonomous congregations clustered in a bewildering array of synods, each going its own way, and each representing a differing shade of conservatism and of Americanization. Since most nineteenth-century German Lutheran immigrants found existing churches too Ameri-

canized to serve their needs, they created their own synodical organizations. Although these groups usually bore
names like Ohio, Missouri, Iowa, or Wisconsin, they were
by no means confined to the geographic limits of those
states. Almost all of these synods had been organized before
the Civil War. Nevertheless, the German language continued to be widely used in most and almost exclusively in
some. One pre-World War I estimate held that about half of
the approximately two million Lutherans in America at
that time conducted worship services in the German language. While some of the synods were thoroughly assimilated organizations that had long ago lost their German
characteristics, others remained essentially immigrant institutions, dedicated to the ingathering of newcomers and
their children. The largest and most dynamic of the latter
was the Lutheran Church—Missouri Synod, known at that
time as the German Evangelical Lutheran Synod of Missouri, Ohio, and Other States.[18]

The Missouri Synod, organized in Chicago in 1845, displayed attitudes and values much like those of the German
Catholics. Though the two churches differed radically in
theology, both were ritualistic and orthodox. As hostile as
the Catholics to secret societies, freethinkers, socialists, and
nativistic advocates of pietistic or puritanical measures
like prohibition, the Missouri Synod also erected a remarkable institutional structure designed to preserve the church
in its doctrine by resisting assimilation. Seminaries and
preparatory schools were founded, as were colleges to supply teachers for the parochial schools the synod urged each
congregation to maintain. By 1910, Missouri Synod
churches operated more than 2,100 elementary schools en-
rolling about 100,000 children. Another 1,000 schools were
maintained by the other synods, notably Ohio, Wisconsin,
and Iowa. The language of the schools, the worship services, the textbooks, theological journals, magazines for the
laity, hymnbooks, and prayerbooks was nearly always German. All materials were produced in the church's publishing house. A full complement of hospitals, orphanages, and

homes for the aged were established by societies within the church. As a substitute for the appeal of lodges, men's societies were organized. And when the fraternal orders began to incorporate attractive life insurance programs, enterprising German Lutherans founded fraternal life insurance organizations whose members were limited to a particular synod. Though it was totally a product of the American environment, the Missouri Synod (and to a lesser extent the other German Lutheran synods) was a compact German-culture group, thoroughly organized for self-perpetuation. Yet its goals were religious. The preservation of German language and culture was conceived of as a means, not an end.[19]

A third German immigrant church, often mistaken for a Lutheran body, was the German Evangelical Synod of North America. Indeed, its external appearance was Lutheran. The vast majority of its 340,000 members worshipped in German-language services, it operated more than three hundred parochial schools, it maintained a teachers college and a seminary, it established the usual philanthropic institutions, and its publishing house prospered. But the Evangelical Synod was fundamentally different in that it was ecumenical or unionistic. Instead of pursuing theological separatism, as many Lutheran synods did, the Evangelicals sought to break it down. Thus, the maintenance of German language and culture among the Evangelicals, extensive though it was, tended to serve a social rather than a religious function. Some years after World War I, the Evangelical Synod merged with the German Reformed Church, a Calvinistic body which in 1916 used German in about one-third of its 1,700 congregations.[20]

Besides the Lutherans and the Evangelicals, there was a wide variety of Protestant denominations with German antecedents. Some organizations, such as the Church of the Brethren (called Dunkers in colonial times) were thoroughly assimilated by the World War I era. The several Mennonite church bodies, though similar in origin and theology to the Church of the Brethren, were much more retentive of German language and culture. This was especially true of the several small groups that had come to America after 1873 from German colonies in Russia along the Volga River and north of the Black Sea. Overwhelmingly rural, the Mennonites maintained tight, exclusive German cultural islands in which separation from the sinful world, as viewed by Mennonite eyes, was an essential part of their faith and life. Intensely pacifistic, the Mennonites felt that some of the requirements of civil law were contrary to the will of God and therefore should not be obeyed. Inevitably they suffered severe persecutions throughout their history.[21]

There were also several Methodistic church bodies with German immigrant origins. The largest of these, the Church of the United Brethren in Christ, was organized in colonial times, and by 1916 represented about 350,000 persons. By the end of the century, however, English had almost completely displaced the use of German in these churches. Hence, late nineteenth-century German immigrants of Arminian theology or pietistic morality were more likely to be attracted to the German-speaking conferences of the Methodist church. Ten such conferences existed in 1915, serving sixty to seventy thousand German-Americans in the German tongue. They established several colleges and other institutions and maintained a theological magazine of high quality. Although German Methodism was entirely an American phenomenon, its commitment to German language and culture was strong. Similar conferences, smaller in size, were to be found in the Presbyterian and Baptist denominations.[22]

German Jews in America were not unlike some of the separatistic Christian denominations. Like German Catholics, German Jews established their own educational agencies (including some full-time elementary schools), benevolent institutions, and other auxiliary organizations within a framework that transcended lines of national origin. Moreover, their first concern was for the preservation of what was Jewish in their heritage rather than what was German in it. By the time of World War I, there were perhaps as many as three million Jews in America. While only a part of this number was German in origin, the leadership of the Jewish community in America was largely in the hands of nineteenth-century emigrants from Germany and their children. Many took pride in their German roots and vicariously shared the triumphs of the new German Empire. During those years native Americans ordinarily did not distinguish them from other persons of German origin. But as the process of Americanization lengthened, Jewish ties with the German community weakened. Nevertheless, there were individual Jews who were intensely proud of their German inheritance and who, as might be expected, suffered much because of it during the oppressive days of World War I.[23]

German language and culture thus served different purposes for different groups among the church Germans. Among the Catholics, Lutherans, and Mennonites, ethnic heritage was used as a weapon to ward off heresy, to prevent losses among the young, or to exclude worldly influences. It helped to buttress the religious identity of the group, to promote its particularity. Instead of uniting German immigrants in America on a foundation of shared culture, the emphasis on the European heritage widened the gulf separating the several German religious groups from each other and from American society. But above all, the maintenance of German language and culture among the church people had nothing whatever to do with the political goals of Imperial Germany.

Among the other German church groups—the Evangelicals, the United Brethren, the German Methodists—attachment to German culture was less intimately tied to religious goals. Much less isolationist, these denominations did not, for example, perceive lodges and secret societies as enemies or competitors of the church; their pietism closely paralleled the value system of the dominant Anglo-Saxon Protestant society; their theologies were less authoritarian or creedal. They were willing to join hands with others in joint endeavors. This meant that for many persons in these churches attachment to things German was comparatively fragile or superficial and that church membership was no hindrance to full assimilation into American society. For others it meant that there was no religious hindrance to full participation in the activities of German societies which stressed German character and culture.

Persons whose bonds with German culture centered in secular societies have been identified as *Vereinsdeutschen* —"club Germans."[24] In contrast to the church people, most of whom lived in rural areas and small towns and who were conservative in their religious, economic, and political beliefs, the club Germans were oriented toward secular values and attitudes. Overwhelmingly urban in residence, they demonstrated a tendency to be liberal or even radical in their politics. Most significantly, they seemed to value, defend, and promote German language and culture as ends in themselves.

The secular organizations were even more diverse than the churches. They included singing societies, shooting clubs, card clubs, fire companies, and vereins for veterans of the German army, to name but a few. Benevolent associations were common. Initially organized as immigrant aid societies, they undertook extensive programs for the assistance of the impoverished in the decades before the first World War. A multitude of mutual benefit societies, much like those maintained by church people, developed in the big cities. Cincinnati alone had as many as seventy in 1915. They were especially important to the laboring classes, who depended upon their insurance-like programs, but there were also clubs for the social elite, such as the Liederkranz in Saint Louis and the Germania Society in Baltimore. In some organizations the cultural emphasis was very strong as in the German-American historical societies, which seemed devoted to the discovery and praise of the great deeds of Germans in this country. In several cities reading societies sprang up whose main goal was the development of subscription libraries of German books. There were also associations of German physicians, lawyers, teachers, editors and publishers, businessmen, brewers, and artisans of various kinds. Still other societies were organized on the basis of the German state or province from which immigrants had come. There were clubs for Hessians, Badenese, Bavarians, Swabians, and many others. The *German-American Address Book* for 1916–1917 lists 6,586 societies in the United States, exclusive of the churches and their innumerable parish organizations.[25]

Some societies were strictly local while others were nationally organized. The most famous of the latter was the association of Turner societies. Brought to this country by the Forty-eighters, the *Turnvereine* had been deeply involved in programs of cultural maintenance. By 1900, however, they had gradually evolved into social organizations for lower-middle class persons. Similarly, a variety of German fraternal orders and secret societies had been established in the mid-nineteenth century. The most famous were the Sons of Hermann and the Order of the Harugari and all pursued goals explicitly related to cultural nationalism. They were of the same spirit that led to the founding of the National German-American Alliance in 1901, an association which by 1917 had come to symbolize for the American people all that was arrogant and distasteful about German ethnocentrism.[26]

For many urban German immigrants, the vereins provided the same kind of social function that churches afforded the *Kirchendeutschen.* The ethnic lodge frequently stood in lieu of a church, especially for the free-thinker. Elaborate club houses and halls were often erected. Some had facilities for theatrical productions, concerts, classes and lectures, celebrations, and bazaars. A variety of services was provided. Food and drink were often served; indeed, profits from the sale of beer kept many vereins on sound financial bases.

Most vereins drew heavily for their memberships from the ranks of the lower middle class: skilled craftsmen, factory workers, clerks, petty merchants, and the less prestigious professional persons. Frequently uncommitted in politics and religion, they cared little about the process of assimilation into American society. They read German-language newspapers, for example, because it was convenient to do so. Their devotion to German culture frequently did not transcend an appreciation for traditional food and drink.[27]

The German-American elite, defined as those persons who enjoyed noteworthy social and economic success, found little in the vereins to attract them. While these better-educated and more richly talented persons would often retain memberships in some of the clubs, they rarely gave them leadership. As upwardly mobile persons, they were generally more interested in developing contacts with established society than in maintaining their bonds with a disintegrating ethnic group. The result was that leadership positions often fell to persons who had recently immigrated, persons for whom German culture remained intensely important.[28]

It is possible to draw too sharp a line of distinction between the church Germans and the club Germans. Not all the societies, of course, were antipathetic to religious institutions. It was more often the other way around. A verein was unacceptable to the church Germans to the extent that it partook of the heritage of the Forty-eighters. That is to say, if the vereins were anticlerical, rationalist, politically active, liberal, or radical; if they tended to give precedence to cultural and social values over religious values; if they advocated German-language instruction in the public schools and opposed parochial schools; or if their leadership and constituency included large numbers of turners and lodge members, then the church Germans were likely to look elsewhere for their associations. Among Catholics, Lutherans, and Mennonites the proportions of persons who also affiliated with one or more of the secular societies were small, probably not more than a fifth. In other German Protestant churches the percentages were significantly higher. At the same time many persons of German stock, perhaps a third of the total, were either apathetic or hostile to both the churches and the vereins and their efforts to organize immigrants on an ethnic basis. No doubt most of these were second-generation Germans who were assimilating rapidly and felt no personal needs for ethnic associational activity.[29]

Despite the great diversity of the German-American population, it had a semblance of unity that was provided primarily by the German-language press. By the 1890s, there were nearly 800 German-language newspapers and journals published in the United States, most of them weeklies. By the time the United States entered the war in 1917, the number had dropped to 522, but even that figure was nearly as great as that of all other foreign-language publications in America combined.[30]

The tone of the German-American press had undergone a subtle change in the years since the 1880s when the immigration had reached its peak. Earlier the German-language press had been highly effective as an agent of Americanization. It had explained American ways to the newcomers and had kept them informed of developments in America, thereby easing their adjustment to life in a strange land. In most respects, the German-language press had differed little in form, style, and even content from English-language publications. But as the years passed, the editors and publishers of many of the more important papers, often persons who were themselves Forty-eighters or who shared their liberal attitudes, were replaced by recruits from Imperial Germany. Much less critical of the Fatherland, the later editors tended to include more news about Germany and often attempted to explain the conduct of the German government and its Kaiser in a favorable light. Expressions of Anglophobia likewise increased. The cultural chauvinism of the earlier period was gradually replaced by a more nationalistic strain.[31]

This shift in emphasis from the American to the German was reinforced by economic factors. Like the churches and the vereins, the German-American press depended upon a steady influx of immigrants. When this source of readers declined sharply after 1890, the newspapers endeavored to sustain a readership among second-generation Germans, few of whom were dependent in a linguistic sense on the German language. The device used by the papers to hold readers was the promotion of German-Americanism, that is, a self-conscious identity as participants in a subsociety equipped with a complete institutional structure expressive of what was perceived to be a superior culture. Thus, in the years before World War I, the German-language press tended to give full, uncritical support to the organizations of the ethnic community, to German opera and theater, to any and all efforts toward the maintenance of language and culture, and to political measures and movements that could be identified broadly as in the German-American interest.[32]

Such efforts were mutually beneficial to the press and the societies. But they seemed to suggest a cohesion that had little basis in fact. An appearance of institutional health was substituted for what in reality was extensive internal division and erosion.[33] In a sense, the German ethnic community was feeding upon itself in order to sustain a considerable economic investment. This was a perfectly natural phenomenon, made possible by the great size of the German population in America.

Other German-American institutions were similarly affected. Proprietors of beer gardens and restaurants, teachers of the German language in public schools, butchers and bakers and shopkeepers, musicians, and clergymen with ethnic clienteles expected to benefit by the maintenance of German identity and by a corresponding slowing of the Americanization process.

Germans have often been the butt of jokes about the high level of their associational activity. Yet their behavior was no different from that of other immigrant groups. At first the enclaves—the high concentrations of immigrant peoples—tended to be integrated on the basis of kinship and acquaintance. Their societies were communally organized and were relatively undifferentiated and stable. But Americanization subsequently brought about a dispersion of the immigrants and their children. As a result, they had to create a network of voluntary associations, usually integrated on the basis of occupation or social status, if ethnic relationships were to be sustained in a mobile society.[34]

That the Germans of the early twentieth century seemed separatistic, clannish, and overorganized, or that they apparently resisted Americanization was not reflective of a national characteristic or ethnic trait. Rather it was related to the numbers in which they came to America, to their religious, linguistic, political, and social diversity, and to the composition and development of the receiving American society at the time when most of the Germans arrived. As the largest non-English speaking ethnic group in nineteenth-century America, the Germans had the numbers to permit a rich range of societies reflective of German heterogeneity. Moreover, as the size and vigor of ethnic voluntary associations increased, so did their capacity for the perpetuation of ethnic identification. German slowness to assimilate was thus primarily a sociological rather than a cultural phenomenon.

And yet culture was a part of it. Many Germans could not forget that they came from a land which they remembered as having a superior culture. This attitude was not mere ethnocentrism. The Germans were the only large nineteenth-century immigrant group in the United States with a cultural heritage equal to the dominant English inheritance. Their literature was superb; German newcomers were proud of Goethe, Lessing, or Schiller even though they may never have read their works. German preeminence in music was unquestioned; Bach, Handel, Haydn, Mozart, and Beethoven were recognized geniuses. German philosophy, as the ordinary immigrant dimly realized, was the more profound because of Leibnitz, Kant, or Hegel. Moreover, he knew that German universities harbored some of the world's foremost scholars and scientists. By contrast, America seemed culturally impoverished. Its schools were decidedly inferior to what the immigrants remembered was standard in Europe. Americans, they thought, were crude, extravagant, materialistic, hypocritical, rootless—quite lacking in the finer qualities of what they called the German spirit.

While it is true that the later German immigrants tended to be less critical of political conditions in the Fatherland than their predecessors had been, it hardly follows that they gave blind approval to the policies and goals of the German Imperial Government. German Lutherans were often intensely anti-Prussian; many of their early leaders had emigrated to escape governmental domination of their church. Catholics, who were the victims of repressive legislation in the 1870s, hardly conceived of Bismarck and the Kaiser as heroes. Few of the thousands of emigrants who had left to escape military service could favor German imperialist ambitions. German Socialists in America were likewise sharp critics of the German government; indeed, some were political refugees. And even those most favorably inclined toward Wilhelmine Germany resented its discouragement and partial prohibition of emigration after the turn of the century.

Few German-Americans ever imagined that American institutions should be remodeled along German lines. Although some of the more nationalistic of their leaders, notably editors of the secular press and officers of various vereins, relied on Germany as a symbol around which they could rally their disintegrating constituency, the majority of the rank and file, especially the church people, felt no strong loyalty for the German government. They had a natural affection for the old country; their friends and relatives continued to live there; and they earnestly desired that America would be able to maintain peaceful if not friendly relations with Germany. But their political allegiance belonged to the United States of America.

The sentiments of most German-Americans were summed up in the aphorism "Germania our mother; Columbia our bride." It was not necessary, they insisted, for a

man to forsake his mother in order to be loyal to his bride.
To use the German language and to cherish German literature, art, and philosophy had nothing to do with Germany
as a political unit. Loyalty to the United States was not
remotely involved. But a few arrogant German-Americans
insisted that their Americanism was best expressed
through the maintenance of German culture and ideals.
America was the land of the free, they asserted; it was a
place where each citizen could develop his own individual-
ity without interference. By cultivating his superior ethi-
cal, artistic, religious, and philosophic ideals, they argued,
the German could contribute to the future higher civilization of America.[35]

The rhetoric of German-American leaders in the early
twentieth century contained frequent assertions of deeply
felt patriotism. Chauvinism was apparent, but it was
uniquely American. For example, some believed that the
American Revolution could not have been won without the
aid of German patriots; that the Republican party was
founded primarily as a result of German-American efforts;
and that Abraham Lincoln's ancestors were German immigrants named Linkhorn. Such sentiments demonstrated
that the Germans yearned for a share in the American historical tradition. By exaggerating the importance of Germans in the American past they were compensating for the
increasing exclusionist attitudes of native Americans as
the nineteenth century drew to a close.[36]

The German-American historical societies, which encouraged these grotesque distortions of the past, were thus
ethnic equivalents of the Daughters of the American Revolution, the Colonial Dames of America, and similar organizations founded by native Americans during the latter part
of the nineteenth century. The Germans were keenly sensitive to what they considered to be slights of their "contributions" to American greatness. They resented the fact that
native Americans never seemed to appreciate properly
their great accomplishments in this country. More significantly, however, these attitudes demonstrated that the Ger-

mans thought of themselves as Americans, not as so-
journers in a strange land.

It is not surprising that they should have held these
views. German-American society and its institutions as
they existed in 1914 were the products of decades of development in this country. They were made in America. When
the immigrants arrived here, they confronted problems
quite unlike anything they had experienced in Europe; circumstances required them to create novel institutions. Immigrant churches, schools, newspapers, the innumerable
organizations for social, economic, and political action—all
were designed to help immigrant minorities succeed in a
society dominated by persons who spoke a different language and whose customs, traditions, and values were in
some degree different from their own. Appearances to the
contrary, immigrant institutions had few organizational
bonds of any kind in Germany and they engendered no
political loyalty for the Fatherland.

Most Germans thought of themselves as Americans totally loyal to American democratic ideals. Indeed, some
considered themselves better custodians of liberal traditions than the puritanical native-born, who seemed determined to impose on unwilling newcomers their
Anglo-Saxon culture with its threat of prohibition, woman
suffrage, Sabbatarianism, and compulsory education laws.
To the Germans, America was not a nation with a uniform
ethnic identity like France, Italy, or Sweden; it was a pluralistic society consisting of many identities. The English, of
course, were the most numerous and had given their language and political institutions to the United States. But
members of other ethnic groups could be just as genuinely
American as persons with English antecedents. The German-born citizen could value his cultural heritage just as
an Anglo-American cherished his. He felt that he could
read the news in a German-language daily, worship in his
German church, deposit his savings in a German-American bank, bask in the warmth of sociability in a German
beer garden, and sing the old songs in his *Sängerverein*. At

the same time, he could vote and even hold public office with as much intelligence, loyalty, and responsibility as any other citizen. In the German-American's view, his cultural heritage created no special loyalty for the German Imperial Government, nor did it inhibit his capacity for patriotic citizenship in his adopted homeland.

Notes

1. Edward A. Steiner, *On the Trail of the Immigrant* (New York: Fleming H. Revell, 1906), p. 101.
2. U.S., Bureau of the Census, *Historical Statistics of the United States, Colonial Times to 1857* (1960), p. 57.
3. Ibid.; Mack Walker, *Germany and the Emigration, 1816–1885* (Cambridge: Harvard University Press, 1964), pp. 175–94; Maldwyn A. Jones, *American Immigration* (Chicago: University of Chicago Press, 1960), pp. 193–96.
4. U.S., Bureau of the Census, *Historical Statistics,* p. 56.
5. U.S., Bureau of the Census, *Thirteenth Census of the United States: 1910. Population* (1913), 1:875–79; Albert B. Faust, *The German Element in the United States,* 2 vols. (Boston: Houghton Mifflin, 1909), 1:577–91.
6. U.S., Bureau of the Census, *Thirteenth Census,* 1:882–957.
7. Audrey L. Olson, "Saint Louis Germans, 1850–1920: The Nature of an Immigrant Community and Its Relation to the Assimilation Process" (Ph.D. diss., University of Kansas, 1970), p. 47.
8. Edward P. Hutchinson, *Immigrants and Their Children, 1850–1950* (New York: John Wiley, 1956), pp. 123–24.
9. Ibid., p. 177.
10. For English-language examples, see Faust, *German Element,* or Rudolf Cronau, *German Achievements in America* (New York: Rudolf Cronau, 1916).
11. Carl Wittke, *We Who Built America,* rev. ed. (Cleveland: The Press of Western Reserve University, 1964), p. 205f.; Carl Wittke, *Refugees of Revolution: The German Forty-Eighters in America* (Philadelphia: University of Pennsylvania Press, 1920), p. 141; Guido A. Dobbert, "The Disintegration of an Im-

migrant Community: The Cincinnati Germans, 1870–1920" (Ph.D. diss., University of Chicago, 1965), pp. 94–98.

12. The division of the German-American population into groups based on religious and secular values is developed in Heinz Kloss, *Um die Einigung des Deutschamerikanertums: Die Geschichte einer unvollendeten Volksgruppe* (Berlin: Volk und Reich Verlag, 1937). Kloss gives briefer exposition to his conceptual scheme in "German-American Language Maintenance Efforts," *Language Loyalty in the United States,* ed. Joshua Fishman (The Hague: Mouton, 1966), pp. 206–52. As an explicit example of the primacy of religious over ethnic values, note the slogan of the Baltimore *Katholische Volkszeitung,* "First Catholic, then German," in Dieter Cunz, *The Maryland Germans* (Princeton: Princeton University Press, 1948), p. 357.

13. Colman Barry, *The Catholic Church and German Americans* (Washington, D.C.: Catholic University of America Press, 1953); U.S., Bureau of the Census, *Religious Bodies, 1916,* 2 vols. (1919), 2:654.

14. U.S., Bureau of the Census, *Religious Bodies, 1906,* 2 vols. (1910), 1:371, 373.

15. A convenient survey of German Catholic institutions may be found in *Das Buch der Deutschen in Amerika,* ed. Max Heinrici (Philadelphia: Walther's Buchdruckerei, 1909), p. 252f. The modern history of the Central-Verein is treated in Philip Gleason, *The Conservative Reformers: German-American Catholics and the Social Order* (Notre Dame: University of Notre Dame Press, 1968).

16. Cunz, *Maryland Germans,* p. 356.

17. Gleason, *Conservative Reformers,* p. 17.

18. U.S., Bureau of the Census, *Religious Bodies, 1916,* 2:348–415; Abdel R. Wentz, *A Basic History of Lutheranism in America* (Philadelphia: Muhlenberg Press, 1955). See also Sydney E. Ahlstrom, *A Religious History of the American People* (New Haven: Yale University Press, 1972), pp. 756–59.

19. I have developed these ideas further in my essay "The Immigrant Condition as a Factor Contributing to the Conservatism of the Lutheran Church—Missouri Synod," *Concordia Historical Institute Quarterly,* 38 (April 1965): 19–28. See also the series of articles by Heinrich H. Maurer entitled "Studies in the Sociology of Religion: The Sociology of Protestantism," a detailed analysis of the Lutheran Church—Missouri Synod, published in *American Journal of Sociology,* 30 (November 1924): 257–86; 31 (July 1925): 39–57; 31 (January 1926): 485–506; 33 (January 1928): 568–85; and 34 (September 1928): 282–95. The actual number of full-time elementary schools maintained by

the several German Protestant denominations is open to question, since pastors often reported part-time educational agencies as full-fledged parochial schools.

20. U.S., Bureau of the Census, *Religious Bodies, 1916,* 2:306–309,
629–34; Carl E. Schneider, *The German Church in the American Frontier* (Saint Louis: Eden Publishing House, 1939); Heinrici, *Das Buch der Deutschen,* p. 242; Ahlstrom, *Religious
History,* p. 755.

21. U.S., Bureau of the Census, *Religious Bodies, 1916,* 2:153–66,
416–45; C. Henry Smith, *The Coming of the Russian Mennonites* (Berne, Ind.: Mennonite Book Concern, 1927); Ahlstrom,
Religious History, pp. 230–50, 753.

22. U.S., Bureau of the Census, *Religious Bodies, 1916,* 1:76; 2:54,
241, 460–61, 559; Paul F. Douglas, *The Story of German Methodism: Biography of an Immigrant Soul* (New York: Methodist
Book Concern, 1939); Heinrici, *Das Buch der Deutschen,* p. 242.

23. Oscar Handlin, *Adventure in Freedom: Three Hundred Years
of Jewish Life in America* (New York: McGraw-Hill, 1954), p.
122; Moses Rischin, *The Promised City: New York's Jews*
(Cambridge: Harvard University Press, 1962), p. 95f.; Dobbert,
"Cincinnati Germans," p. 260.

24. Kloss, *Um die Einigung,* pp. 20–49.

25. Harry W. Pfund, *A History of the German Society of Pennsyl-
vania* (Philadelphia: German Society of Pennsylvania, 1944);
Dobbert, "Cincinnati Germans," p. 11; Olson, "Saint Louis Ger-
mans," pp. 257, 276; Cunz, *Maryland Germans,* pp. 321–27;
Heinrici, *Das Buch der Deutschen,* p. 682f.; Wittke, *Refugees of
Revolution,* pp. 282, 315; Robert E. Park, *Immigrant Press and
Its Control* (New York: Harper, 1922), p. 128.

26. *Jahrbücher der Deutsch-Amerikanischen Turnerei* contain
much information on the Turner societies. See especially vol.
3 (October 1894): 243–72. Wittke, *Refugees of Revolution,* pp.
151, 156, 283; Wittke, *We Who Built America,* pp. 213–14; Heinrici, *Das Buch der Deutschen,* p. 747.

27. Dobbert, "Cincinnati Germans," p. 279; Wilhelm Hense-Jensen
and Ernest Bruncken, *Wisconsin's Deutsch-Amerikaner bis
zum Schluss des neunzehnten Jahrhunderts,* 2 vols. (Milwaukee: Im Verlage der Deutschen Gesellschaft, 1902), 2:208; Olson, "Saint Louis Germans," p. 162.

28. Hermann Hagedorn, *The Hyphenated Family: An American
Saga* (New York: Macmillan, 1960), p. 42; Dobbert, "Cincinnati
Germans," p. 279; Olson, "Saint Louis Germans," p. 254f.

29. Hense-Jensen and Bruncken, *Wisconsin's Deutsch-Amerikaner,* 2:208; Kloss, "Language Maintenance Efforts," p. 230f.;
Wittke, *Refugees of Revolution,* pp. 122, 134, 137; Olson, "Saint

Louis Germans," pp. 147, 197; Dobbert, "Cincinnati Germans," p. 254f.

30. Park, *Immigrant Press,* p. 310.
31. Ibid., pp. 267, 352f.; Dobbert, "Cincinnati Germans," pp. 49, 163; Carl Wittke, *The German-language Press in America* (Lexington: University of Kentucky Press, 1957), pp. 199–201, 217.
32. Gleason, *Conservative Reformers,* pp. 11, 46; Park, *Immigrant Press,* p. 364f.; Olson, "Saint Louis Germans," p. 112.
33. Dobbert notes that the German-language press deliberately ignored discord within the ethnic community in order to preserve the appearance of unity. "Cincinnati Germans," pp. 266–70.
34. Guido A. Dobbert, "German-Americans between New and Old Fatherland, 1870–1914," *American Quarterly,* 19 (Winter 1967):663–80. Olson, "Saint Louis Germans," analyzes the horizontal mobility of Germans within the city.
35. For example, see Julius Goebel, *Der Kampf um deutsche Kultur in Amerika* (Leipzig: Verlag der Durr'schen Buchhandlung, 1914), pp. 11–13.
36. Dobbert, "Cincinnati Germans," pp. 11, 89, 92; Julius Goebel, *Das Deutschtum in den Vereingten Staaten von Nord-Amerika* (Munich: J. F. Lehmanns Verlag, 1904), p. 59 n.; Faust, *German Element,* 2:475; Oscar Handlin, *The American People in the Twentieth Century* (Boston: Beacon Press, 1963), p. 80.

CHAPTER THREE

The Sauerkraut Question

The image German immigrants held of themselves as citizens of the American democracy bore slight resemblance to the stereotypes through which Americans perceived them. Americans naturally caricatured all ethnic groups, investing each with traits that appeared unusual or dramatically different from commonly accepted values or standards of behavior. The Germans were no exception.

Hugo Muensterberg, an eminent psychologist who was a professor at Harvard during the prewar decades, described an incident that illustrates the tenacity with which an American friend clung to one stereotype of the German. Muensterberg had been a guest at a luncheon featuring German food, including sauerkraut. The German-born Muensterberg confessed that he had never before seen or tasted the stuff. His host, who had never been outside the United States, replied that Muensterberg evidently knew nothing of Germany, since sauerkraut, as everyone knows, is the favorite dish of every Prussian.[1]

The sauerkraut question, unimportant in itself, symbolizes the larger differences of perception between natives and immigrants and the ways in which their cultures clashed socially and politically. Of course, there was no uniform or consistent content to the stereotype of the German. Wealthy and educated Americans, for example, generally registered more favorable impressions than did the lower classes. Their exposures to German immigrants were often either superficial or limited to favorable circumstances. Rarely rubbing shoulders with ordinary newcomers, these Americans more often encountered persons who, like themselves, were educated and successful and who had adapted quickly to American ways and attitudes. Thus cultural friction, the source of negative impressions, was minimized for them.

Upper-class impressions of the Germans were also conditioned by the preeminence of German universities and learning in the nineteenth century. While images of Germany, its people, and institutions must be distinguished from ideas about German-Americans, the former were rarely separated from the latter except in rigorous or analytical thought. The vast majority of the nearly ten thousand Americans who studied in German universities in the nineteenth century were deeply influenced by their European experiences. They discovered a quality of scholarship, a depth of thought, and an appreciation of learning and academic freedom that led them to place Germany on a cultural pedestal. When they returned to America, they brought with them well-developed notions of how universities should be organized and operated, how research should be conducted, and how books should be written.[2]

The German-trained American scholars often commented on their high regard for German culture. From the historian George Bancroft, one of the first Americans to study in Germany, to the economist Richard T. Ely, most perceived the German mind as intellectually independent, utterly systematic and thorough in method, and rigorous in the development of ideas. Admiration for German forms spread as Americans imported the concept of the university as a research-oriented institution. Johns Hopkins University, founded in 1876, was based frankly on the German model, and such leaders in higher education as Andrew Dickson White of Cornell, Nicholas Murray Butler of Columbia, and Charles W. Eliot of Harvard, repeatedly expressed their indebtedness to the German example.[3]

As the nineteenth century drew to a close, the warm regard for the German university began to cool. The growing distrust stemmed in part from the recognition that German scholarship was also authoritarian, elitist, and ponderous, if not pompous. Some American students began to feel that the Germans lacked a sense of beauty and that their emphasis on specialization might actually result in the elevation of minutiae. At the same time, many American employers of academic talent, especially those associated with denominational colleges, found that the products of German universities were unduly skeptical in their theology. Suspicion was augmented by the belief that drinking and fencing were traditional and common among German students. Such behavior clashed with the pietistic attitudes of nativist Protestants whose program of coercive reform climaxed in the enactment of nationwide prohibition during the World War I period.[4]

The ordinary American of the nineteenth century, however, had little contact with the products of German universities and still less with their books or essays. He gained his impressions of things German chiefly from the immigrants who lived next door or on a nearby farm, worked in the same factory, shopped in his store, clipped his beard, repaired his shoes, or deposited savings in his bank.

Perhaps the most prominent elements in the American stereotype of German immigrants were industriousness, thrift, and honesty—admirable virtues in the American value system. Despite a frequently noted tendency toward ethnic separatism, the newcomers fitted into American society easily and well. The German was apparently strongly attached to his family; he was orderly, disciplined, stable. A bit too authoritarian by American standards, he was nonetheless admired for his ability to achieve material success through hard work. Similarly attractive was his minor reputation for mechanical ingenuity. The Germans were usually perceived as an intelligent people, though somewhat plodding in their mental processes. And if they tended to be unimaginatively thorough, they sometimes also seemed extraordinarily stubborn and graceless in manner.

Unlike the educated elite of Germany, who may indeed have been famed for their rationality, the German-American farmer or laborer was better known for his emotionalism and sentimentality.[5]

The German *Hausfrau* was commonly recognized as a model of cleanliness and efficiency and her daughter was valued as a reliable house servant or maid. While some native Americans thought the Germans treated their women badly, on the whole they considered these newcomers desirable additions to the American population. German immigrants seemed to have many of the same qualities they associated with themselves.

Although some Americans were impressed by the apparent ease with which most German immigrants fit into American society, others felt that the Germans were unwarrantably proud of their origins and culture. The native-born could not understand why they seemed to retain their loyalty to their Fatherland (had they not deserted it for a better land?), to their language (a guttural, unlovely speech), and to their religions (even German Protestantism was either unseemly in its enthusiasm or unbearably liturgical and dogmatic). Ignorant of the sociology of immigration, some Americans concluded that clannishness was an ethnic characteristic and that the Germans were naturally exclusive as well as arrogant.

Americans had ambivalent feelings about German festivities. It seemed as though the Germans had a celebration for every occasion, complete with parades and contests both athletic and cultural. They danced and sang and recited poetry. Even their church affairs often took on a festive air. And they consumed vast quantities of beer. All this was delightful and admirable to some Americans, who freely admitted that the Germans taught them to enjoy life. But others were distressed, for such behavior smacked of hedonism, immorality, and a remarkably degenerate sense of values. They were especially offended by the abandoned dancing and boorish swilling of beer that occurred on the Sabbath, the day God had wisely set aside for worship, rest, and spiritual contemplation.[6]

Clashes between native and immigrant cultures produced some of the most potent political issues of the late nineteenth century. Although many German immigrants were interested in political reform, economic development, and the tariff and currency questions, they responded more strongly to issues related to ethnocultural conflict. In addition to political and economic liberties they wanted social and cultural freedom. They deeply resented the efforts of some Americans to impose upon them by political means a morality foreign to their own heritage.

By the 189Cs prohibition had become the dominant political manifestation of cultural conflict. Advocates of coercive reform throughout the country were fighting for temperance legislation. They sought prohibition by state constitutional amendment as the ideal; where that was impossible, county-option laws and Sunday-closing ordinances were substituted as transitional measures. Woman suffrage was also wielded as a formidable weapon by the prohibitionists. It received great support not merely because Americans were influenced by the arguments of the feminists but also because the extension of the franchise to women would double the political power of those sturdy defenders of Anglo-Saxon Protestant culture who saw their value system threatened by hordes of immigrants, of whom the Germans were the most numerous. Prohibitionists assumed that because of the role most immigrant groups ascribed to their women, the size of the ethnic vote would not be correspondingly enlarged.

Efforts to enforce conformity occurred in education as well. Economic conditions had often caused immigrant parents to put their children to work at ages when, by American standards, they should have been in school. American political philosophy assumed that democracy could not function without a literate citizenry. It was therefore doubly important for immigrant children to be in school, learning the English language and American ways. Even more threatening to the nativist mind was the growth of parochial schools among Catholics and German Lutherans, especially since the 1880s. It seemed that such foreign-language institutions could only perpetuate alien cultures and delay the process by which the immigrant young could become useful citizens, that is to say, perceive political issues in the same terms as the native-born. In the early 1890s, many states considered and several legislatures enacted compulsory school attendance laws along with legislation aimed at regulating parochial schools. The combined effect of prohibition, woman suffrage, Sabbatarianism, and education legislation was a remarkable, though temporary, degree of unity among German-American voters under the Democratic banner during the 1890s.[7]

Ethnocultural politics was not without its impact on nativist attitudes. Awareness of ethnic group identities was greatly intensified among immigrants and nativists alike. Thinking in stereotypes and symbols was encouraged; tolerance and understanding diminished. The live-and-let-live attitudes common in earlier decades were weakened by organized political action. Richard Bartholdt, a German-born Republican congressman from Missouri, expressed the point of view of the immigrants: "New organizations grew up like mushrooms, just as if the devil had traveled over the country and sown poisoned seeds everywhere. There were those who wanted to put up bars against immigration, others crusaded against the good cheer of the social cup. The Puritans begrudged us our laughter and innocent enjoyments because they want all pleasures postponed until we get to heaven."[8] Perhaps the most publicized organization was the stridently anti-Catholic American Protective Association, which during its brief life in the 1890s experienced an extraordinary growth. Its contemporary, the Immigration Restriction League, was more effective among the elite. Both groups were popularly associated with the Republican party. The activities of these and similar organizations stimulated the growth of many religious and ethnic associations, which made new efforts to unite their constituencies on a national scale and to expand their political activities. Among these were the Personal Rights League, the Immigration Protective League, and the National German-American Alliance.

Nativist antipathies for German immigrants were augmented also by the activities of socialist labor agitators in
the industrial centers of the North and East. These persons,
who achieved notoriety during the labor strife of the 1880s,
especially in Chicago's Haymarket Riot, were German-
born almost to the man. Nor was the image of the German-
Americans enhanced by the apostles of anarchism, of
whom Johann Most was the best known. Such purveyors of
alien ideologies were inevitably typed as threats to American democratic values.

Changes in American attitudes toward race and ethnicity
at the end of the century further encouraged the tendency
to sort out and identify the separate components of the immigrant stream. Americans in the past maintained their
confidence in the ability of their fluid, cosmopolitan society
to absorb and transform all newcomers into a distinctively
American type. Though the virus of xenophobia occasionally swept the land, as in the Know-Nothing era of the
1850s, it had not generally led Americans to identify ethnic
causes for the evils or threats they perceived. Their habit
of mind was altered as enormous numbers of immigrants
arrived in the 1880s and as the sources of emigration
shifted from Protestant, Teutonic, and Scandinavian nations of Europe to Latin, Slavic, Catholic, and Jewish peoples.

This attitudinal evolution was fostered by the thinking of
some of the most respected social scientists of the day. In
general, their study of the immigration question led them
to conclude that socially undesirable characteristics were
hereditary or inborn and were more common among some
ethnic nativity groups than others. The qualities, both positive and negative, of each ethnic group were thus thought
to be fixed or rigid. Armed with this biological assumption,
many of these men began to demand a curtailment of the
nation's free immigration policy by means of a literacy test.

Still, as such ideas gained currency during the 1890s and
the first decades of the twentieth century, the German-
Americans fared well among American intellectuals. A
few made unfavorable comments: Francis Amasa Walker,

an eminent statistician, demographer, and educator, grumbled about "wretched beer guzzlers"; Richmond Mayo-Smith, a well-known sociologist, deplored German-American views on liquor consumption, socialism, and anarchism. As a general rule, however, the educated elite of America considered the Germans a desirable people. Prescott Hall of the Immigration Restriction Society reflected the common view, which was based on presumably scientific notions of Aryan or Teutonic superiority. Did Americans, he asked, "want this country to be peopled by British, German, and Scandinavian stock, historically free, energetic, progressive, or by Slav, Italian, and Asiatic races, historically down-trodden, atavistic, and stagnant?"[9] Similar sentiments found expression in the writings of such commentators as Josiah Strong, Edward A. Ross, John R. Commons, Henry Cabot Lodge, and Woodrow Wilson.

American historians swelled the chorus. While Edward Channing did not hesitate to endow separate nationalities with distinctive character traits, others such as Albert Bushnell Hart taught that the Teutonic race, broadly defined, combined the greatest love of personal freedom with the greatest respect for law. No scholar championed the Germans more vigorously than John W. Burgess. Once a student at the University of Göttingen, Burgess insisted that the German element, which in his definition included the Dutch and the Scandinavians, was the most numerous group in the United States. He considered the Germans the elite of Caucasian peoples, unique in their application of reason to political activities. Even Frederick Jackson Turner, who had fought Teutonist notions as a student at Johns Hopkins, wrote that German-Americans contributed "a conservatism and steady persistence and solidarity useful in moderating the nervous energy of the Native Americans."[10]

The assumptions undergirding such views of race and ethnicity received their fullest development in the famous reports of the Immigration Commission, popularly known as the Dillingham Commission, after the senator who served as its chairman. Created by an act of Congress in 1907, it sponsored a comprehensive analysis of immigrant peoples in the United States; its findings, published in 1911, filled forty-one impressive volumes.[11] The commission accumulated an immense quantity of data, most of it based on the assumption that country of origin was the most important variable associated with immigrant life in America. If a particular ethnic group consistently ranked low on a variety of criteria, one could assume that it was biologically inferior to other races and that immigration from the country in question ought to be restricted. Ethnicity was related in this way to illiteracy, crime, disease, occupation, income, and a host of other factors. Even though the amassed data did not warrant it, the commission concluded that peoples from western and northern Europe, including the German-born, ranked higher than immigrants from southern and eastern Europe. The idea that Teutonic peoples, Germans among them, were superior to others now seemed grounded on scientific evidence.[12]

Other studies lent further support to the favorable estimate of Germans in America. According to the census of 1910, the male-to-female ratio among German immigrants was the most desirable of all ethnic groups save the Irish. In a Nebraska study, the Germans were shown to have had the highest percentage of all nationalities in the completion of naturalization proceedings. The illiteracy rate among Germans during the first decade of the twentieth century was 5.1 percent compared to 26.7 percent for all immigrants. Another study showed that 25.8 percent of German immigrants owned their own homes compared to 5.7 percent of the native-born. Similarly, the income of the German-born among 10,000 males eighteen years of age and over averaged $613 per year, compared to $595 for the native-born. A study of Boston's immigrants indicated that the proportion of Germans in the city's almshouses was half that of the English. Moreover, the Germans had the lowest incidence of alcoholism of all north European peoples. German-American tendency toward crime, the sociologist Edward A. Ross reported, was about the same as that of the native-born population—slightly below average for crimes of violence, slightly above average for crimes involving gainful offenses.[13]

Perhaps the most favorable picture of the German-Americans in the literature of the day appeared in the *American Journal of Sociology* in 1916.[14] Extraordinarily naive by modern standards, this ostensibly scientific study is valuable for the summation it provides of stereotypic thinking in the World War I era. The author, Howard Woolston, sought to rate ten ethnic groups on the basis of ten personal traits, none of which was defined in any way. Ratings were gathered from sociologists, psychologists, journalists, and social workers. On the basis of this data, Woolston devised an overall rating for each ethnic group in which native Americans placed first and Germans second, ahead of the English. Germans were ranked first in self-control, moral integrity, and perseverance; second in physical vigor, intellectual ability, cooperation, and efficiency. Not surprising is the fact that Negroes were rated last in every category save sympathy, a place assigned to the English. As part of a society that was thinking increasingly in terms of race, German-Americans inevitably received these statistics with much satisfaction. Hard data again seemed to validate their own notions of ethnic superiority. The benign climate of opinion encouraged them to push their claims with new boldness.

But the Anglo-American race thinkers of the day were hardly prepared to accept the Germans as their equals. While it was assumed that both the Germans and English descended from the same noble barbarians who roamed the forests of northern Europe, the latter-day Anglo-Saxon was identified as the finest product of the evolutionary process. Just as plants and animals were engaged in a struggle for existence in which the fittest survived and the weak were purged, so races and civilizations competed with one another to preserve the best biological and cultural elements and to eliminate or subjugate the inferior. Especially after the Spanish-American War, the attitudes of Anglophiles spread in a way that had been impossible earlier when there was a residue of anti-British feeling from the revolutionary and early national experience. Many Americans of English antecedents joined in a new effort to discover the Anglo-Saxon origins of their culture. The Brahmin leadership of New England participated most strongly in this refined form of ancestor worship.[15]

Anglo-Americans thus indulged in a cultural chauvinism much like that of the Germans and the other immigrant groups. But there was a difference. Because Americans of English origin had always been numerically dominant, their assertions of cultural superiority implied that their own way of living defined what was American, and that all newcomers were expected to conform to these standards. As the historian Oscar Handlin has pointed out, the demand for Anglo-American conformity rested on the assumption that a distinctively American style of life actually existed, and that social and cultural homogeneity was desirable.[16] By contrast, Americans of an earlier day had tended to see themselves as a new people whose character was not fixed but was emerging from the blend of many peoples in the new environment of America. Naturally immigrants from non-English-speaking countries were easily aroused by the changing attitudes. Each new sign of resurgent nativism or Anglo-Saxon superiority evoked an equally militant immigrant response.

Reactions were especially common among the Germans in America. Although other ethnic groups behaved similarly, the Germans, because of their numbers and distribution, received much more public attention. The proliferation of local alliances, leagues, lodges, and German-language publications was accompanied by the appearance of numerous German immigrant reminiscences and histories, including the famed two-volume work by Albert B. Faust, *The German Element in the United States,* first published in 1909 as the winner of a prize offered by a wealthy Chicago woman for the best monograph on Germans in America.[17] German-American cultural chauvinism of the prewar period was further manifested by local societies that erected statues of Goethe, Schiller, and other German cultural figures in the public parks of American cities.

Meanwhile the political involvement of the innumerable social, cultural, and economic agencies of the German-American community broadened to encompass action on a national scale. Ethno-political issues usually had been limited to the local and state level. But with the systematic agitation for national immigration restriction in the 1890s and the stronger, more urgent demands for national prohibition and woman suffrage in the early 1900s, some Germans felt obliged to organize their group on a similar scale. Thus the National German-American Alliance was founded in 1901 and received a national charter from Congress in 1907. Political action even began to cross ethnic lines as, for example, when the National German-American Alliance signed an agreement in 1907 with the Ancient Order of Hibernians to oppose all forms of immigration restriction being considered by Congress.[18]

Native Americans noticed the change and invented a term to describe it—"hyphenism." Hyphenated expressions such as "Irish-American" or "German-American" had been current for decades. In ordinary usage they had been neutral in tone and simply referred to specific ethnic identities in American society. At most they implied a distinctive way of life, different from the native American style, but tolerable nonetheless. Gradually, however, these labels acquired a pejorative nuance. As early as 1894 Theodore Roosevelt proclaimed that this nation had no need for German-Americans, but for Americans only. As he used the hyphen, it signified divided political loyalties, as though the pursuit of ethnic group goals was somehow un-American and based on a deep-seated political loyalty to the immigrants' native land. More than any other public figure, Roosevelt popularized the term "hyphenate" to refer to immigrants whose sense of ethnic identity remained strong and "hyphenism" as the pursuit of ethnopolitical goals of allegedly un-American character. "Some Americans need hyphens in their names," thundered TR, "because only part of them have come over. But when the whole man has come over, heart and thought and all, the hyphen drops of its own weight out of his name."[19]

Charles Nagel of Saint Louis, who had served as secretary of commerce and labor in the Taft Administration, advised his fellow German-Americans in 1915 to avoid using the hyphen whenever possible "because the transition from the descriptive sense to a doubtful purpose is so easy." While Nagel supported societies "calculated to keep alive traditions, sweet customs, language or songs" of Germany, he declined membership in any organization that savored of politics. He resented the Rooseveltian usage of the term "German-American" to represent dual allegiance, yet he shared fully TR's conviction that the American citizens of German origin should never segregate themselves politically.[20] Despite the new American sensitivity to hyphenism, German immigrants in the main continued to enjoy high levels of acceptance, probably because of the huge numbers of Italians, Poles, Russian Jews, and other "new immigrants" whose variance from native American norms was much greater than their own.

American estimates of Imperial Germany, by contrast, steadily deteriorated during the prewar decades. Public sentiment in America had been decidedly pro-German in 1870 when Bismarck used his momentous victories over the French to create the German Empire. But thereafter friction developed as both Germany and the United States underwent rapid industrialization. There was competition, not only in manufactured goods, but in foodstuffs as well. In 1879 Germany erected tariff barriers against a variety of American goods. A series of retaliatory measures led to the virtual exclusion of allegedly contaminated American meats from German markets, to the distinct irritation of the American government.[21]

In 1890, the aggressive young Kaiser Wilhelm II put his venerable warhorse of a chancellor, Bismarck, to pasture and guided Germany on a new course—a militaristic, imperialistic *Weltpolitik* not unlike the ambitious policies of other major powers of the time. International friction was inevitable. American and German interests had already clashed in the Samoan Islands of the South Pacific more than a decade earlier, resulting in distrust and suspicion. In American eyes Germany had exercised raw power in a high-handed fashion. This image was later strengthened by German activity in China and the Philippines. In 1898, when a German fleet was dispatched to Manila Bay, allegedly to protect German interests during the Spanish-American War, diplomatic relations between the two nations were strained nearly to the breaking point. A series of German actions in the Caribbean several years later intensified American distrust and dislike of German diplomacy and military methods. In a debt collection controversy with Venezuela in 1904, Americans generally suspected that those Teutonic intruders had as their real objective the permanent occupation of South American territory, despite disclaimers by the Germans. Rumors of a German plot in Brazil further excited these fears. The large number of German immigrants to the southern provinces of Santa Catarina and Rio Grande do Sul were presumably to serve as a nucleus for the Germanization of Brazil. According to some American Cassandras, including Secretary of War Elihu Root, Germany intended to seize these provinces and convert them into German protectorates at some future date when the United States was distracted by a foreign war.[22]

American suspicions thrived on the belief that the German government regularly made secret use of German immigrant organizations in America and elsewhere to achieve its imperialistic goals. Even John Hay, secretary of state under Presidents McKinley and Roosevelt, was convinced that paid German agents organized societies in America for the specific purpose of substituting German imperialism for American democratic ideals.[23] The alleged coordinating agency in Germany for this conspiratorial activity was the Pan-German League. Capitalizing on a growing hatred of Britain at the end of the nineteenth century, the League endeavored to unite the fanatic fringes of German superpatriotism. By 1901, it had attracted a membership of 21,000 persons, most of whom were small businessmen, academics, physicians, lawyers, and other professionals. The organization was a symptom rather than a cause of the extreme nationalism of the times. Its publications and sponsored lectures emphasized above all the racial and cultural kinship of Germans everywhere, and they promoted a loyalty to the state based on the crudest forms of racism. While the Pan-German League applauded Germany's superior achievements, it also deplored alleged weaknesses in the armed might of the nation and demanded improvements. The League was vociferous in agitating for a colonial empire, for a bigger navy, for the preservation of German language and culture in the German diaspora, and for the sword as the means to defend national honor.[24]

In the American view the Pan-German League was a gigantic propaganda machine distributing millions of tracts and newspapers to German expatriates, polluting their loyalty to their adoptive homelands and converting them into sinister agents for German world domination—all at the behest of the German Imperial Government. Yet there is no documentary evidence to confirm a connection between the League and the official regime. Indeed, the latter dismissed the superpatriots as unimportant but noisy nuisances. In 1909 Count von Bernstorff, the German ambassador to the United States, denounced the "flights of fancy of the so-called Pan-Germanists" who "stir up ill-feeling abroad against Germany by putting forth questions and aims which are quite beyond the scope of practical politics." As for its propaganda efforts in the United States, League records show that the high point was reached in 1910 when 200 free copies of its weekly journal, the *Alldeut-*

sche Blätter, were sent to sixteen American communities, almost all of which were the locations of small German Lutheran colleges or preparatory schools.[25] Ridiculed by progressive elements of German society, the Pan-German League was no more representative of German public opinion and no more influential with the German government than was the John Birch Society with the American government in the 1960s.

To say that French, English, and American writers grossly exaggerated the importance of the Pan-German League is not to deny the existence of a strong spirit of chauvinistic nationalism in Germany in the prewar period. It was there just as it was in France, England, and the United States. Moreover, it was mobilized effectively by other organizations such as the Navy League, founded in 1898 by Admiral von Tirpitz. That organization enlisted a million members during its first decade and won the ardent support of Germany's vastly important industrial elite. Yet American perceptions were as important as the German reality. When German-American associations such as the National Alliance undertook to organize themselves for effective political action in domestic as well as foreign affairs, many American citizens naturally linked them and their political goals with Pan-Germanism.

The German *Weltpolitik* was also served by racist notions. Just as some native Americans rummaged through their Anglo-Saxon heritage for past glories, so many Germans sought "scientific" explanation for what they perceived to be the transcendent superiority of their "race" and its culture. Others supposed that war waged by culturally preeminent nations like Germany against inferior peoples (the Poles and the French, among others) was vital for the advancement of civilization. Thus, the German war machine, dignified as the hand maiden of progress, began to rival eminent figures of German culture as the great source of national pride.[26]

During the two decades before the war, Germany repeatedly enlarged its army and navy, but not without notice in the American press. Earlier, in the nineteenth century, Americans had tended to interpret German military prowess as a favorable aspect of national efficiency and strength. But now they were sharply critical of German militarism with its compulsory service, its unbending rules and regulations, and its disciplinary excesses. Americans were not impressed by a *Kultur* that approved of brutalities inflicted by army officers on soldiers for trivial offenses. Moreover, editorial comment frequently noted contrasts between the German and American political ideologies. In the German system, it was observed, the individual existed for the state, while in America a democratic government existed for the protection and development of the individual.[27]

For Americans the symbol of German autocracy, imperialism, and militarism was Kaiser Wilhelm II. He behaved the way nationalistic Germans of the time expected their monarch to behave: punctilious in manner, resplendently uniformed, and ceremonial as a peacock. The Emperor seemed to be a latter-day exponent of the divine right of kings. Though he regarded himself as "the instrument of the Lord" he was more often a cross to be borne by German diplomacy. American newspapers caricatured him savagely, elaborating upon his Jehovah complex. His pronouncements on militarism and imperialism were usually greeted with suspicion or sarcasm. There seemed to be no niche in the American value system for what the Kaiser symbolized, no tolerance for manners so different.[28]

Wilhelm II and his ministers were quite aware of this debasement in American opinion and they made some efforts to repair the image. German ambassadors to Washington were carefully chosen for their abilities and for their understanding of and sympathy for the United States. Exchange professorships between Harvard, Columbia, and the University of Berlin were created. A statue of Frederick the Great was presented to the American government and artifacts from German museums were donated to American colleges and universities. Prominent American citizens were received ostentatiously at the German court. A minor vessel in the German navy was christened "Alice Roosevelt." The initial bid in this policy of smiles and bouquets was the highly publicized visit of Prince Henry, the Emperor's brother, on a good-will tour of the United States in 1902. But Americans were suspicious of Germans bearing gifts and the prince's benevolent words fell most softly on German-American ears. As an attempt to counter the growing estrangement between the two countries, the royal mission was a failure, along with the rest of the Kaiser's "American policy."[29]

American perceptions of Imperial Germany became most negative during the years immediately preceding the outbreak of hostilities in 1914. The leadership of the Pan-German League had passed to persons more militant and superpatriotic than their predecessors. Pan-German ideology was meanwhile promoted by other chauvinist organizations and by several prominent German newspapers as well. American observers reported the trend; it was given much publicity by historian Roland G. Usher in his book *Pan-Germanism,* published in 1913.[30] Usher ignored organizations like the League as he painted a larger canvas intended to depict the German view of international power relationships. Usher's moderate tone and apparent objectivity enhanced the effectiveness of the book as anti-German propaganda.

In the same year that Usher's book was published, anti-German sentiment fed ravenously on the so-called Zabern affair. German troops garrisoned in the Alsatian village of Zabern had by their imperious manners caused much tension among the civilian population. An unusually arrogant German lieutenant named Förstner threatened, in a speech to a group of army recruits, to shoot anyone who assailed him. His tirade was reported to the townspeople, who then singled him out for ridicule as he strode the streets of the village. On one occasion Förstner was unable to control his emotions. He drew his sword, lashed out at his antagonists, and wounded an allegedly unoffending spectator who, by chance, was a cripple. The incident received world-wide

Carter in *New York Evening Sun*

"Laws? I Make My Own Laws"

Kaiser Wilhelm II was savagely attacked in the American press.

publicity and the lieutenant was quickly court martialed. German chauvinist sentiment was outraged by the action of the court and it contributed to a subsequent reversal of the decision by a higher tribunal. The German Reichstag thereupon censured the military by an overwhelming vote for its mishandling of the case, but the Kaiser, as though determined to justify vicious behavior, responded by pardoning the officer. In the American view, the affair began with German brutality and ended with imperial approbation. The Kaiser was again denounced in the American press and German militarism was vigorously attacked.[31]

American suspicions of German motives were greatly stimulated also in 1913, when the Reichstag passed the Delbrücke law, which seemed to push the concept of dual citizenship to new limits. It provided that a German emigrant could by application retain his German citizenship while gaining citizenship in the country to which he had moved. Uneasy Americans perceived the law as new evidence that the German government hoped to retain the political allegiance of its expatriates in the United States for imperialist, Pan-German purposes. Actually, the Delbrücke Law was no threat, since the American formula for naturalization included the express renunciation of all other allegiances.[32]

The image of Germany as an ominous military power bent on world domination was strengthened immensely by the publication of *Germany and the Next War* by General Friedrich von Bernhardi, an officer on active service in the German army. Originally published in Germany in 1911, it appeared in an English-language edition in 1913. This stridently bellicose work was a vulgarization of ideas drawn from the philosopher Nietzsche and the historian Treitschke. Bernhardi viewed war as a social necessity for a strong and flourishing nation and as an indispensable expression of cultural strength. Although Bernhardi was chiefly concerned with French power as an obstacle to German imperialism, he offered world domination as the sole alternative to national destruction. Of the same genre as jingoist tracts produced in Britain, France, and the United

States, Bernhardi's book caused a greater stir in those countries than it did in Germany. American newspapers frequently referred to it and printed extracts from it to document their charges that Germany was incurably aggressive, martial, and imperialistic.[33]

Other books also contributed to the growing fear and hatred of Germany. When war broke out in the summer of 1914, prominent American publishers rushed a variety of materials into print. These ranged from irresponsible propaganda tracts to substantial efforts to understand Germany and its emperor. Sample titles reveal their temper: *Germany's Madness,* by Emil Reich; *Builder and Blunderer,* by George Saunders; *The Real Kaiser,* by an anonymous writer; *Men around the Kaiser,* by Frederick Wile; *The German Emperor as Shown in His Public Utterances,* by Christian Gauss. The figure of Kaiser Wilhelm dominates these books. Generally depicted as a man of keen intelligence and imagination, well-informed, a powerful orator and administrator, he appeared all the more menacing because of his considerable abilities. But he was also seen as autocratic, vain, cruel, and unscrupulous—a perfect symbol of threatening German imperialism.

By 1914 most of the ingredients for an explosive mix were present. The rapidly assimilating German element in America, properly proud of their cultural heritage, had been encouraged in their ethnic chauvinism by the stereotypes native Americans had generally held of them. Negative elements in the image were more than compensated for by the pseudo-scientific racist thinking of the time, which gave high marks to the Germans. While Anglo-Saxonists were not prepared to accept Germans as equals, circumstances prompted the chauvinistic among German-Americans to promote their heritage as a counter culture to the dominant one. This was a dangerous course in a period of resurgent nativism. Deviations from American norms were but lightly tolerated in the prewar period by persons unwilling or unable to distinguish cultural chauvinism from the political or nationalist variety. Meanwhile, American perceptions of Wilhelmine Germany grew increasingly unfavorable. Pan-German thinking was freely attributed to the Imperial Government; Germany's behavior in international affairs convinced troubled Americans that world domination was the Kaiser's ultimate goal. They suspected that Wilhelm II was prepared to employ any available means, including German-American citizens and their organizations to achieve his objective. But the German-American community, by this time dominated by its second generation, took its Americanism seriously. To many German-Americans this meant that political action was an entirely appropriate means to defend their culture from Anglo-American dominance. Unfortunately, as they became so involved, they convinced other Americans that they were the willing dupes of the Kaiser's nefarious schemes.

Thinking in terms of stereotypes, symbols, and slogans became a habit of mind for many Americans, old stock as well as new. The result was that individual differences were obscured; the realities of interpersonal relationships between natives and newcomers were beclouded. Personal idiosyncracies or behavior patterns were not taken at face value but were interpreted within a network of preconceived notions. For the German-American who valued his cultural heritage this meant, at best, that he was a second-class citizen, inferior to Americans of English antecedents; at worst it meant that he was perceived as the agent of a foreign despot. Any emphasis, therefore, of the Anglo-Saxon character of the American nation implied a social humiliation for the German-Americans. In compensation, he tended to assert his Germanness all the more vigorously.

When war came in 1914, discordant ethnic relationships were laid bare. It was not a new circumstance. Instead, sensitivities, antipathies, and fears of long standing were intensified.

Notes

1. Hugo Munsterberg, *American Traits from the Point of View of a German* (Boston: Houghton Mifflin, 1901), p. 7.
2. Charles F. Thwing, *The American and German University: One Hundred Years of History* (New York: Macmillan, 1928), p. 40; Walter P. Metzger, *Academic Freedom in the Age of the University* (New York: Columbia University Press, 1955), pp. 93, 95, 104–7.
3. Edward N. Saveth, *American Historians and European Immigrants, 1875–1925* (New York: Columbia University Press, 1948), pp. 13–31; Thwing, *American and German University,* pp. 46, 106, 149, 154; Benjamin G. Rader, *The Academic Mind and Reform: The Influence of Richard T. Ely in American Life* (Lexington: University of Kentucky Press, 1966), p. 15; John A. Walz, *German Influence in American Education and Culture* (Philadelphia: Carl Schurz Memorial Foundation, 1936); Metzger, *Academic Freedom,* pp. 100–103, 119–24.
4. Clara E. Schieber, *The Transformation of American Sentiment toward Germany, 1870–1914* (Boston: Cornhill Publishing Co., 1923), p. 256.
5. Josiah Flynt, "The German and the German-American," *Atlantic Monthly,* 78 (November 1896): 655–64; Edward A. Ross, *The Old World in the New: The Significance of the Past and Present Immigration to the American People* (New York: Century, 1914), pp. 63, 65; Prescott F. Hall, *Immigration and Its Effects upon the United States,* 2d ed., rev. (New York: Henry Holt, 1913), p. 47; Barbara Miller Solomon, *Ancestors and Immigrants: A Changing New England Tradition* (New York: John Wiley, 1956), pp. 155–59.

6. John Higham, *Strangers in the Land: Patterns of American Nativism 1860–1925* (New York: Atheneum, 1965), p. 25. As an example of a negative reaction to the German life style by a churchman, see Howard B. Grose, *Aliens or Americans?* (New York: Eaton & Mains; Cincinnati: Jennings & Graham, 1906), p. 252.

7. A considerable literature has developed in recent years on ethnopolitical conflict in the last decades of the nineteenth century. See especially Paul Kleppner, *The Cross of Culture: A Social Analysis of Midwestern Politics, 1850–1900* (New York: Free Press, 1970); Richard J. Jensen, *The Winning of the Midwest: Social and Political Conflict, 1888–1896* (Chicago: University of Chicago Press, 1971); and Frederick C. Luebke, *Immigrants and Politics: The Germans of Nebraska, 1880–1900* (Lincoln: University of Nebraska Press, 1969).

8. Richard Bartholdt, *From Steerage to Congress: Reminiscences and Reflections* (Philadelphia: Dorrance, 1930), p. 81.

9. Quoted in Solomon, *Ancestors and Immigrants,* p. 111. See also pp. 71, 80.

10. Saveth, *Historians and Immigrants,* pp. 42–51, 198; Turner is quoted on p. 135; Edward McNall Burns, *The American Idea of Mission: Concepts of National Purpose and Destiny* (New Brunswick: Rutgers University Press, 1957), p. 200.

11. U.S., Congress, Senate, *Reports of the Immigration Commission,* 41 vols., 61st Cong., 3d sess. (1911).

12. Oscar Handlin has analyzed the reports in his critical essay "Old Immigrants and New," in *Race and Nationality in American Life* (Garden City, N.Y.: Doubleday Anchor, 1957), pp. 74–110.

13. U.S., Bureau of the Census, *Thirteenth Census, 1910, Abstract* (1913), p. 191; Hattie Plum Williams, "The Road to Citizenship: A Study of Naturalization in a Nebraska County," *Political Science Quarterly,* 27 (1912): 399–427; Jeremiah Jenks and W. Jett Lauck, *The Immigration Problem: A Study of American Immigration Conditions and Needs,* 5th ed., rev. and enl. (New York & London: Funk & Wagnalls, 1922), p. 35; Frederick Bushee, *Ethnic Factors in the Population of Boston* (New York: Macmillan, 1903), p. 154; Ross, *Old World in the New,* p. 61.

14. Howard B. Woolston, "Rating the Nations: A Study in the Statistics of Opinion," *American Journal of Sociology,* 22 (November 1916): 381–90.

15. Solomon, *Ancestors and Immigrants,* pp. 59–81; Saveth, *Historians and Immigrants,* p. 58; Higham, *Strangers in the Land,* pp. 133–44.

16. Oscar Handlin, *The American People in the Twentieth Century* (Boston: Beacon Press, 1963), p. 98.
17. Albert B. Faust, *The German Element in the United States,* 2 vols. (Boston: Houghton Mifflin, 1909).
18. Higham, *Strangers in the Land,* p. 123.
19. Theodore Roosevelt, "What 'Americanism' Means," *Forum,* 17 (April 1894): 202.
20. Charles Nagel, *Charles Nagel: Speeches and Writings, 1890–1928,* ed. Otto Heller (New York & London: G. P. Putnam's Sons, 1931), 2:83.
21. Price Collier, *Germany and the Germans from an American Point of View* (New York: Charles Scribner's Sons, 1914); R. G. Steinmeyer, "Certain Aspects of German Public Opinion toward the United States (1914–1917)," (Ph.D. diss., American University, 1935), p. 15.
22. Schieber, *Transformation of American Sentiment,* pp. 88, 136, 171, 177, 178.
23. William Roscoe Thayer, *The Life and Letters of John Hay,* 2 vols. (Boston: Houghton Mifflin, 1915), 2:291.
24. Mildred S. Wertheimer, *The Pan-German League, 1890–1914,* Studies in History, Economics, and Public Law, vol. 112 (New York: Columbia University, 1924), pp. 65, 74, 117, 126f.
25. Ibid., pp. 118–20, 159, 196, 208, 215. Bernstorff is quoted on p. 151.
26. Ibid., p. 17.
27. Schieber, *Transformation of American Sentiment,* pp. 222, 228; Ruth Miller Elson, *Guardians of Tradition: American Schoolbooks of the Nineteenth Century* (Lincoln: University of Nebraska Press, 1964), p. 143f.
28. Schieber, *Transformation of American Sentiment,* pp. 209, 214, 216.
29. Saveth, *Historians and Immigrants,* p. 48; Schieber, *Transformation of American Sentiment,* p. 261.
30. Roland G. Usher, *Pan-Germanism* (Boston: Houghton Mifflin, 1913). By 1915 Usher's book had gone into a second edition, revised and enlarged.
31. Schieber, *Transformation of American Sentiment,* p. 230; *Literary Digest,* 48 (3 January 1914): 9–10; 48 (31 January 1914): 195–96; 48 (7 February 1914): 249–50.
32. Schieber, *Transformation of American Sentiment,* p. 208.
33. Richard O'Connor, *The German-Americans: An Informal History* (Boston: Little, Brown, 1968), p. 378f.; Robert E. Osgood, *Ideals and Self-Interest in America's Foreign Relations* (Chicago: University of Chicago Press, 1953), p. 131.

CHAPTER FOUR

The Sound of Distant Guns

LATE SUMMER AND FALL 1914

Europe was still a remote place to Americans in 1914. Although problems of rapid transatlantic communication had been solved years earlier, the ocean remained a formidable physical barrier between the Old World and the New. Transatlantic liners like the *Titanic* and the *Lusitania* had reduced passage time to a few days, but old attitudes based on centuries of experience remained. Americans still perceived their land as a world apart, far removed from the national rivalries and petty squabbles of Europe.

The murder of the Austrian archduke at the end of June 1914 stimulated few anxieties. It was a regrettable incident, to be sure, but entirely typical, in the American view, of the anarchy endemic in that unfortunate part of the world. Few European observers, for that matter, recognized the assassination as an event that could trigger the first world war since the Napoleonic era. Even when the guns of August began to boom five weeks later, most Americans saw no possibility of American involvement. President Woodrow Wilson was right, they thought, it was not our affair. They continued in their preoccupation with domestic concerns despite the horrors revealed by the war dispatches that began to crowd the front pages of their daily newspapers. War in Europe was fundamentally a spectacle to be viewed from the sidelines. Some persons whose concern for personal advantage was paramount simply did not care at all about the war or its outcome. Others whose loyalties were enlisted in extravagant partisanship observed the new carnage with fascination or revulsion. Yet they, too, could agree with Wilson that their country's remoteness would protect it from direct involvement and that Americans must try to be neutral in thought as well as in action.[1]

But the American people could not be emotionally impartial or neutral in their sentiments, any more than Wilson himself. The war naturally evoked sympathies for one or the other side, though it hardly followed that American intervention would be favored. The majority naturally perceived the cause of Britain and her allies as worthy and just. Most persons of English antecedents, no matter how many generations removed from the British Isles, tended to feel an emotional bond with their ancestral home. They lived in an era when ethnocultural ties (as well as tensions) were strong. The values and attitudes associated with Anglo-Saxon Protestantism were identified as those of American society in general; cultural characteristics diverging from this standard were expected to be discarded or remodeled. The Anglo-Americans, still the largest ethnic group in the country, were proud that they had provided the United States with its dominant language, political institutions, religion, and democratic ideals. Many pro-Ally observers were willing to admit that not all virtues reposed on the British side and that stubbornness and ineptitude could be ascribed to Allied leaders as well as to others. Yet they quickly came to believe that this war was a threat to cherished ideals and values, ill-defined though they were. Anglo-American imagination magnified German militarism and autocracy, German devotion to power based on brute strength, and German efficiency and technical brilliance. Notions of Anglo-Saxon superiority, it seemed, were being put to the test. Perhaps old-stock Americans could be neutral in their outward behavior, but their emotions were not so easily suppressed.

Such persons did not need British propaganda to convince them. But before the first month of the war had passed, they read lurid stories of German brutality. The world was told how innocent Belgium had been wantonly raped and pillaged: the cultural treasures of Louvain had been destroyed, defenseless civilians had been massacred, fiends in German uniforms had amputated the breasts of Belgian women with the stroke of a sword, Belgian children had been bayoneted, and babies had had their hands chopped off. By no means were these tales of German atrocities—some fabricated, others distorted and embellished—accepted without question in the United States. American correspondents who accompanied the German armies sharply rejected the stories in September, and soon the Germans were spreading comparable fictions about horrors wrought by the Belgians and the French. Yet countless, uncritical persons in the United States accepted the reports of German brutality as unassailable fact, and their attitudes toward all things German were modified accordingly.[2]

Perhaps more convincing than atrocity propaganda were the numbing accounts of observers such as the famous reporter, Richard Harding Davis, who described a tidal wave of grey-clad German soldiers, marching, goose-stepping with precision, hour after hour, through the streets of Brussels.[3] Equally chilling were the photographs, especially those printed in the Sunday supplements: the arrogant Kaiser and his six sons, all resplendently uniformed; the endless columns of German soldiers; the ruins of Louvain. Maps of Belgium, planted squarely on the front pages of the newspapers, charted the daily progress of the Kaiser's hordes as they swept across that little land into northern France. Most old-stock Americans were immeasurably alienated by the German invasion of Belgium, which was perceived as a harmless neutral trapped by geography. They instinctively identified the Belgians as gallant defenders of hearth and home against the ruthless German giant.

The actions of the German government during the first weeks of the war greatly strengthened a new stereotype that had been evolving in America during the preceding decade. What was left of the old image of thrift, energy, and geniality, of preeminence in music, philosophy, and science gave way to a harsh picture of unyielding efficiency and strength, of arrogant militarism and imperialism. Some observers believed that the agent of change was the Hohenzollern dynasty. In forty years, the *New York Times* editorialized in 1915, the German people had been "transformed from a nation worthy of the world's esteem and admiration into a people who stand apart from other nations, distrusted and feared, disturbers of the peace, a menace to the general security, and now pursuing their ends by the hideous atrocities perpetrated in Belgium and France, by deeds of monstrous inhumanity. ... Their ideals have been abased and their intellectual development stifled, they have been bred away from the high and noble things of life."[4]

Statements of this kind blurred the distinction, given wide currency by President Wilson and supported editorially by many distinguished newspapers, between the German people and the German government. To maintain the distinction was, like Wilson's exhortation to neutral thought and conduct, a matter of the head rather than of the heart. If the people of Germany had indeed been transformed by Hohenzollern autocracy, was it not possible that Germans elsewhere had similarly been converted into agents of German might? If German-Americans talked and acted like the subjects of the Kaiser, might not one fairly conclude that Pan-Germanism was a reality and that the first loyalties of German-Americans were to a foreign potentate whose values, ideals, and goals were all too often antithetic to those of America?

The German-American response to war in Europe was strong, though it was hardly what nativistic Americans suspected. For two decades social forces had been operating to weaken the cohesion of the immigrant community. German ethnic leaders had resisted the trend and had become increasingly chauvinistic in their promotion of *Deutsch-*

Strongly pro-Ally in sentiment, *Life* published much atrocity propaganda that depicted the Germans as base and brutal.

---

tum as a culture counter to the dominant one based on English foundations. Now, in the late summer and early fall of 1914, newspapers and magazines overflowed with war dispatches, almost all of which had been cleared by British censors. Not surprisingly, advocates of German culture in the United States overreacted as they used every possible device to promote ethnic solidarity and enlisted every plausible argument to justify Germany's position. But their crusade was not, as most German-American chauvinists themselves believed it to be, a fight for fair and impartial treatment of the Kaiser, his government, and his armies, nor was it a battle against British imperialism in favor of a German variety. Actually, it was more a matter of defending the status of Germans in the American social structure. Each war dispatch, anti-German editorial, and partisan pronouncement by an Allied government regarding the origin of war served indirectly to emphasize the Anglo-Saxon character of the American nation and to erode the position of the German group in the society. For years the chauvinists had extolled the virtues of German culture and now, it appeared, the American people were being told that all things German were sinister, base, and brutal. Each day's news, as reported in most American newspapers, became a source of humiliation for many German-Americans. Their pride wounded, they were determined to fight back and, as one of them expressed it, "to protect the good name of everything German."⁵

But there were others, less sensitive, who exulted in the initial German victories as indisputable proofs of German superiority. If Germans would not be loved in America, they thought, at least they would be respected. In very few cases, however, did Germany replace the United States as the primary object of their political loyalty. Rather, the Kaiser and his empire were cultural symbols. His victories and defeats were important, not in themselves, but for the implications they carried for German-American life and success in America, for social deprivation or status improvement, real or imaginary.

German-American reaction to the war was by no means as uniform as perceived by most American observers. In general, the American press made the understandable error of assuming that the editors of German-language newspapers and the officers of German-American associations accurately reflected group opinion. The fact that these ethnic leaders had much to gain through a pro-German line was ignored. Indeed, it is even possible that a majority of persons of German stock in the United States in 1914 were either indifferent to the war in Europe or actually hostile to the German government and its goals. For every reservist of the German army in the United States who responded to his government's call to arms there were others who hastened to initiate or to complete the process of becoming an

American citizen. For every German immigrant whose pulse quickened at sounds of the anthem, *"Deutschland über Alles,"* there were others who were alienated from German culture and sought to obscure the marks of their origin. For them anonymity and silence, if not vocal opposition to Germany, were virtues.

Nevertheless, champions of German ethnocultural separatism were taken to represent the collective attitudes and opinions of Germans in America. They formed a solid front. A detailed examination of the German-language press during World War I shows remarkable uniformity of thought. Almost without exception, the German-American editors accepted uncritically the official German explanation for the outbreak of war, and many predicted a quick and decisive victory for German arms. They were dismayed, however, when during the first week following the several declarations of war the British cut the German transatlantic cable to the United States somewhere east of the Azores. German sources of war news were almost completely blocked and in the weeks and months that followed, most items published in the American press reflected the heavy editing of Allied censorship.[6]

German-American newspapers immediately denounced the pro-Ally bias of the news coverage. The editors, in cooperation with local chapters of the National German-American Alliance, the Turnerbund, and other ethnic societies, organized protest meetings in several major cities, including Washington, Boston, and Saint Louis. These usually well-attended gatherings heard vehement demands for "fair play" and balanced reporting. Threats were made, including the possibility of boycotts against offending newspapers. Some speakers were remarkably indiscreet, but most voiced reasonable complaints about the suppression of news favorable to Germany, about ignorance of conditions in Germany, and especially about anti-German editorials and biased headlines. Charles J. Hexamer, president of the National German-American Alliance, urged the establishment of press vigilance committees throughout the country to watch for and to denounce all expressions of anti-German sentiment. Within the month, New York Germans responded by creating the German-American Literary Defense Committee. It served effectively as a clearinghouse for letters of protest and by September and October 1914, it became a major center for the preparation and distribution of thousands of pro-German tracts and pamphlets throughout the United States.[7]

German-born Congressman Richard Bartholdt of Missouri, speaking at a rally in Washington, D.C., implicitly related the war issue to anxiety over the status of his ethnic group. Better treatment of Germany could have been expected in the American press, he said, "in view of the conduct in this country of German-American citizens and considering the great services German-Americans have rendered in this country." Sensitive to charges of this kind, several prominent newspapers tried to exonerate the German people and to place the blame for war and alleged war crimes on the Kaiser and his government. The *New York Times,* for example, asked, "Why should Germans who have sought homes on this Republic resent American criticism of European militarism and European absolutism?" But most German-American spokesmen rejected the distinction between the Kaiser and the German people as specious. The *New Yorker Staats-Zeitung* dismissed it as "groundless folly." Such efforts, it said, could only lead to an undesirable weakening of friendship between the German and the American peoples. Others rejected the idea because of its implication that Germany had started the war. This was not the case, they claimed, since war had been forced upon Germany by a greedy England and by a vengeful France. Professor Hugo Muensterberg of Harvard, in a widely published letter to the *Boston Herald,* described the war as a great, inevitable clash between the forces of civilization, represented by Teutonic Germany, and the forces of barbarism, headed by Slavic Russia. Another Harvard professor, Kuno Francke, argued that the Kaiser had been a devoted champion of peace for decades and could not reasonably be expected to destroy everything that his life had stood for. In this dovish view the vaunted German military machine was transformed into a powerful agent of peace. Many German-American editorialists pleaded that the army was necessary for defensive purposes. Besides, asserted the president of the German-American Peace Society, the German army was a citizen army, and since the German people were kind souls, German soldiers must be also. Imperial Germany was not an autocracy, he claimed further, but a democracy. The Kaiser was merely a figurehead, chimed in George Sylvester Viereck, since the real power to govern resided in the Bundesrat.[8]

Viereck very quickly became the best known American defender of Germany in 1914. Although he had been born in Munich, he had lived most of his life in America, and loyalties for the two cultures contended strongly in this brilliant, energetic, and rather neurotic young man. By 1914 he had achieved some distinction in literary circles as a poet. He had also been an editor and publisher who assiduously cultivated the friendship of influential persons. When war came he saw an opportunity to harmonize his affections for Germany and America by publishing an English-language weekly newspaper, the *Fatherland*. He would use it to educate Americans in the virtues of the German position, to disclose the malevolence of the Allies, and to encourage the German-Americans, especially the second generation, to united action. The first issue, dated 10 August 1914, was snapped up from the newsstands. By October more than 100,000 copies were in circulation.[9] Vehement, insulting, sardonic, articulate, the *Fatherland* was widely quoted by friend and foe. It contributed greatly to the image of the German-Americans as arrogant partisans of the Kaiser's government.

Viereck's paper, as well as the several hundred German-language dailies and weeklies published in the United States at that time, delighted in reprinting pro-German articles penned by native or old-stock Americans. These pieces, welcomed as evidence that espousal of the German

The front page of an early issue of George Sylvester Viereck's pro-German propaganda sheet.

position on the war was not merely ethnocentrism, suggested that the German-American arguments had a validity and respectability of their own. The Teutophile historian John W. Burgess was one of the most prominent of such contributors. The newspapers used any other ready means to get their message to the public. Free copies were distributed in some cities; columns of war news, allegedly free of Allied bias, were printed in English for the benefit of persons unable to read the German language.[10]

Such pro-German versions of the war were normally as distorted as anything that appeared in the English-language press. The destruction of Louvain, for example, was coolly justified on military grounds. The German forces were always described as irresistible; apparently they could lose no battles, although the German generals could order strategic retreats. Even when the French halted the German advance at the Marne River in September 1914, one German-American paper described the event as being in conformance with the battle plans of the German General Staff. Tales of German atrocities were regularly denied, but editors frequently repeated equally outrageous stories about the behavior of Allied troops. They tapped historical sources for a further supply of anti-British propaganda items. Thomas Jefferson's celebrated catalog of British misdeeds incorporated into the Declaration of Independence, the burning of Washington in 1814, the *Trent* affair and other evidences of unneutral conduct by the British in the American Civil War—all were revived to demonstrate that, then as now, the interests of "perfidious Albion" were antithetical to those of the United States.[11]

Chauvinist editors also used their columns to promote the sale of German war bonds (while denouncing as unneutral loans to the Allied powers) and to urge German-Americans to make donations to the German Red Cross to aid war relief efforts for German war widows and orphans. In order to demonstrate their solidarity, they exhorted their readers to purchase German-language publications, patronize the

Fatherland, 21 July 1915

Advertisements for German and Austrian war bonds frequently appeared in both the English and German languages in German-American newspapers and periodicals.

German-language theater, attend churches that continued to use the German language, and participate actively in the German clubs and societies.[12] In short, the German-American press utilized the war as a means of rallying the disintegrating ethnic community to united action. An editorial writer of the *Saint Louis Westliche Post* exemplified this spirit. Pleased by the great demonstration of German-Americans in his city in August 1914, he asserted that in their anger over the way Germany was being abused in the American press, German-Americans were finding themselves and were wiping away old divisions and differences. "We must hold on tenaciously," he wrote, "so that we will not have to put up with the old disharmony and thus destroy the work of this sacred hour."[13] The gathering had indeed been a significant achievement, sponsored as it was by such disparate and antipathetic organizations as the Catholic Union, the Turnerbund, the Sängerbund, and the Saint Louis branch of the German-American Alliance.

Chauvinism had its rewards. Even though large numbers of Americans of German birth or descent were unmoved by these appeals, the fact remains that the sound of distant guns produced new levels of cooperation and institutional vigor. German-language publications enjoyed notable increases in circulation, and countless societies experienced a surge of new interest.

And yet the response of German-Americans often fell short of their leaders' expectations. Inflated goals for relief collections were reduced to more realistic figures and new fund-raising methods were devised. In New York the German Historical Society, for example, inaugurated a war relief fund by selling rings bearing the famous German Iron Cross. According to newspaper accounts, thousands of New Yorkers donated money, jewels, watches, and other valuables in return for the rings, which carried the inscription: "To show my loyalty to the old Fatherland, I brought it gold in time of trouble for this piece of iron." In Saint Louis the German societies followed up their August rally with a two-day festival in October. Income from concession

Fatherland, 3 March 1915

German-American cultural chauvinists exploited the war in Europe to revitalize their disintegrating ethnic community.

stands, the sale of foaming liquid refreshments, and admission fees to concerts, dramatic presentations and gymnastic displays was combined with profits from sales of Iron Crosses. Allegedly $20,000 was gathered from the 25,000 persons who attended.[14]

Similar festivals and bazaars were sponsored in other major cities. They attracted much attention in the American press and created an illusion that the masses of German-Americans were as chauvinist and as partisan as their leaders. The press understandably reported the activities of what they believed were the largest and most representative of German ethnic associations. The most extreme statements were the most newsworthy; the most divergent opinions were the most extensively noted. Organizations or persons who disagreed remained silent. Unfortu-

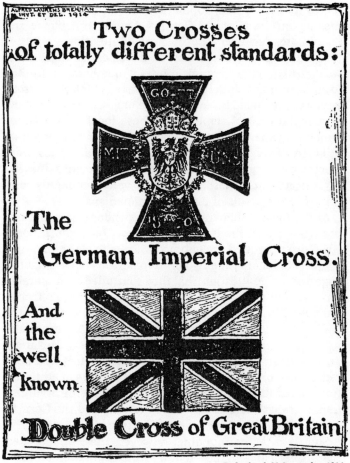

Fatherland, 30 September 1914

George Sylvester Viereck and other apologists for Germany's cause tried to neutralize pro-British propaganda in the United States.

nately for the German population in the United States, this meant that the National German-American Alliance and its affiliates received a lion's share of attention.

Actually the *Nationalbund,* as it was called in German, was mostly a paper organization. Its membership, limited to citizens of the United States, consisted chiefly of persons who were included because they belonged to a local society or a social club of some kind. These local organizations banded together in a city alliance (*Stadtverband*) or a state alliance (*Staatverband*). Officers of the alliances were elected by delegates chosen by the local societies. Inevitably, the delegates chose leaders who were thoroughly committed to the ideals of cultural nationalism.

At the top of this pyramid of independent state and city branches rested the National Alliance. Its organizational structure permitted the national officers to claim that they represented more than two million persons of German lineage and, by implication, that they controlled a comparably large bloc of public opinion, if not votes. With an effective membership scarcely a tenth of the size it claimed, the National Alliance was dominated by its leaders, especially its founder and long-time president, Charles J. Hexamer, an American-born engineer of Philadelphia. It had been established originally to further the objectives of ethnocultural separatism and was part of the surge of organizational strength and expansion which infused the German community in the first years of the twentieth century.[15]

Shortly after its founding, however, the National German-American Alliance acquired the reputation of being concerned almost exclusively with opposition to the prohibition movement. It developed into an ethnic counterorganization to the Anti-Saloon League. When prohibition threatened a certain state or locality, the National Alliance would organize branches there, which in turn would become politically active, attempting to form and lead public opinion, approving candidates for public office, and marshaling the so-called German vote in behalf of the anti-prohibition cause. Congress had granted the national orga-

nization a federal charter in 1907, and for that reason it was
not permitted to engage actively in politics. But since it was
preeminently a political agency (its stated objectives to the
contrary), the National Alliance normally carried out its
political goals through the state organizations, which operated under no such restrictions. Like the Anti-Saloon
League, it was a classic example of a pressure group, basically no different from hundreds of other organizations except that it was ethnically based. It was this difference, of
course, that made it seem un-American to the apostles of
Anglo-Saxon conformity.

To assert that "the German vote floated on an ocean of
beer," as George Sylvester Viereck impishly claimed in
1924, or to interpret the program of the National Alliance
as an assault upon the governmental system by "a great
debauching and overweening brewery trust," as one of its
enemies declared in 1910, is to misunderstand the immigrant mind in politics. Prohibition was more than a mere
issue to most German-born voters. It was the political symbol of a general clash of cultures which confronted many
immigrants as they adjusted to American society. As they
saw it, prohibition was cut from the same cloth as woman
suffrage, Sabbatarian legislation, and governmental regulation of parochial schools. It was true that the National
Alliance was heavily subsidized by the brewing industry, as
its enemies charged, but that fact failed to bother the cultural chauvinists. To them the important thing was that
prohibition was a type of legislation that threatened their
life style and value system. It was vitally necessary, they
thought, to fight all such encroachments on personal liberty
everywhere and in every way possible. Germanism had to
be advanced as a more generous, tolerant, and liberal cultural alternative to the dominant Anglo-Saxonism, which
they perceived as "narrow hearted, dark knownothingism,"
as "zealotry which sprang from England," and as "the slav-
ery of puritanism."[16]

The advent of war in 1914 required no changes in attitude
on the part of the National German-American Alliance.

According to an article in the organization's official bulletin, the world had been plunged into a great war by that same British element that was the fountainhead of prohibition.[17] Battling British war propaganda and exposing British imperialism as inimical to American interest was merely another aspect of the struggle against Anglo-Saxonism, as they understood it.

The most widely publicized summary statement of German-American cultural chauvinism during the neutrality period was made by Charles J. Hexamer in Milwaukee on 22 November 1915. Extensively quoted, it later achieved sufficient notoriety to be singled out for special condemnation in the investigation into the activities of the National German-American Alliance conducted by the United States Senate in 1918. In his address, Hexamer had stressed the importance of German-American unity and resistance to assimilation. "No one," he said, using words that infuriated his nativistic critics, "will find us prepared to step down to a lesser *Kultur;* no, we have made it our aim to draw the other up to us." After describing the German home and family in unusually maudlin terms, Hexamer asserted that it was the duty of the German-Americans "to transmit to the American people the depth of German feeling, that seeking after all that is good, beautiful, and true." He predicted that even though German-Americans, like Washington and Lincoln before them, were being slandered, history would later praise and prize them "because they [will] have saved the land from the claws of English tyranny." Hexamer closed his speech with a master flourish:

No people is so modest and no people is so ready to recognize the good in others as the Germans. . . . But we will not permit our kultur of two thousand years to be trodden down in this land. . . . [We can give our German kultur to America] only if we stand together and conquer that dark spirit of muckerdom [bigotry] and prohibition just as Siegfried once slew the dragon.[18]

The ethnocentrism displayed by Hexamer and by dozens of other persons prominent in the National German-American Alliance thus contributed mightily to a polarization of popular opinion during the several months following the outbreak of war in Europe. Every challenge by opponents of the German cause was met with impassioned rhetoric, while advocates of the British cause were denounced. German-Americans were exhorted, cajoled, and pressured toward an appearance of unity by the cultural chauvinists, whose tantrums meanwhile succeeded in alienating persons whose emotions lay on the other side of the war issue. Voices of moderation were commonly lost in the uproar. There is no way to discover how many people shared the sentiments of one German-American, for example, who in a letter to the editor of the *New York Times* advised his fellow ethnics to adopt a low profile. He objected to the public display of partisanship, and in order to avoid challenging the subjects of other nations, he advised them to celebrate their victories privately in German beer gardens. Moreover, he noted the "better class" of German-Americans wouldn't think of participating in such affairs as the demonstrations that had been staged by the German reservists in the streets of New York. In response to such appeals for moderation, the chauvinists castigated all who would shed their German cultural heritage. In Hexamer's lexicon the moderates were rascals and deserters—contemptible dogs unworthy even to be spat upon.[19]

The most obvious dissenters from the dominant attitude were the German-American socialists. Enjoying extensive support among the laborers and skilled workers of industrial centers like New York, Cleveland, Chicago, Milwaukee, and Saint Louis, most socialist leaders emphasized their Marxist doctrine that the war was the consequence of ruling-class ambition and avarice. They taught that war was a conspiracy of kings and capitalists against the laboring masses of all countries and that the capitalist quest for raw materials and markets inevitably meant imperialism and militarism. The masses were being exploited; their lives sacrificed on altars of greed. German-American socialists were devoid of sympathy for the Fatherland. To them, the German Kaiser and German capitalists were just as guilty as their counterparts in France and Britain. Moreover, predicted one socialist editor, American capitalists would soon try to force this country into the conflict because they would find it easier to rob the people under the flag of war. In Saint Louis, socialists organized an International Anti-War and Peace Demonstration on 16 August 1914. As many as 2,000 persons attended this meeting, revealing that numerous Americans held strongly divergent opinions of the war, its causes, and implications.[20]

For most leaders of the German-American churches, the European war was not a subject calling for partisan comment. The churches as ethnic institutions had no interest in a German victory comparable to their concern for the unhampered maintenance of German language and culture. There were, of course, eager advocates of the Kaiser's cause among German-American clergymen, but such persons commonly spoke as individuals rather than as representatives of an ecclesiastical body. In general, church officials refrained from endorsing either side in the conflict. As German culture came increasingly under attack, however, many reacted strongly. How could the church perform its mission, they asked, if it was denied its means of communication? How could the church retain its youthful members if its cultural symbols were debased?

In few German-American churches was the identification with the German government so weak and the retention of German language and culture so strong as in the Lutheran Church—Missouri Synod, the largest and most conservative of German Lutheran organizations in the United States. From the outset it adopted a remarkably neutral stance on the war issue in its official publications. Their most frequent observation was that the war was the hand of God chastening a sinful world. Each nation was guilty of irreligion, jealousy, and greed: the French were atheistic, frivolous, and licentious; the English were grasping, materialistic, supercilious manipulators; Russians embraced colossal ignorance, superstition, and imperial ambition. But Germany was also sharply criticized. Writing in the *Lutheran Witness,* the English-language organ of the Missouri Synod, Theodore Graebner asserted that Germany was "immeasurably puffed up with pride of its learning and culture, [and] now as in the days when the Lord sent Bonaparte to chastise it with a rod of iron, [it is] given to rationalism and rankest materialism, an apostate nation, spreading the fogs of its unbelief to every land of the globe." The *Lutheran Witness* regularly deplored the war as utter folly, exacting a frightful toll in money and men. Graebner noted that there was no adequate justification for the conflict; each nation insisted that it was driven to war by the others and hence had no choice in the matter. Yet Graebner was somewhat defensive of the Kaiser. The idea that Wilhelm II thirsted for war he dismissed as "too ridiculous to be seriously discussed."[21]

A similar editorial stance was presented by *Der Lutheraner,* the official German-language publication of the synod. Its editor also asserted that the German people should accept the war as punishment from God, repent, and return "to God and His Word." *Der Lutheraner* went one step further as it defined the meaning of neutrality. To be neutral did not mean to be completely nonpartisan. "We may sympathize ... we may participate in the efforts to relieve the suffering of persons trapped in these unprecedented misfortunes of war." It was also permissible, according to this journal, to discuss the war dispatches, the alleged origins of the war, and the possibilities of its outcome in private conversation, in public speeches, and in the press. Yet, cautioned *Der Lutheraner,* church members must be very careful never to take a stand in opposition to the neutrality declaration of the government (the authority which God had placed over them) and they must avoid passionate discussions of the war capable of inflaming public opinion for one side or the other. Throughout the fall of 1914, *Der Lutheraner* did not deviate from this neutralist stance. It admitted to great interest in the war and its outcome but refrained from expressing any support for the German government, and never attacked the American press for the alleged bias of its reporting.[22]

Not all German Lutheran editors and publishers were as circumspect as those of the Missouri Synod. The official publication of the German Nebraska and Wartburg synods, for example, vehemently denounced Great Britain as it defended American neutrality in terms of an arms embargo. Similarly, the American-born Rev. G. C. Berkemeier achieved considerable notoriety for the unrestrained pro-German line he followed in *Der Deutsche Lutheraner,* the German-language organ of the General Council of Lutheran synods. His campaign resembled that of *Die Abendschule,* a popular home magazine which catered to a German Lutheran readership. As chauvinist as any of the large German-American daily newspapers, *Die Abendschule* crowded its pages with pictures of the Kaiser, the German army in action, and German battleships, generals and admirals. Special summaries of war news from the German point of view appeared in each issue. It called for a unified German-American stand against the alleged prejudices and intrigue of the American press and it echoed Hexamer's plea for press vigilance committees. Form letters to United States congressmen were prepared in English for readers to copy and send. The magazine advertised pro-German pamphlets and books and offered portraits of the Kaiser's family as bonuses to accompany purchases and subscriptions. Like the German-American newspapers, *Die Abendschule* happily announced that its editorial policies had resulted in a spurt in circulation.[23]

Most English-language Lutheran publications differed only slightly from other products of the Protestant press. The occasional touches of pro-German sentiment were offset by items like the comment in the *Lutheran Observer* that Germany "is literally possessed with the devil of Militarism, and her victory would fasten that curse upon the world." In general, the Lutheran churches were sensitive and judicious in their behavior regarding the war. Although there were exceptions, these churches usually did not permit their agencies or publications to become instruments of pro-Germanism.[24]

What the pastors, professors, and editors of the German Lutheran churches did as private citizens was another matter. Although most tended to keep the secular societies at arm's length, some became very active in the German-American effort to state the German case in 1914 and 1915. A notable example was Professor Friedrich Bente, editor of the Missouri Synod's theological journal. Although his intense partisanship seldom found explicit expression in his own magazine, it was clearly evident in his private life. Bente spoke at numerous rallies and demonstrations, wrote many articles for the German-language press, and even gained an interview with President Wilson in 1916 to protest what he considered to be an unneutral foreign policy. Occasionally, German Lutheran pastors would act in the names of their congregations, as when several from Philadelphia jointly dispatched a letter to the Kaiser to convey their hopes for a German victory.[25]

It is almost impossible to determine the response of ordinary church people to the advice of their leaders. No doubt many attended the rallies and bazaars sponsored by the cultural militants. Contributions for the relief of German and of Austrian victims of war are a matter of record. For example, during the first three months following the outbreak of war, the Lutheran Church—Missouri Synod channeled $4,336 to the German ambassador. But this was scarcely an enthusiastic outpouring; it was a mere 6 percent of the charitable gifts processed by the synodical treasurer.[26]

The responses of other German-American Protestant churches were much the same as the Lutheran. Some clergymen were notoriously pro-German, but the majority, who placed the interest of the church ahead of their devotion to *das Deutschtum,* were more often quiet about their sentiments or were genuinely neutral. Public attention was inevitably drawn to the extremists like Pastor Hans Haupt of Cincinnati, whose unrestrained chauvinism seems to have led him to direct public prayers to his Fatherland rather than to his God. Even the pacifistic Mennonites, who

commonly lived in tight, rural colonies to insulate themselves from worldly influences, were not without pro-German publicists. Abraham L. Schellenberg, editor of a
journal designed for his coreligionists in Hillsboro, Kansas,
was an outspoken defender of Germany who carped persis-
tently about the Anglophile character of Wilson's foreign
policy. A more moderate note was struck by the eminent
German Baptist theologian Walter Rauschenbusch of
Rochester, New York. In a widely noted article, he asked for
fairness in the public discussion of Germany's ethics in the
war. His arguments were not new, but his efforts to place
the discussion in historical and comparative perspectives
were rational rather than bitter. And there were also German-American Protestant publications that were sharply
critical of Germany. A noteworthy example is *Der Christ-
liche Apologete* of the German Methodist conferences, edited by Wilhelm Nast. According to this journal the war was
incompatible with the principles of Christianity and culture, and the responsibility for the catastrophe could properly be placed on German militarism.[27]

The reaction of the numerous German Catholics in the
United States to the war in Europe presents a different
problem of analysis because there was no separate church
structure for them, as was the case among the Protestant
denominations. Their status as a minority group within the
Roman Catholic Church (itself a lightly tolerated religious
body) heightened the defensive, conservative mentality
common to many immigrants. They were jealous of their
cultural strengths and sensitive to criticism from sources
both within and from without Catholicism. That they
tended to be strongly pro-German is due as much to their
social circumstance as it was to their cultural heritage. In
general, their response was not unlike that of the German
Lutherans.

The Roman Catholic bishops of German antecedents
were especially careful never to compromise the interests
of their church by espousing Germany's cause or, indeed,
any form of neutralism that others could identify as pro-

German. The records of Archbishops Henry Moeller of Cincinnati and Sebastian Messmer of Milwaukee and of lesser figures in the hierarchy clearly reveal their great caution throughout the neutrality period. The bishops had no desire to test the fragile bond that held the many ethnic groups together in the Catholic church. They remembered well the Cahenslyite controversy that had raged a generation earlier when German-American Catholics had unsuccessfully battled for the creation of dioceses organized on an ethnic rather than a territorial basis. The war issue, they knew, could easily reopen old wounds.[28]

The Roman Catholic clergy were less circumspect. According to one contemporary estimate, as many as one-third bore names of German origin; no doubt a substantial proportion sympathized with Germany. Many priests made public displays of their feelings, some participating as organizers or speakers for the German-American rallies and demonstrations. Others revealed their sentiments as editors of Catholic publications.

The American Catholic press was numerous and varied because of its heterogeneous constituency. Hence, it reveals the full range of editorial opinion on the war issue from the pro-Ally stance of the *Catholic World,* for example, to the pro-Germanism of the *Indiana Catholic.* One extensive sampling of Catholic publications shows that the majority were either genuinely nonpartisan or neutral with muted sympathy for Germany.[29] This was especially true of journals with a national circulation like *Our Sunday Visitor* or of distinguished diocesan papers like the *Boston Pilot.* In general, the tendency to endorse the German position was strongest in cities or regions where there were large numbers of German-stock Catholics. The presence of Irish Catholics naturally strengthened this bias because of their intense and long-lived hatred of the British.[30]

But there were also Catholic publications in the German language. Some were closely connected to the institutional structure of Catholicism, while others were independent ventures published by laymen for German Catholic readers. The most influential was *Die Amerika* [of St. Louis], edited by Frederick Kenkel, an ambitious and dynamic convert to Catholicism. Although Kenkel understood that nationalistic chauvinism could undermine the influence of the church, he consistently defended the German viewpoint in the war. Joseph Matt of Saint Paul, Minnesota, publisher of *Der Wanderer,* was similarly committed. In his view a German victory would benefit the Catholic church. The great cultural heritage of Germany and Austria served to protect religion, he believed, while that of France and England was basically anti-Catholic. Father Joseph Och of the Columbus, Ohio, *Josephinum Weekly,* English-language paper for German Catholics, expended much space and emotion on discussions of "all the subjects upon which the German people have been slandered and misrepresented." Most German-Catholic journals evinced some measure of support for the Fatherland, and some were unrestrained in their partisanship.[31]

German Catholic response to the war in Europe may also be noted in the activities of the German Roman Catholic Central-Verein of North America. Originally established in 1854 as a national alliance of parish mutual aid societies, the Central-Verein underwent extensive reorganization in the early years of the twentieth century. Chiefly as a result of Joseph Matt's leadership, the Central-Verein was transformed into a well-knit national union of state federations. It became the bureaucratized backbone of Catholic *Deutschtum* in America, similar in structure to the secular National German-American Alliance.[32]

The relations between these two national organizations were cool. Catholics, like Lutherans, perceived the National Alliance as the latter-day manifestation of the old anticlerical, rationalistic liberalism of the Forty-eighters. Hence, despite the persistent, friendly overtures of Charles J. Hexamer and others, the Central-Verein remained aloof. Leaders like Matt and Kenkel insisted that ideological differences precluded the possibilities of meaningful cooperation, and their view generally prevailed. But there were

Fatherland, 19 May 1915

The willingness to exploit chauvinist sentiment for economic gain was not limited to German-American businessmen.

others like Joseph Frey, an affable New York businessman who became president of the Central-Verein in 1911, who were less sensitive to ideology and hoped for a rapprochement with the alliance. Shortly after the war began, Frey issued a statement declaring that German Catholics would stand solidly with their ethnic kindred.[33]

Frey's remarks were made at the annual convention of the Central-Verein, held that year in Pittsburgh. Ethnic loyalty was much in evidence. The huge assembly of delegates and guests, estimated at more than 7,000 persons, lustily sang *"Die Wacht am Rhein."* Speakers expressed their hopes for German success in the war and Frey guided the convention to adopt a series of resolutions which deplored the European resort to arms, supported American efforts at mediation, proposed a relief campaign for war sufferers, and protested the "intentional malicious publication of flagrant falsehoods" in the Anglo-American press.[34]

During the months that followed, prominent Catholic German-American leaders continued to make public display of their sympathies. Despite the disapprobation of lay leaders like Matt and Kenkel, the Central-Verein increasingly involved itself in the activities of the National Alliance. German Catholic support was given to numerous joint German-American endeavors, including the formation of the American Independence Union, the American Neutrality League, and other antiwar or pro-German interest groups.[35]

There were fundamental differences in the ways the varied groups of German-Americans reacted to the crisis of world war in 1914. But these distinctions were not readily discerned by the ordinary native American. What was there to distinguish the reported activities of the church Germans from those of the secular-minded, culturally militant club Germans? While the Catholic hierarchy and other persons who were closely identified with the churches as institutions sought to maintain a strictly nonpartisan and nonpolitical position, some of the lesser clergy and lay leaders, more exuberant in their ethnicity, unwittingly eroded the important difference between cultural maintenance and nationalistic chauvinism. Like the secular leaders who believed that they had much to gain through a resurgence of ethnic solidarity, the churchmen also tried to uphold and defend all things German, including the political and military goals of Kaiser Wilhelm II and his government. These thoughtless efforts to withstand status deprivation placed a heavy strain on the willingness of the dominant society to tolerate divergent attitudes and behavior.

Notes

1. See the President's proclamation of 19 August 1914, in Woodrow Wilson, *The Public Papers of Woodrow Wilson,* ed. Ray Stannard Baker and William E. Dodd, 6 vols. (New York: Harpers, 1925–27), 3:157–59.
2. James M. Read, *Atrocity Propaganda, 1914–1919* (New Haven: Yale University Press, 1941), pp. 29–34, 285; Horace C. Peterson, *Propaganda for War: The Campaign against American Neutrality, 1914–1917* (1939; reprinted, Port Washington, N.Y.: Kennikat Press, 1968), pp 51–70; Arthur S. Link, *Wilson,* vol. 3: *The Struggle for Neutrality, 1914–1915* (Princeton: Princeton University Press, 1960), p. 41.
3. From the *New York Tribune,* quoted in Mark Sullivan, *Our Times: The United States. 1900–1915,* 6 vols. (New York: Scribner, 1927–1936), 5:21–26.
4. *New York Times,* 1 June 1915.
5. *Washington Post,* 13 August 1914.
6. Carl Wittke, *The German-language Press in America* (Lexington: University of Kentucky Press, 1957), pp. 237–41; Carl Wittke, *German-Americans and the World War* (Columbus: Ohio State Archaeological and Historical Society, 1936), pp. 6–13; Peterson, *Propaganda for War,* p. 138; *Washington Post,* 7, 8, 13 August 1914. See also the systematic analysis of newspaper reports in Edwin Costell, *How Maine Viewed the War, 1914–1917,* University of Maine Studies, 2d series, no. 49 (Orono: University Press, 1940), pp. 14–16.
7 *New York Times,* 30 August 1914; *Washington Post,* 11 August 1914; Guido A. Dobbert, "The Disintegration of an Immigrant Community: The Cincinnati Germans, 1870–1920" (Ph.D. diss., University of Chicago, 1965), p. 191; Audrey L. Olson, "Saint

Louis Germans, 1885–1920: The Nature of an Immigrant Community and Its Relation to the Assimilation Process" (Ph.D. diss., University of Kansas, 1970), p. 183; John C. Crighton, *Missouri and the World War, 1914–1917: A Study in Public Opinion* (Columbia: University of Missouri, 1947), p. 28; Wittke, *German-Americans and the World War*, p. 23f.; Clifton J. Child, *The German-Americans in Politics, 1914–1917* (Madison: University of Wisconsin Press, 1939), pp. 24–29.

8. *Washington Post,* 12 August 1914; *Literary Digest,* 49 (22 August 1914): 293–94.

9. Niel M. Johnson, *George Sylvester Viereck* (Urbana: University of Illinois Press, 1972), p. 23.

10. See also the examples of Herbert Sanborn of Vanderbilt University, "Why the Teuton Fights," *Fatherland* 1 (24 August 1914): 6–8, and 1 (30 August 1914): 6–8, and Benjamin Wheeler, president of the University of California, in *Fatherland* 1 (18 November 1914): 3–4.

11. *Literary Digest,* 49 (22 August 1914): 300; 49 (5 September 1914): 400; 49 (12 September 1914): 442; Wittke, *German-Americans and the World War*, p. 19; *Die Abendschule* (Saint Louis) 61 (18 February 1915): 460.

12. See the example of the *Cincinnati Volksblatt,* quoted in Dobbert, "Cincinnati Germans," p. 200.

13. Quoted in Olson, "Saint Louis Germans," p. 178.

14. *New York Times,* 22 August 1914, 18 October 1914; Olson, "Saint Louis Germans," p. 183. During the years 1914–1917, the National German-American Alliance remitted a total of $866,670 to the German and Austrian ambassadors for relief purposes. U.S., Congress, Senate, Committee on the Judiciary, *Hearings on the National German-American Alliance,* (65th Cong., 2d sess., 1918), p. 266.

15. Child, *German-Americans in Politics,* pp. 1–21.

16. Ibid., p. 19. See also Frederick C. Luebke, "The German-American Alliance in Nebraska, 1910–1917," *Nebraska History,* 49 (Summer 1968): 174.

17. Child, *German-Americans in Politics,* p. 19.

18. *Hearings on the National German-American Alliance,* pp. 25–27.

19. *New York Times,* 30 August 1914; *Hearings on the National German-American Alliance,* p. 25.

20. Wittke, *German-Americans and the World War,* p. 8; Crighton, *Missouri and the World War,* pp. 29, 32–33, 37; David A. Shannon, *The Socialist Party of America* (New York: Macmillan, 1955), pp. 81–98.

21. *Lutheran Witness,* 33 (11 August 1914): 133–34; 33 (25 August 1914): 138; 33 (8 September 1914): 145.

22. *Der Lutheraner* 70 (18 August 1914): 270; 70 (1 September 1914): 281.
23. David L. Scheidt, "Some Effects of World War I on the General Synod and General Council," *Concordia Historical Institute Quarterly,* 42 (May 1970): 85–87. Virtually every issue of *Die Abendschule,* 61 (1914–1915) contains material in praise of Kaiser Wilhelm II and Germany.
24. *Literary Digest,* 49 (26 September 1914): 578.
25. Josephine H. Bente, *Biography of Dr. Friedrich Bente* (Saint Louis: Concordia Publishing House, 1936), pp. 40–44; *Die Abendschule,* 61 (24 June 1915); Link, *Wilson,* 3: 169f.; Scheidt, "Some Effects," p. 87.
26. *Der Lutheraner* 70 (10 November 1914): 373–374, 389, 392.
27. Dobbert, "Cincinnati Germans," p. 185; James C. Juhnke, "The Political Acculturation of the Kansas Mennonites, 1870–1940" (Ph.D. diss., Indiana University, 1966), pp. 130–47; *Literary Digest,* 49 (7 November 1914): 892.
28. Edward Cuddy, "Pro-Germanism and American Catholicism, 1914–1917," *Catholic Historical Review,* 54 (October 1968): 447; Philip Gleason, *The Conservative Reformers: German-American Catholics and the Social Order* (Notre Dame: Notre Dame University Press), pp. 169, 173.
29. Cuddy, "Pro-Germanism and American Catholicism," p. 447.
30. Ibid., p. 442; Dean R. Esslinger, "American German and Irish Attitudes toward Neutrality, 1914–1917: A Study of Catholic Minorities," *Catholic Historical Review,* 53 (July 1967): 200–206.
31. Gleason, *Conservative Reformers,* 160–65; Esslinger, "American German Attitudes," p. 203.
32. Gleason, *Conservative Reformers,* p. 57.
33. Ibid., pp. 154–59.
34. Ibid., p. 160f.; *Washington Post,* 10 August 1914.
35. Gleason, *Conservative Reformers,* pp. 161–71.

CHAPTER FIVE

Neutrality with an Accent

1915

On 4 July 1915, Americans were shocked to read of an attempted assassination of the financier, J. P. Morgan, Jr., at his home in Glen Cove, Long Island. His assailant, according to first reports, was Frank Holt, a Cornell University instructor of German who had just the month before earned his Ph.D. Newspaper accounts alleged that Holt, acting independently, had first detonated a bomb in the United States Capitol in Washington and then raced to New York and to the Morgan estate. Armed with two revolvers and a stick of dynamite, the amateur terrorist gained access to the mansion, where he confronted the famous banker, who had been breakfasting with guests, including the British ambassador to the United States. Before Holt could be overpowered, he shot Morgan twice, but neither wound was serious.[1]

The prisoner was not entirely coherent as he explained his intentions. He insisted that he had hoped to induce the powerful banker to use his influence to stop the manufacture and shipment of arms and munitions to Europe and to half American loans to the Allied powers. Later he asserted that he had intended to hold Mrs. Morgan as a hostage until her husband complied with his demands. In any case, it is doubtful that he had actually intended to kill Morgan. The next day Holt was identified as Erich Muenter, a German-born former Harvard professor who had disappeared in 1906 after being charged with the arsenic poisoning of his wife. Long before he could be brought to trial for his assault on Morgan, Muenter took his own life in prison by leaping headlong onto a concrete floor twenty feet below. That he was mentally deranged was commonly acknowledged. The *New York Times,* for example, agreed that Muenter was mad and that it would be improper to hold the German-American community responsible for his acts. Yet, the *Times* charged, the effect of the excessive partisanship of the German-American press "is to breed mischief in such ill-balanced minds as that of the man who attacked Morgan."[2]

The charges were not without substance. German-American newspapers had indeed been immoderate during the first year of the war. Ethnocentric editors, demanding fair play when they were unwilling to grant it to others, had been as blind in their pro-German partisanship as their pro-British detractors had been in theirs. The language they used had often been vehement, insulting, and uncompromising, yet they were extremely sensitive to criticism of any kind. The writers were especially intolerant of dissent within their own ethnic group and desperately sought to create an appearance of solidarity.

The American public was as ready to accept the illusion of German-American unity as the cultural nationalists were to foster it. The German-American press displayed a remarkable consensus on each of the issues that arose: the unfair reporting of a pro-British press, the alleged German atrocities in Belgium and France, the manufacture and sale of war materiel to the Allied powers, the embargo, the safety of American passengers on the vessels of belligerent states, and loans to the British and French governments.

The German-Americans and the administration differed sharply in their conceptions of neutrality. They argued over the meaning of international law and whether the government's policies were likely to preserve or endanger

American neutrality. Despite his unmistakably pro-British sentiments, Wilson pursued a course which he honestly believed would keep the country out of war. The German-Americans were equally convinced that his policies were essentially unneutral and that they would surely draw the United States into the European holocaust. In their view, the Wilson Administration was untrue to the President's own balanced and high-minded counsel of 19 August 1914 that the nation "must be impartial in thought as well as in action."[3]

German-American suspicions were aroused during the second week of the war by the administration's assuming control of the short-wave radio stations erected by the Germans at Sayville, Long Island, and Tuckerton, New Jersey. Beset by technical difficulties, these two stations operated only intermittently in August 1914. Nevertheless, the German-Americans believed them to be an important means of acquiring the German version of the war news since the British had cut the German cable to America. Charges of unfairness were leveled at the Wilson government when it subjected the two stations to censorship by the Navy Department, while no comparable surveillance was imposed upon British dispatches arriving via the cable from England.[4]

The German-Americans were also offended by Wilson's personal reception of a Belgian commission sent to Washington in September 1914, to protest against German atrocities. To counter the presumed Belgian influence, a self-appointed delegation of German-Americans headed by Horace Brand of Chicago, the publisher of the *Illinois Staats-Zeitung,* journeyed to the national capital to provide the President with a German version of the incidents. But Wilson refused to see them. Stung by the fact that the President withheld courtesies from American citizens that he had extended to foreigners, German-Americans deluged the White House with petitions and letters of protest. They insisted that, since Belgium was a belligerent, the President seriously compromised American neutrality by permitting the commission the freedom in the United States to elicit sympathy for the Allies and hatred for Germany.[5]

Meanwhile, Germany's sympathizers in the United States began to take notice of new purchases of American arms and ammunition, as well as foodstuffs, by Allied countries. Germany would also have taken the opportunity to buy American goods had it not been for the British navy, which was sovereign of the seas. Had Germany been able to trade with the United States as easily as the Allied powers there probably would not have been a debate. As it was, German-Americans argued that because circumstances naturally favored the British, relations with Germany were bound to deteriorate and therefore threaten the neutrality of the United States.

President Wilson held tenaciously to traditional concepts of neutrality rights. An extensive body of international law, established by a series of multilateral treaties among maritime nations, was reiterated in the official Proclamation of Neutrality of 4 August 1914, a routine statement which outlined what acts were forbidden by the laws and treaties of the United States.[6] By international agreement a neutral government was prohibited from supplying implements of war or making loans of money to belligerent nations. A neutral government, on the other hand, was not responsible for any commerce in arms and munitions which private citizens or corporations might engage in. Traders in contraband were required to assume all risks without the protection of their government; this meant that the enforcement of the restriction against neutral trade in military goods was left to the cruisers of the warring nations. The rules further specified that the search for contraband on neutral vessels was to be carried on as part of a recognized, legal blockade. In order to be legitimate, a blockade could not exist beyond enemy ports and coasts and it could not bar access to neutral harbors.

By the time the United States entered the war in 1917, all of these regulations (and others as well) had broken down.

Blockades had been extended, and interpretations of continuous voyage and ultimate destination had virtually ended all American trade with European neutrals, save that permitted by the British. International law had simply not kept pace with technological advances. There were no provisions, for example, to govern the activities of submarines. Were they on that account not to be used? Were the rules developed for cruisers to be applied to these fragile vessels? Given the inadequacy of international law, should a belligerent unilaterally announce the conditions it intended to impose upon neutral shipping?

During the fall of 1914 the debate centered on the manufacture and sale of munitions to the Allies. Already in September the State Department responded to German-American criticism by announcing that it would be unwise to impose restrictions upon American commerce in deference to the sympathies of one element of the population. A month later it published a document on the subject which stressed the legality of the trade in arms. The government, it said, had no authority to prevent sales that were permitted by international law and custom. Germany had the right to prevent the trade if it could, but her inability to do so placed no obligation on the United States to forbid it. If the government were to impose restrictions, thereby changing the rules after the game had started, it would be guilty of an unneutral act that could only be interpreted as unfriendly by the Allied powers.[7]

To many German-Americans the administration's argument merely betrayed its pro-British sympathies. It was true, they argued, that international law permitted the trade, but it hardly followed that it could not be restricted for that reason. Genuine neutrality in harmony with the spirit of the law meant taking whatever steps were necessary to treat both sides equally. Under present circumstances adhering to the letter of the law meant favoring the British side. It was obvious, the German-Americans thought, that Germany would have to take steps to hinder American aid to the Allies and that war would then be a real possibility. If the State Department could find no legal basis for regulating the merchants of death, the proper procedure, it seemed, was to enact appropriate legislation. Hence, German-American energies were next directed toward the passage of an embargo act that would prohibit the sale of war goods to any belligerent. On 7 December Representatives Richard Bartholdt of Missouri and Henry Vollmer of Iowa introduced into the House of Representatives nearly identical measures to enact an embargo. Senator Gilbert M. Hitchcock of Nebraska sponsored another in the Senate. The measures were mild, proposing only that the President be given the authority to stop the exportation of arms at his own discretion.[8]

Sentiment in favor of an arms embargo was broadly based among all segments of the population, especially in the midwestern states. Though not in the majority, its supporters were by no means limited to German-Americans. They were joined by other ethnic groups (notably the Irish and to some extent the Scandinavians), pacifists and socialists, and many intellectuals, especially economists who feared the artificial prosperity stimulated by the munitions industry. At the congressional committee hearings, testimony was offered almost exclusively by advocates of restriction, which led German-Americans to overestimate their chances of success.[9]

Unusual efforts were made to generate support for the embargo bills. Demonstrations were organized in some cities with prominent speakers addressing mass meetings. A variety of German-American church groups drafted resolutions condemning the allegedly unneutral attitude of the administration and demanding an end to "the unholy traffic in arms." Dozens of foreign-language newspapers printed an appeal to the American people to support the embargo. An avalanche of telegrams, letters, and petitions descended upon Washington. Complaints were registered with the secretary of state, and congressmen were polled regarding their stand on the matter. The German-American rhetoric frequently included threats "to visit political retributions upon those in our eyes guilty of such evasion and infraction of the ethics of neutrality," as one publicist put it.[10] At the same time, new organizations were created to concentrate pressure on the government. Among the best known were the American Independence Union, Labor's National Peace Council, the League of American Women for Strict Neutrality, and the Friends of Peace.

Despite the furor, the militant German-American leaders were not very effective. They demonstrated a considerable ability to mobilize the faithful but they failed to win much support among those native Americans who were willing to consider the merits of an embargo. It was partly a matter of style; the German-Americans lacked subtlety and tact. Instead of trying to win support for their point of view, they insisted on overpowering the opposition with logic or words or numbers. Their appeal was too obviously ethnocentric. At the mass meeting held in Saint Louis in January 1915, for example, sympathy for Germany pervaded the proceedings. The German flag was prominently displayed and a rousing chorus of *"Deutschland über Alles"* set the tone. As the speakers attempted to define a truly American neutrality they could not resist making intemperate attacks on British and American statesmanship.[11]

The German-Americans had little success in influencing the decision makers in Washington, except perhaps in a negative sense. The mountains of petitions, telegrams, and letters (invariably signed by persons or organizations with German names), were monotonously alike in wording, uniformly harsh in tone, and repititious in argument. President Wilson's tolerance wore thin and his propensity to lecture those who misbehaved was encouraged. Others in government overestimated the degree of unity and militance among German-Americans, whose loyalty and patriotism they failed to take seriously. More pathetically, their apparent success in organizing the ethnic community stimulated the German-American chauvinists to new excesses.

They knew that what they were doing was legal, but they failed to understand the extent to which they had exceeded the limits of acceptable behavior in American society.

No event illustrates this lack of comprehension better than a well-publicized conference in support of the embargo held in Washington, D.C. on 30 January 1915, under the guidance of Representative Richard Bartholdt. More than fifty prominent German-Americans participated. The majority were publishers and editors of the German-American press, including Bernard and Victor Ridder, Horace Brand, and George Sylvester Viereck. Hexamer was there, along with other cultural nationalists. Church leaders were also invited, among them Joseph Frey of the Catholic Central-Verein and the Rev. G. C. Berkemeier, the editor of the pro-German *Deutsche Lutheraner*. Several academicians were present, including Hugo Muensterberg and Edmund von Mach of Harvard and Albert B. Faust of Cornell. Non-Germans, such as Professor William R. Shepherd of Columbia, also came. The purpose of the conference was to plan a shift from defensive tactics to a positive program of political action in favor of "genuine American neutrality . . . free from commercial, financial, and political subservience to foreign powers." By the end of the day the assembly decided to found an organization, subsequently known as the American Independence Union, to carry on the fight. In addition to routine propaganda activities, the new agency was to support only those candidates for public office, irrespective of party, who promised to place "American interests above those of any other country" and who would help "to eliminate all undue foreign influence from official life."[12]

Americans who shared the Wilsonian view perceived this as sheer effrontery. The *New York Times* flayed the German-Americans mercilessly: "Never since the foundation of the Republic has a body of men assembled here who were so completely subservient to a foreign power and to foreign influence and none ever proclaimed the un-American spirit so openly." Denounced by the *Times* as "agents of German propaganda" who were "emboldened by the good-natured tolerance of the American public," the conference participants were accused of having violated their oath of allegiance when they supported the embargo through political action. The *Nation* allowed that citizens can form societies for any benevolent purpose; they may even organize to foster radical changes in the form of government or "to induce it to change its foreign policy" so long as "they are actuated by patriotic American motives. ... But when this organizing is plainly in the interest of a foreign government, ... those who undertake it are playing with extremely dangerous fire."[13]

A meaningful exchange of ideas had ceased. The German-Americans considered their patriotism as authentic as that of the *Times* or the *Nation.* They were loyal American citizens who earnestly wished to preserve American neutrality and to escape entanglement in a war foreign to American interests. Their reading of American history placed them in the mainstream tradition established by Washington and carried on by Jefferson and Lincoln. The fact that their version of strict neutrality would work to the advantage of Germany did not detract from their devotion to American interests; it was as incidental as the fact that Wilsonian neutrality tended to favor Britain. The important thing, as they saw it, was that the President's policies could only end in war with Germany, whereas their proposals were calculated to preserve peace. They resented anyone impugning their patriotism, just as Wilson was offended by German-American charges that his neutrality was tantamount to a subservience to British interests.

Only a few German-American leaders, among them Professor Kuno Francke of Harvard, understood that American society was still unsure of its ability to tolerate political activity organized on an ethnic basis, legal though it was. As one who had written much in support of the German view in 1914, Francke had also been invited to the organizing conference of the American Independence Union. However, instead of attending, he dispatched a letter to the *New York Times* in which he deplored the effort to organize the Germans politically.[14] Such an attempt, he wrote, would lead "to the degradation of the German name in this country. It would foster hatred instead of sympathy; and only by gaining the sympathy of the majority . . . can we German-Americans help the cause of our mother country." Though Francke freely admitted his enthusiasm for Germany's cause, he was more deeply concerned about the status of his fellow ethnics in American society. He argued that nothing "is more prejudicial to our position as American citizens than the clamor for recognition which is so often heard at German mass meetings. Nothing would be more fatal to our standing in the community than the insistence of racial contrasts and demands."[15]

The embargo resolutions had almost no chance of adoption in Congress even though they were supported editorially by perhaps as many as 40 percent of American newspapers. They enjoyed powerful bipartisan support, but the administration was clearly opposed to them. In January each of the bills was pigeonholed by the committee to which it had been assigned. Moreover, Germany itself had complicated matters by acknowledging the legality of the munitions trade early in December. Then, on 4 February 1915, the Kaiser's government announced that it was creating a war zone around the British Isles in which all enemy vessels would be subject to submarine attack after 18 February. Because of the British practice of displaying American flags on its ships, it was becoming increasingly difficult to distinguish neutral vessels from those of the enemy. Germany therefore warned the world that it could not be held responsible for sinkings due to false identification. On the day the war zone was to go into effect, Senator Hitchcock moved to attach his embargo bill as an amendment to the ship purchase bill being debated by the Senate at that time. Although Hitchcock's desperate maneuver was defeated by a vote of fifty-one to thirty-six, a majority of midwestern senators supported him, indicating further that the appeal of the embargo extended well beyond the German-American community.[16]

Despite this legislative defeat, the German-Americans went ahead with organizing the American Independence Union on 20 February 1915. Richard Bartholdt, who was ending his long career as a congressman, served as president. Non-German names were prominent among the officers and directors—an effort to obscure the essentially German-American character of the group. The organizers also specified that membership was to be restricted to American citizens whose loyalty "would remain absolutely unshaken and undiminished in case of war between the United States and any other country on the face of the globe." During the weeks and months that followed, the union carried on the usual propaganda activities in its support of an embargo and strict neutrality, organizing mass meetings in various cities, and scheduling speakers.[17]

The American Independence Union was one of many similar organizations established during 1914 and 1915. Among the most controversial was the German University League. Intended to enlist the support of American intellectuals who studied in Germany, it never amounted to anything more than another German-American agency to defend the Kaiser and German culture, to maintain the status of Germans in America, and to neutralize pro-British sentiment.[18]

Other organizations were more cynical in character. The Citizens' Committee for Food Shipments, organized by Edmund von Mach, was a response to the British blockade of Germany, which by 1 March 1915, had placed food on the contraband list. According to George Sylvester Viereck, this organization wished to focus public attention on the illegal practice of interfering with American mail by promoting shipments of dried milk to Germany via first class mail. Through this device, images of starving German babies were to provoke a confrontation between Britain and the United States. The agitation subsided when the German government quietly protested to German-Americans that the campaign created a negative impression of conditions within Germany. Nevertheless, Von Mach's effort set off a barrage of criticism against the Wilson Administration, which seemed willing enough to permit the shipment of guns and ammunition but allegedly obstructed the export of milk for undernourished children. Another organization, Labor's National Peace Council, was intended to mobilize the sentiment of workers against the manufacture and shipment of arms to the Allies. Actually, it functioned as a sort of labor union financed by German treasury notes. Full wages were allegedly promised to longshoremen who refused to handle war goods destined for Europe.[19]

The activities of these and kindred organizations contributed to a rejuvenation of German ethnic life in America. An exciting sense of cohesion seemed to develop as the circulation of German-language publications spiraled upward, languishing societies revived, and interest in German culture was renewed. Meanwhile, beer-philistines, as some of the coarser cultural militants were called, reveled in their command of an enlarged audience. Circumstances encouraged them to flaunt pro-German sympathies, just as editors of the German-language press became increasingly vituperative in their pronouncements. When speakers at mass meetings would mention Wilson or Secretary of State Bryan by name, loud hisses and hoots would often rise from the crowd. References to the Kaiser or to the German General Hindenburg would evoke cheers. Nor was it unusual for especially aggressive German-Americans to disrupt pro-Allied rallies by booing and by interrupting speakers. Others ostentatiously read their German-language newspapers in public places and displayed headlines announcing German victories. Sometimes pro-German meetings were held in city parks so that lusty renditions of *"Die Wacht am Rhein"* would reach the public at large.[20]

This new sense of ethnic solidarity, real enough in some quarters, disturbed and alienated other Americans of German origin. In Saint Louis a Lutheran clergyman denounced the open display of pro-German sentiment since it would inevitably result in the forfeiture of all American support. In Toledo a German-born federal jurist, less measured in his judgment, announced that "it was all the same to him if someone showered a thousand bombs upon the Kaiser's head." Others complained bitterly in letters to the press that the attitudes of many German-Americans were being misrepresented, as one writer suggested, by the noisy pro-Wilhelmists in league with "Germany's wonderful and efficient spy system."[21]

More seriously, the apparent cohesion of the German-American community was accomplished at a time when the definition of national loyalty was narrowing. Tolerance for divergent behavior was weakening as America became entangled in the far-reaching consequences of European war. Patriotic sentiment increasingly stressed the need for national unity, and slogans like "United States above all" or "Be an American first" became common.

Suspicions of German-Americans were greatly augmented by the activities of several official representatives of the German government in the United States. The ambassador, Count Johann von Bernstorff, was a skilled diplomat with a fine understanding of America and its relationship to Germany. Unfortunately for Germany's cause, he had at best only partial control over such men as Franz von Papen, the military attaché, and Karl Boy-Ed, the naval attaché, about whom many stories of intrigue circulated. Others who acquired notoriety included Dr. Bernhard Dernburg, ostensibly representing the German Red Cross but actually engaged in propaganda work, and Dr. Heinrich Albert, a privy councillor who had been assigned the task of purchasing goods for the German government. Dernburg and Albert, along with several others, were stationed in New York and were not attached to the German embassy.[22]

Bernstorff's ambassadorial task was especially difficult. Berlin did not always heed his counsel and, by his account, he was not always informed of the instructions and activities of German agents in America. This was especially true of the few genuine spies and saboteurs in America. Their activities, unlike those of Dernburg and Albert, were often illegal because they involved the destruction of property.

As a purchasing agent, Dr. Albert had a large sum of German money at his disposal. He succeeded in making a few intelligent purchases but, as the months wore on, the realities of the British naval blockade required him to find other ways to dispense his funds, which were later estimated at $38 million. He apparently arranged secret subsidies for several of the pro-German organizations (such as Labor's National Peace Council) and financed the propaganda activities of the private and unofficial German Information Service, a hastily organized press bureau in New York. There he and Dernburg met and planned with George Sylvester Viereck, William Bayard Hale, and other American instruments of German propaganda.[23]

Dernburg was a whirlwind of activity. Fluent in English, he authored numerous pamphlets, brochures, and newspaper articles and delivered dozens of speeches, mostly to German-American audiences. His forceful expositions of Germany's position did much to tighten the ranks of German-Americans, but little to convert opponents or to win the wavering. Indeed, Dernburg's defense of Germany's actions was so impolitic and the resentment it aroused was so strong that Bernstorff ultimately arranged for his "voluntary" return to Germany. He had come to symbolize all that was cold and inhuman about the German submarine policy.[24]

The problem of the submarine and its relationship to neutral rights gradually pushed other questions aside after Germany established its war zone in February. President Wilson informed the German government that the United States intended to hold it strictly accountable for any loss of American life or property.[25] There were several incidents early in 1915, but only two of them involved submarine warfare. On 28 March 1915, a German submarine sank the small, unarmed British liner *Falaba,* causing the death of an American citizen. A month later the American oil tanker *Gulflight* was torpedoed, and although the vessel did not sink, the attack resulted in the deaths of three Americans.

The *Falaba* case stimulated a vehement argument within the State Department over the alleged right of American citizens to travel in safety on the merchant ships of belligerent nations. During April 1915, Wilson sought to formulate a policy capable of preventing a breakdown in relations with Germany without abandoning neutral rights. Secretary of State Bryan, a man deeply committed to pacifist ideals, insisted that the conflict of interests could be resolved if the United States would acquiesce to German submarine warfare as it had to the British blockade and if it would warn its citizens against traveling on belligerent vessels. Other advisors, notably Robert Lansing, the counselor of the State Department, were unwilling to abandon neutral rights so readily. They tried to convince Wilson that the German policy of sinking unarmed passenger vessels was such a flagrant violation of international law that the United States had to devise a policy to cover future violations. National honor and duty, they insisted, required the government to hold Germany in "strict accountability." But the President was indecisive. Before he could make up his mind the issue was complicated by the even more serious *Gulflight* case.[26]

Bernstorff meanwhile waxed aggressive. On 9 April he submitted a memorandum to the State Department that bitterly attacked the Wilson government for its failure to protect American trade in noncontraband goods with Germany and for its refusal to restrict the exportation of arms and munitions to Britain. Hoping to influence American public opinion, Bernstorff then unilaterally released his note to the American press. Cries of astonishment greeted its publication. A flood of anti-German editorials condemned the ambassador's behavior as "insulting" and "impudent." Bernstorff's undiplomatic procedure and sledge-hammer style tended to obscure the considerable truths contained in his note.[27]

This blunder was succeeded by a much graver one. The German ambassador was genuinely concerned about the safety of American citizens on board British ships, believing that their presence clearly menaced the peace. Since

OCEAN TRAVEL.	OCEAN TRAVEL.

NOTICE!

TRAVELLERS intending to embark on the Atlantic voyage are reminded that a state of war exists between Germany and her allies and Great Britian and her allies; that the zone of war includes the waters adjacent to the British Isles; that, in accordance with formal notice given by the Imperial German Government, vessels flying the flag of Great Britian, or of any of her allies, are liable to destruction in those waters and that travellers sailing in the war zone on ships of Great Britian or her allies do so at their own risk.

IMPERIAL GERMAN EMBASSY,
WASHINGTON, D. C., APRIL 22, 1915.

CUNARD

EUROPE VIA LIVERPOOL

LUSITANIA

Fastest and Largest Steamer
now in Atlantic Service Sails
SATURDAY, MAY 1, 10 A. M.

Transylvania - Fri , May 7, 5 P.M.
Orduna, - - - Tues., May 18, 10 A.M.
Tuscania, - - - Fri., May 21, 5 P.M.
LUSITANIA, - Sat., May 29, 10 A.M.
Transylvania, - - - - - 5 P.M.

Literary Digest, 22 May 1915

The German Embassy placed this warning, called the "Death Notice" by the *Literary Digest,* next to the Cunard advertisement. It appeared in the *New York Times* on the day the *Lusitania* sailed for Europe.

the American government refused to forbid or even to discourage such "guardian angels," as the Germans called them, Bernstorff decided to place notices in major newspapers reminding American travelers that Allied vessels in the German war zone were liable to destruction and that persons who took passage on such ships did so at their own risk. Intended as a general warning, the announcement first appeared in New York papers on the very day the great British transatlantic liner *Lusitania* embarked for Liverpool.[28] Nearly a week later, as the proud ship skirted the southern coast of Ireland, a German submarine commander, without warning, dispatched the *Lusitania* to the bottom of the sea. Nearly 1,200 persons, including 124 American citizens, lost their lives.

No event in World War I stirred American emotions more profoundly. Appalled by the destruction of civilian life, most Americans condemned the sinking as a revolting crime against humanity. Their censure of the act and of the German policy that permitted it was limited only by the restrictions of the English language. A Presbyterian publication, for example, called the sinking the "worst crime of responsible government since the crucifixion of Christ." Recalling the German embassy's warning, some journalists concluded that it was a case of premeditated murder by an uncivilized and outlaw nation. Atrocity charges against Germany seemed more credible, especially when they were confirmed in the report published five days after the sinking by a British investigation headed by James Bryce, the highly respected former ambassador to the United States. Some Americans, such as Theodore Roosevelt, were convinced that it was in the American interest to intervene, and they used the tragedy to agitate for war against Germany. The prevailing sentiment, however, was to keep the peace, even though diplomatic relations with Germany were strained nearly to the breaking point.[29]

The German-American responses to the *Lusitania* catastrophe were as varied as the German element itself. A great many persons shared the commonly expressed horror: a German-born professor at the University of Rochester called it a "slap in the face of humanity" and in protest refused to conduct his classes; a prominent German-American businessman of New York, who refused to believe that the Berlin government had actually sanctioned the attack, labeled it a "wanton murder;" and Professor Hugo Muensterberg suffered such a loss of self-confidence that he withdrew from active involvement in the issues raised by the war. There was also a four-fold increase in the number of applications of German aliens in New York to acquire

New York Herald, 8 May 1915

"VELL, VE VARNED 'EM!"

This cartoon, which appeared the day after the *Lusitania* sinking, refers to the warning by the German Embassy against travel in the war zone.

American citizenship. One group of eight formed a street band to play the "Star-Spangled Banner" in front of the Federal Building in New York, then marched into the office of the chief clerk, renounced their allegiance to the Kaiser, and received their first naturalization papers. German-American Socialist opinion represented another variation. The *New York Volkszeitung,* for example, declared that the sinking of the *Lusitania,* like the war itself, was inexcusable but emphasized that American involvement must be avoided at all costs.[30]

Most German-American newspapers adopted a neutralist stance with moderately pro-German overtones, although a few applauded the sinking at first. The *Cincinnati Volksblatt,* for example, gleefully exclaimed that "the torpedoing of the *Lusitania* was a shot straight into the heart of England." But the majority deplored the tragedy. Their first concern was that the United States would keep out of the war, but they also sought to excuse Germany in the affair. Many repeated the argument of the German government that the regrettable loss of lives was the direct result of the illegal British blockade (designed to starve millions of Germans into submission), and that Germany had no choice but to retaliate with submarine warfare. Others reiterated that the American victims had foolishly ignored German warnings about travel on British ships. Most of the Kaiser's apologists also claimed that the *Lusitania* was fair game for a German torpedo because it was in the British naval reserve, because it was actually an armed vessel commanded by a captain who was also an active naval officer, and because its cargo of more than 5,000 cases of ammunition was in absolute violation of international law. Some German-Americans attributed the loss of American lives to British negligence. Britain had done nothing to protect the great liner—not a single escort vessel had been sent to accompany it through the war zone. Furthermore, the captain had performed none of the routine safety measures and antisubmarine maneuvers. A few journalists were arrogant enough to argue that the 1,200 who died had to be compared to the 100,000 German soldiers who could have been slaughtered by the bullets that sank with the *Lusitania.* Still others tried to fix the blame on Congress for refusing to enact an arms embargo and on the Wilson Administration for failing to forbid American citizens from taking passage on belligerent vessels. Finally, the most imaginative of Germany's partisans charged that the British deliberately permitted the *Lusitania* to be sunk so that the United States would be drawn into the conflict.[31]

Fear of war naturally led some journalists to question the loyalty of German-American citizens. Wild rumors circulated that several hundred thousand German-Americans living in the New York area intended to seize the city in the name of the Fatherland. Other reports alleged that German-Americans were preparing for a German invasion by secretly constructing concrete foundations for German artillery installations in New York, Washington, and other major cities. Such stories were dismissed as "malicious poppycock" by the *Outlook* which stated flatly that the "German-Americans would be loyal to the last man" in case of war with Germany. The *New York Times* was equally sensible in its evaluation of German-American loyalty. It urged Americans to recognize the painful position into which German-Americans had been thrust. Under no conceivable circumstances would any portion of the German-American element become enemy or alien; although it was natural that some dissident voices would be heard, asserted the *Times,* the marvel of it was that there were so few among the Germans in America.[32]

The German-Americans understood that the *Lusitania* crisis greatly reduced the tolerance American society had for divergent opinion. The new climate of persecution which they sensed was partly imagined, but real enough in some cases. The National German-American Alliance became one target, with its president, Charles J. Hexamer, receiving threatening letters from many parts of the country. Other German-American leaders were subjected to surveillance by private detectives. Isolated individuals relieved the tension by repudiating their German ethnicity, but many German-American publications and societies reinforced their position with outward displays of loyalty. The *Saint Paul Volkszeitung,* for example, observed that "no matter how great the suffering and mental agony that German-Americans would undergo, there can be no question about their loyalty to the Stars and Stripes." The president of the German Veterans Alliance of North America announced that German-Americans would unhesitatingly take up arms against their old Fatherland. The German Catholic Union of Baltimore resolved in convention to express its undivided loyalty to the American flag. The Massachusetts branch of the National German-American Alliance, among others, adopted similar resolutions.[33]

But there were other German-Americans who responded to the new intensity of anti-German feeling by encouraging an even greater sense of ethnic solidarity and its attendant separatism. The *Chicagoer Presse,* published by Horace Brand, charged that Americans were discriminating against German-American businessmen, especially grocers and butchers. Hence, this paper suggested, German-Americans should counter the boycott by patronizing only German-American establishments. Others hoped to sustain ethnic unity by organizing more mass demonstrations. Madison Square Garden in New York was the scene of a great rally on 24 June 1915. Its chief sponsor, Henry Weismann of the New York branch of the National German-American Alliance, won the cooperation of Socialist, Catholic, and Irish organizations in promoting the venture. A huge crowd of more than 70,000 persons participated, far more than could be accommodated within the building, making additional outdoor sessions necessary.[34]

German-Americans waited and watched anxiously during the summer of 1915. Many were thoroughly frightened by the talk of war. According to Ambassador von Bernstorff, they were terror-stricken by the violence of the American reaction to the *Lusitania* sinking. Although President Wilson had been deeply shaken by the *Lusitania* tragedy, he clearly intended to resolve the crisis without resorting to armed conflict. Three days after the sinking, in an address to 4,000 newly naturalized citizens in Philadelphia, he extemporized that one could be "too proud to fight," that a nation could be "so right that it doesn't need to convince others by force that it is right." Wilson later regretted having uttered these words, subject as they were to gross misinterpretation. In contrast to that speech, his several notes to the German government defended neutrality rights in the strongest terms, so strong, indeed, that Secretary of State Bryan resigned his post rather than sign the note of 9 June. Convinced that Wilson's course would ultimately plunge the nation into war because of its innately pro-Allied character, Bryan quixotically believed that he could do more for the cause of peace by making speeches as a private citizen than by making decisions as secretary of state.[35]

At first German-Americans generally approved of Wilson's conduct in the crisis. The extremists, of course, were obdurate. Henry Weismann denounced Wilson as the dupe of Wall Street pirates; the Wisconsin branch of the National German-American Alliance voted to censure the President; and Professor Edmund von Mach of Harvard ridiculed Wilson's refusal to recognize that the submarine was a new weapon that required new rules. But expressions of confidence in Wilson were more common. The president of the German-American Press Association said that Wilson's "handling of an extremely delicate situation [had] been admirable." Henry Kersting, president of the Saint Louis branch of the National German-American Alliance, praised the frankness and manner of the President's "statesmanlike note" and observed that "it deserved to take high rank among American state papers." The *Saint Paul Volkszeitung* rejoiced "to see the President take such a strong stand for upholding the rights of American citizens." Even *Die Abendschule* of Saint Louis, which had been unremitting in its German partisanship, suggested that its readers contemplate a reversal of roles: suppose Germany was a neutral and America a belligerent; would the Kaiser have done anything less than Wilson, it asked, if many German citizens had drowned because they had been passengers on a belligerent vessel sunk by the United States?[36]

As the summer wore on, it became apparent that the United States would not go to war with Germany over the *Lusitania* incident. Thereafter German-American editorial support for Wilson gradually weakened.[37] It became increasingly difficult for the chauvinists to repair the deepening cracks in the facade of German-American unity. They were even rebuffed at the biennial convention of the National German-American Alliance held early in August in San Francisco. Six officers, including four vice-presidents, threatened to resign their posts if the convention gave its approval to a letter for President Wilson that had been drafted by some of his severest critics. America's "criminally pernicious" traffic in munitions, the letter said, had caused Americans to be pilloried "before the world as consummate hypocrites." It demanded that the President restore America's "reputation, its honor, its fair and unsullied name." The convention ultimately adopted, with Charles J. Hexamer's support, a letter much milder in tone. Meanwhile, the pro-German Labor's National Peace Council suffered a blow as its first vice-president resigned, charging that the organization was a propagandistic front subsidized by the German government and that its character as a labor group was fraudulent.[38]

Similar problems plagued an effort to rally the faithful at a national Friends of Peace congress, held in Chicago early in September. The organizers of this affair sought to broaden the base of support for their version of neutrality by inviting the support of labor unions, pacifist societies, the Socialist party, Catholic organizations, and Irish ethnic leaders. William Jennings Bryan and Washington Gladden, a prominent Protestant clergyman, were scheduled to address the assembly. But the pro-Germanism of the sponsors (including Henry Weismann, Congressman Henry Vollmer, the Lutheran clergyman G. C. Berkemeier, the Catholic lay leader Alphonse Koelble, and Jeremiah O'Leary, the Irish-American firebrand) was too well known for this attempt at exploitation of pacifist sentiment to succeed. Samuel Gompers, the president of the American Federation of Labor, discouraged labor union participation. Pacifists and socialists refused to send delegations. Gladden failed to appear in Chicago and Bryan, who did show up, was noticeably embarrassed by the proceedings. Poorly attended, the congress merely confirmed the prejudices of both the participants and their enemies. Hostility was so intense that the Chicago police were called out to maintain order.[39]

The failure of the Friends of Peace demonstration and its strong anti-Wilson rhetoric was due partly to the success of the President's diplomacy. On 1 September Bernstorff had assured Robert Lansing, the newly appointed secretary of state, that his government had ordered the cessation of submarine attacks on passenger ships without warning, provided the liners did not offer resistance or try to escape. This concession came after Wilson's negotiations with the German government had reached a new crisis with the torpedoing of the liner *Arabic* on 19 August. Two Americans had been among the fifty persons killed. Wilson and Lansing thereupon resolved to force the issue, and after several days of anxious consultation, the Germans decided to abandon unrestricted submarine warfare as not worth the risk of American intervention.[40]

Ambassador von Bernstorff played the key role in the negotiations. Sensitive to shifts in American opinion, he had urgently warned his superiors in Berlin that if a breach was to be avoided some action must be taken to pacify public attitudes. The situation at the end of August had become critical because of a series of articles published in the *New York World* exposing German propaganda efforts in the United States. The revelations were based on documents found in a portfolio stolen from Dr. Heinrich Albert, the

German propagandist and financial agent in New York. One day late in July, Albert, accompanied by George Sylvester Viereck, was on his way home on the Sixth Avenue Elevated train. Viereck left at Twenty-third Street and Albert continued on alone. Soon after, the clicking and swaying of the train lulled him to sleep. He awoke with a start at the Fiftieth Street station, where he wanted to leave the train, and dashing from the car, he left his precious briefcase behind. He came to his senses on the platform, returned to the train, and frantically tried to retrieve his documents. He never saw them again. The portfolio had been snatched up by Frank Burke, one of several Secret Service agents assigned by order of the President to shadow German officials in the United States.[41]

The materials were brought to the attention of Secretary of the Treasury William G. McAdoo, the administrator responsible for the Secret Service, who recognized immediately that they gave substance to many rumors and accusations that had filled the air for several months. German efforts to influence the American press and to control an important daily newspaper, subsidies for Viereck's *Fatherland,* support for professional lecturers, the publication of pro-German books and pamphlets, the financing of the movement to halt the arms trade, attempts to purchase munitions factories and otherwise prevent shipments of supplies to the Allies—all were revealed in sensational detail. Yet all of the documented activities were legal, in contrast to the theft of the portfolio by an official agent of the United States government. Eager to discredit the German propaganda effort without impeaching the integrity of the administration, McAdoo secretly released the choicest materials to the loyal Wilson supporter Frank I. Cobb, editor of the *New York World,* who began to publish them on 15 August, four days before the *Arabic* was sunk.[42]

The Albert papers were widely reprinted and did much to stimulate anti-German feeling, especially in the eastern states. The exposé was published at a time when the country was on the brink of war and even though the German propaganda was legal, it was decried as "subsidized sedition," "double-faced treachery," and "unscrupulous and colossal machination." The *World* passionately asserted that the German purpose was "to destroy American neutrality, sacrifice American interests, and annihilate American rights for the advancement of German arms." Some papers even raised the cry of treason. Ironically, the implicated German-Americans had done nothing more than what partisans of the Allied cause were doing.[43]

A spate of books, articles, and tracts published in 1915 also raised the pitch of feeling against German-Americans. During April and May several articles appeared in British publications which attacked German-Americans in general and the National German-American Alliance in particular. Obvious examples of British propaganda, these pieces were occasionally reprinted in America or served as sources for domestically produced diatribes. In the summer of 1915 *The German-American Plot,* authored by the journalist Frederic W. Wile, appeared. Though published in London, the book received wide distribution and favorable reviews in the United States. Seeing pro-German intrigues everywhere, the author hurled wild charges of disloyalty against German-Americans, especially those of the Midwest. In October a similar volume, *German Conspiracies in America,* ostensibly written by an American "from an American point of view," was produced in England by William Skaggs. This hastily assembled smear concentrated on German-American political activities. In the same month a prominent Indianapolis attorney, Lucius B. Swift, wrote a pamphlet entitled "Germans in America" which sold forty thousand copies, mostly in Indiana.[44]

By the fall of 1915 a full-scale assault on "hyphenism" was underway. The term was by no means new to public debate but in the context of a world war that threatened to engulf the United States it acquired a new currency, especially in the rhetoric of Theodore Roosevelt. A frank advocate of American intervention, TR raged at anyone whose

Ireland in *Columbus Dispatch*

HALF-WAY AMERICANS NOT WANTED

The campaign against "hyphenism" was under way by fall, 1915.

---

concept of Americanism differed from his own. He defined a hyphenate as a person whose loyalties were divided between America and the old country or, as he put it in a letter to Viereck, "an American citizen [who] is really doing everything to subordinate the interests and duty of the United States to the interests of a foreign land." In practice this meant that any German-born American citizen who advocated, for example, an embargo on the munitions trade or restrictions on neutrals traveling on belligerent vessels was a hyphenate. As historian Merle Curti has pointed out, there is no evidence that Roosevelt ever developed a standard for testing policies he favored as being genuinely in the national interest (and therefore patriotic) or as merely corresponding to his own temperament and class preferences.[45] Thus, even though TR repeatedly endeavored to distinguish Americans of German origins from "professional German-Americans"—such as Hexamer, Weismann, Viereck, Brand, and the Ridders—the distinction was meaningless. Anyone who retained ties with German culture could be accused of disloyalty.

Wilson's role in the antihyphen campaign of 1915 was more subtle than Roosevelt's. Instead of attacking the German-Americans directly, the President spoke in general terms, as in his famous "too-proud-to-fight" speech, delivered to a group of newly naturalized citizens of Philadelphia several days after the *Lusitania* catastrophe:

You cannot become thorough Americans if you think of yourselves in groups. America does not consist of groups. A man who thinks of himself as belonging to a particular national group in America has not yet become an American, and the man who goes among you to trade upon your nationality is no worthy son to live under the Stars and Stripes. ... and the man who seeks to divide man from man, group from group, interest from interest, in this great Union is striking at its very heart.[46]

Although Wilson's remarks were clearly aimed at his German- and Irish-American critics, they are more important for the insight they offer into the President's conception of American society. In denying its pluralistic or group character, his words imply a loss of confidence in the country's capacity to assimilate the millions of immigrants who had arrived in the preceding decade. Wilson, like many old-stock Americans, appeared disturbed because the heat generated by the European war seemed to retard rather than to hasten the fusion process of the "melting pot." The effect of Wilson's position was to deny the legitimacy of policies or politics aimed at satisfying the particular needs or desires of newly arrived ethnic groups if they differed

Kirby in *New York World*

"THAT MAN WILSON IS CRAZY!"

markedly from those of older, better established Americans. Ironically, it was Wilson himself who, in the name of national unity, unwittingly drew invidious distinctions between men, groups, and interests and reduced new Americans to second-class citizenship.

Despite the frequent assertions of undivided loyalty by German-Americans and declarations of confidence in their patriotism by many old-stock Americans in the summer of 1915, Wilson retained deep suspicions. In July he learned of the activities in America of Captain Franz von Rintelen, a

German spy. He secretly feared some kind of German-American collusion and therefore directed government investigators to follow up every clue. But nothing involving American citizens that threatened national security was discovered. At the time of the Albert disclosures he consulted with his close friend, Colonel Edward M. House, on what to expect in case of war with Germany. House, on the basis of no discernible evidence, advised Wilson on 26 August 1915, that "attempts will likely be made to blow up waterworks, electric light and gas plants, subways and bridges in cities like New York." House further assured the President that he did not "look for any organized rebellion or outbreak, but merely some degree of frightfulness in order to intimidate the country."[47]

The events of August and September evidently convinced Wilson of the need to speak out publicly against "hyphenism." On 11 October 1915, he addressed the Daughters of the American Revolution in Washington. After affirming his belief in the patriotism of the vast majority of foreign-born citizens, he declared that he wanted "an opportunity to have a line-up and let the men who are thinking first of other countries stand on one side . . . and all those that are for America, first, last, and all the time on the other side." The tone of this message harmonized perfectly with the trumpeting of Theodore Roosevelt, who declared to the Kinghts of Columbus in New York the next day that "there is no room in this country for hyphenated Americanism." Roosevelt, with a characteristic lack of moderation, saw treason in the activities of "those hyphenated Americans who terrorize American politicians by threats of the foreign vote." Widely noted in the American press, these two speeches set the pitch for an ensuing chorus of intolerance.[48]

Three weeks later President Wilson addressed the Manhattan Club in New York. Although his main theme was military preparedness, hyphenism provided the counterpoint. "Very loud and very clamorous" voices have been raised in recent months, he declaimed, which professed "to be the voices of Americans [but] were not indeed and in truth American, but which spoke alien sympathies." They "were partisans of other causes than that of America," the President said, and it was "high time that the nation should call [them] to a reckoning."[49]

It is hardly appropriate to attribute the wave of intolerance that inundated the United States in the fall of 1915 to the rhetoric of Theodore Roosevelt and Woodrow Wilson. These men merely rode its crest and sanctioned it with their moral authority. A sequence of events had created a heightened sense of national crisis: the *Lusitania* tragedy in May, the assault on J. P. Morgan, Jr., in July, the exposés provided by Dr. Albert's portfolio and the sinking of the *Arabic* in August. Then, early in September, came news of intrigue by Dr. Konstantin Dumba, the ambassador of Austria-Hungary to the United States. Dumba had warned Austrian subjects in the United States that they would be considered guilty of treason if they worked in factories supplying arms and ammunition for their homeland's enemies. Dumba was then charged with fomenting strikes and walkouts, and Wilson requested his recall by the Vienna government. A few days later the government leaked reports of Rintelen's espionage. Disclosures appeared intermittently through November in the *New York World,* and were widely reprinted. By the end of 1915 hundreds of stories were circulating in the national press about German bomb plots, intrigues, and conspiracies, often linked with unnamed German-Americans. Meanwhile, the German military and naval attachés, Von Papen and Boy-Ed, were also identified with numerous intrigues (not without basis in fact), and in December Wilson decided to request their recall also.[50]

Cartoonists, columnists, and well-meaning clergymen united in the campaign against the hyphen. Attacks were not made specifically on German cultural traits, but rather on "immigrants of divided loyalties," a category sufficiently vague to include any German-American who dissented from majority opinion. Sinister tales of espionage and sabotage reinforced the image of the German-American as the advance agent of a Pan-German conspiracy, as the willing tool of the Kaiser, and as the subverter of national solidarity.[51]

President Wilson provided the capstone for the anti-hyphenate movement in his State of the Union message of 7 December 1915. Again the main emphasis of his address was on preparedness, but he rambled on at some length about those "infinitely malignant" hyphenates, "creatures of passion ... and anarchy" who "preach and practice disloyalty." Wilson leveled unsubstantiated charges against unnamed Americans:

There are citizens of the United States, ... born under other flags but welcomed under our generous naturalization laws to the full freedom and opportunity of America, who have poured the poison of disloyalty into the very arteries of our national life; who have sought to bring the authority and good name of our Government into contempt, to destroy our industries wherever they thought it effective for their vindictive purposes to strike at them, and to debase our politics to the uses of foreign intrigue.[52]

Such men, the President further advised Congress, "must be crushed out ... the hand of our power should close over them at once." The House of Representatives immediately responded with a resolution asking the President to be specific in his charges. He refused to comply, believing that "it would seriously interfere with the ends of justice."[53]

The President's annual message drove a deeper wedge between "hyphenated Americans" and other groups making up the nation. His denunciation of allegedly disloyal citizens elicited enthusiastic applause from many leading American newspapers, but the German-American journalists knew the President had them in mind and they fiercely resented it.[54] Some persons were frightened and withdrew from any action or opinion that could implicate them. Others were goaded to defensive postures and nervously reiterated their undivided loyalty to their adopted homeland. But the vocal minority, too deeply committed to back off, continued to supplement their professions of patriotism with at-

Bradley in *Chicago Daily News*

HIS SHELTER

German-American citizens were accused of bomb plots, intrigues, and conspiracies.

tacks on Wilson's pro-Allied neutrality with its arms trade, neutral passengers aboard belligerent vessels, and loans to the British and French governments.

As the antihyphen movement got under way, the German-American chauvinists began to concentrate on the question of loans. They felt that Wilson's shifts on this question, like others, betrayed his strongly pro-Allied sympathies. In August 1914, the Department of State had declared that loans to belligerent countries were incompatible with a true spirit of neutrality. Cash and carry was to be the rule.

Pro-Ally publications tended to denounce definitions of the American interest by German-born citizens as disloyal to American institutions.

Two months later, however, as British and French orders for war goods began to stream in to American manufacturers, Wilson approved a distinction between credits and loans: the former were permitted, the latter were not. Under these arrangements the Allied powers had purchased enormous quantities of arms and ammunition by August 1915, but had paid for little more than a third of them. The British deficit alone had reached nearly $1 billion by 30 June 1915, and promised to more than double by the end of the year. Full payment, however, would have imperiled not only British solvency but American prosperity as well, since all further orders would have had to cease. Although German-Americans contemplated that possibility with considerable pleasure, American bankers were alarmed. By mid-August, the British pound began seriously to decline in value. The only answer appeared to be a gigantic American loan of a half billion dollars. Secretary of the Treasury McAdoo, who was Wilson's son-in-law, argued persuasively for the loan as beneficial for the American economy. But, as historian Arthur S. Link has noted, Wilson was inclined to change his policy also because of his conception of strict neutrality. If preventing belligerents from purchasing war goods in America would be an unneutral act, preventing loans to belligerents for those purchases would be equally unneutral. Thus, as the nation came close to war over the *Arabic* crisis at the end of August, the administration let it be known informally that it would not object to a British loan.[55]

Two weeks later an Allied commission arrived in New York to negotiate the transaction. Arrangements were completed by 28 September for floating a loan of $500 million, half of what the commissioners had hoped to get. Despite the unofficial endorsement of the administration, however, the bonds found few buyers, and ultimately the underwriting banks had to assume more than 60 percent of the amount. The spectacular failure of the bonds to sell was due to many factors, not the least being German-American opposition.[56]

The commissioners had hardly disembarked when Charles J. Hexamer sounded the alarm. He dispatched a memorandum to all state and local branches of the National German-American Alliance denouncing the loan as a conspiracy to rob the people of their savings. He urged alliance members to register their objections with their bankers in every way possible and to threaten withdrawal of deposits if they discovered participation in the venture. The response was nationwide. In New York a committee of a hundred persons, representing enormous deposits by German-Americans, applied pressure to that city's financial institutions. The Minnesota Alliance advised its members to put their money only in those banks which gave positive assurance that no funds were invested in Allied securities. In Saint Louis, the local alliance organized a special committee to investigate bankers' attitudes toward the loan. In Milwaukee all banks refused to purchase any of the bonds. Protest meetings were conducted and the usual letters and telegrams were sent to Washington. Many German-language newspapers joined in the hue and cry. The *New Yorker Herold,* for example, printed its attack in English with the headline, "Why buy British bonds when Confederate bonds are cheaper and just as good?"[57]

Despite the intensity of feeling against all things German that had developed by the end of 1915, there is little evidence that German-Americans, even the most avid pro-German propagandists, suffered active persecution. In September 1915, the Union League of Chicago allegedly barred Horace Brand, the chauvinistic editor of the *Illinois Staats-Zeitung,* from membership because of allegedly un-American utterances.[58] Other isolated instances of discrimination occurred, but harassment of German-Americans clearly was not a major problem during the neutrality period. Occasionally the noisiest of German partisans complained that they were not treated fairly. This is understandable because their identities, indeed, their means of livelihood, were intimately tied to ethnic solidarity. But the great majority did not feel persecuted in a personal way.

Anti-Germanism was more subtle than simple harassment. German-Americans sensed it in whispers and rumors, in glances charged with suspicions, in offhand remarks and in the heated eloquence of impersonal editorials, speeches, and sermons. A vague, generalized feeling, it was the more insidious because it lacked specificity. British propaganda roasted the Germans as cruel beasts, criminal barbarians, and lying Huns. Prussianism, Kaiserism, and Pan-Germanism were converted into pejorative terms. Finally, as historian Horace C. Peterson has pointed out, "the word German itself came to signify all that was base" and "pro-German" became the superlative epithet.[59] Anti-Germanism easily corroded the self-esteem of German-Americans and goaded many to compensate by strengthening their ethnocultural loyalties and by making new demands that their rights be respected and their views recognized. They felt they were misunderstood even when they were not. Ironically, two opposing forces had worked to isolate the German-Americans from the rest of society. The chauvinistic leaders of the ethnic community bombarded them with exhortations to cultural separatism and militant solidarity even as Wilson, Roosevelt, and other national spokesmen cut them off as disloyal hyphenates. Frustration mingled with fear as they asserted their patriotism and defended their conception of neutrality.

Notes

1. *New York Times,* 4 July 1915.
2. Ibid., 5, 6, 7 July 1915. See also *Literary Digest,* 51 (17 July 1915): 95–97.
3. Woodrow Wilson, *The Public Papers of Woodrow Wilson,* ed. Ray Stannard Baker and William E. Dodd, 6 vols. (New York: Harpers, 1925–1927), 3: 159.
4. *New York Times,* 6, 7, 14, 21, 31 August 1915, 17 September 1915; Clifton J. Child, *The German-Americans in Politics, 1914–1917* (Madison: University of Wisconsin Press, 1939), p. 31.
5. Child, *German-Americans in Politics,* p. 65; Michael Singer, "Deutschamerika in den Kriegsjahren," *Jahrbuch der Deutschamerikaner für das Jahr 1918,* ed. Michael Singer (Chicago: German Yearbook Publishing Co., 1917), p. 170; Carl Wittke, *German-Americans and the World War* (Columbus: Ohio State Archaeological and Historical Society, 1936), p. 46.
6. Wilson, *Public Papers,* 3:151–56.
7. Child, *German-Americans in Politics,* p. 45; "Neutrality and Trade in Contraband," issued by the Department of State, 15 October 1914, reprinted in *Congressional Record,* 63rd Cong., 2d sess., 1914, 51, pt. 16: 16814.
8. *Literary Digest,* 50 (2 January 1915): 3; *Fatherland* 1 (28 October 1915): 3–4; Singer, "Deutschamerika in den Kriegsjahren," p. 171; Child, *German-Americans in Politics,* pp. 48–49; *Congressional Record,* 63rd Cong., 3d sess., 1914, 52 pt. 1: 6, 12.
9. *New York Times,* 15 December 1914; *Literary Digest,* 49 (26 December 1914): 1259f., 50 (6 February 1915): 225–26, 274f.; Child, *German-Americans in Politics,* pp. 49, 55.
10. Wittke, *German-Americans and the World War,* pp. 59–62; Child, *German-Americans in Politics,* pp. 51–52; Gustavus Oh-

linger, "German Propaganda in the United States," *Atlantic Monthly,* 117 (April 1916): 539; Frederick F. Schrader, "We Demand Real Neutrality," *Fatherland,* 1 (30 December 1914): 11.

11. John C. Crighton, *Missouri and the World War, 1914–1917: A Study in Public Opinion* (Columbia: University of Missouri, 1947), pp. 90–91.

12. *New York Times,* 31 January 1915; Child, *German-Americans in Politics,* pp. 52–55.

13. *New York Times,* 1 February 1915; *Nation,* 119 (10 February 1915): 133–34. See also *Literary Digest,* 50 (13 Feburary 1915): 299–301.

14. *New York Times,* 3 February 1915.

15. Francke's letter evoked widespread response. See *New York Times,* 5 February 1915; *Nation,* 100 (11 February 1915): 156; *Independent,* 81 (22 February 1915): 265; *Literary Digest,* 50 (13 February 1915): 299–301.

16. *Literary Digest,* 50 (6 February 1915): 225–26, 274f.; Child, *German-Americans in Politics,* p. 57; Count Johann Bernstorff, *My Three Years in America* (New York: Scribners, 1920), pp. 73–75; John M. Cooper, Jr., *The Vanity of Power: American Isolationism and the First World War, 1914–1917* (Westport, Conn.: Greenwood, 1969), pp. 28–32; Wittke, *German-Americans and the World War,* p. 68; *Congressional Record,* 63rd Cong., 3d sess., 1915, 52, pt. 4:4016.

17. *New York Times,* 21 February 1915; Richard Bartholdt, *From Steerage to Congress: Reminiscences and Reflections* (Philadelphia: Dorrance, 1930), pp. 1376–77; *Fatherland,* 2 (3 March 1915): 15.

18. *New York Times,* 13, 24 January 1915; A. Busse, "Der deutsche Akademikerbund," in *Jahrbuch der Deutschamerikaner für das Jahr 1918,* ed. Michael Singer (Chicago: German Yearbook Publishing Company, 1917), pp. 319–26; George S. Viereck, *Spreading Germs of Hate* (New York: Horace Liveright, 1930), pp. 94, 99.

19. Viereck, *Spreading Germs,* pp. 95–97, 99; Wittke, *German-Americans and the World War,* p. 51.

20. *New York Times,* 22 February 1915; Crighton, *Missouri and the World War,* p. 91; Guido A. Dobbert, "The Disintegration of an Immigrant Community: The Cincinnati Germans, 1870–1920" (Ph.D. diss., University of Chicago, 1965), pp. 225f.

21. Crighton, *Missouri and the World War,* p. 91; Child, *German-Americans in Politics,* p. 32; *New York Times,* 3 August 1915.

22. Horace C. Peterson, *Propaganda for War: The Campaign against American Neutrality, 1914–1917* (Norman: University of Oklahoma Press, 1939), p. 147; Bernstorff, *My Three Years,*

pp. 31, 40–42; Walter Millis, *The Road to War: America 1914–1917* (Boston: Houghton Mifflin, 1935), pp. 70–73, 147–48.

23. Peterson, *Propaganda for War*, p. 143; Bernstorff, *My Three Years*, pp. 47–50; Millis, *Road to War*, pp. 73, 147, 203, 205; Viereck, *Spreading Germs*, p. 43–59.

24. Viereck, *Spreading Germs*, pp. 56–58, and *passim;* Bernstorff, *My Three Years*, p. 140, 145f.; *New York Times*, 12 June 1915.

25. Arthur S. Link, *Wilson*, vol. 3: *The Struggle for Neutrality, 1914–1915* (Princeton: Princeton University Press, 1960), pp. 320–24.

26. Ibid,. pp. 358–67; Paolo Coletta, *William Jennings Bryan*, vol. 2: *Progressive Politician and Moral Statesman, 1909–1915* (Lincoln: University of Nebraska Press, 1969), pp. 301–7, 310.

27. Link, *Wilson*, 3:350–53; Bernstorff, *My Three Years*, pp. 75–77; *Literary Digest*, 59 (17 April 1915): 861; 50 (24 April 1915): 937.

28. Bernstorff, *My Three Years*, p. 137–39; *New York Times*, 1 May 1915.

29. *Literary Digest*, 50 (15 May 1915): 1133–35; 50 (22 May 1915): 1197–99, 1218; Bernstorff, *My Three Years*, p. 140.

30. *Outlook*, 110 (19 May 1915): 112; Phyllis Keller, "German-America and the First World War" (Ph.D. diss., University of Pennsylvania, 1969), pp. 137, 270; *New York Times*, 12 May 1915, 8 June 1915. *Literary Digest*, 50 (22 May 1915): 1219 provides pro-German statements made by German-American clergymen.

31. Wittke, *German-Americans and the World War*, pp. 72–73; *Outlook*, 110 (19 May 1915): 116; *Nation*, 100 (20 May 1915): 549; *Literary Digest*, 50 (15 May 1915): 1134; 50 (22 May 1915): 1200f.; 50 (29 May 1915): 1262–64; *Die Abendschule* 61 (27 May 1915): 678; Child, *German-Americans in Politics*, 67–71.

32. *Outlook*, 110 (9 June 1915): 307; *New York Times*, 15, 16, 17 May 1915. See also "German-American Loyalty," *Literary Digest*, 50 (29 May 1915): 1262f.

33. Child, *German-Americans in Politics*, p. 68, *Literary Digest*, 50 (30 May 1915): 1262–64; *New York Times*, 16, 17, 24 May 1915.

34. *New York Times*, 11 May 1915; Child, *German-Americans in Politics*, p. 76.

35. Bernstorff, *My Three Years*, p. 144; Wilson, *Public Papers*, 3:318–22, 323, 329, 341–46; Coletta, *Bryan*, 2: 329–61; Lawrence W. Levine, *Defender of the Faith, William Jennings Bryan: The Last Decade, 1915–1925* (New York: Oxford University Press, 1965), pp. 14–21.

36. Child, *German-Americans in Politics*, p. 78; *New York Times*, 12 June 1915, 15 May 1915; *Literary Digest*, 50 (29 May 1915): 1263; *Die Abendschule* 61 (27 May 1915): 675.

37. *Literary Digest,* 51 (24 July 1915): 142.
38. Child, *German-Americans in Politics,* pp. 79–80; *Outlook,* 110 (18 August 1915): 880–81.
39. Andrew J. Townsend, "The Germans of Chicago" (Ph.D. diss., University of Chicago, 1927), p. 172; Child, *German-Americans in Politics,* pp. 81–83; *New York Times,* 3, 4 September 1915.
40. *New York Times,* 2 September 1915; Link, *Wilson,* 3: 565–85.
41. Link, *Wilson,* 3: 554–56, 579, 582–84; Viereck, *Spreading Germs,* pp. 68–71; Millis, *Road to War,* pp. 207–8; Mark Sullivan, *Our Times: The United States, 1900–1925,* vol. 5: *Over Here, 1914–1918* (New York: Scribner's, 1933), pp. 184–87.
42. Peterson, *Propaganda for War,* p. 154; Millis, *Road to War,* p. 214.
43. *Literary Digest,* 51 (28 August 1915): 338; *Outlook,* 110 (25 August 1915): 934.
44. Child, *German-Americans in the War,* p. 99; Richard O'Connor, *The German-Americans: An Informal History* (Boston: Little, Brown, 1968), p. 392f.; Cedric C. Cummins, *Indiana Public Opinion and World War, 1914–1917* (Indianapolis: Indiana Historical Bureau, 1945), p. 148. See also the series of articles by Frank P. Olds in the *Milwaukee Journal,* starting 15 October 1915.
45. Theodore Roosevelt to George Sylvester Viereck, *The Letters of Theodore Roosevelt,* ed. Elting E. Morison, 8 vols. (Cambridge: Harvard University Press, 1954), 8: 911; Merle Curti, *The Roots of American Loyalty* (New York: Columbia University Press, 1946), p. 197.
46. Wilson, *Public Papers,* 3: 319–20.
47. Link, *Wilson,* 3: 563; Charles Seymour, *The Intimate Papers of Colonel House,* 4 vols. (Boston: Houghton Mifflin, 1926–1928), 2: 34–35.
48. Wilson, *Public Papers,* 3: 379; *New York Times,* 13 October 1915; *Current Opinion,* 59 (December 1915): 376–77.
49. Wilson, *Public Papers,* 3:390–91.
50. Link, *Wilson,* 3:646–50; Arthur S. Link, *Wilson,* vol. 4: *Confusions and Crises, 1915–1916* (Princeton: Princeton University Press, 1964), pp. 56–59; *Literary Digest,* 51 (6 November 1915): 993–95; 51 (27 November 1915): 1207–9.
51. Child, *German-Americans in Politics,* pp. 87–88; John Higham, *Strangers in the Land: Patterns of American Nativism, 1860–1925,* 2d ed. (New York: Atheneum, 1963), p. 197; "A 'Swat the Hyphen' Movement," *Literary Digest,* 51 (30 October 1915): 943–44.
52. Wilson, *Public Papers,* 3: 423–24.

53. [James D. Richardson, ed.], *Messages and Papers of the Presidents,* 22 vols. (New York: Bureau of National Literature, 1897–1929), 17:8120.
54. *Literary Digest,* 51 (18 December 1915): 1412.
55. Child, *German-Americans in Politics,* pp. 58–62; Link, *Wilson,* 3:622–25.
56. Link, *Wilson,* 3:625–28.
57. Child, *German-Americans in Politics,* pp. 59–60; *Literary Digest,* 51 (25 September 1915): 647–49; Singer, "Deutschamerika in den Kriegsjahren," pp. 186–87; *New York Times,* 16, 19, 20, 24 September 1915; Crighton, *Missouri and the World War,* p. 61; Link, *Wilson,* 3: 627; *Literary Digest,* 51 (9 October 1915): 760; O'Connor, *German-Americans,* p. 391. See also George Sylvester Viereck's attacks on loans to the Allies in *Fatherland,* 3, beginning 1 September 1915.
58. Townsend, "Germans of Chicago," p. 136.
59. Peterson, *Propaganda for War,* p. 68.

CHAPTER SIX

Furor Teutonicus

THE ELECTION OF 1916

By January 1916 the attitudes and arguments of both the German-American ethnic group and the apostles of super-patriotism were fully developed. The latter continued to define neutrality, patriotism, and Americanism in terms deemed unreasonable by their ethnic antagonists. They made no serious effort to understand the problems of German immigrants in American society at a time when war with Germany threatened. Nor could they comprehend that, even though most ethnic citizens conformed superficially to American standards of behavior, they were still a long way from full assimilation into the structure of American society and therefore had strong psychological needs which dictated the retention of emotional ties with their mother culture. War in Europe had stimulated superpatriots to utter many intolerant expressions of Anglo-conformity, but few matched the "fundamental conviction" of Walter Hines Page, the United States ambassador to Great Britain, who wrote privately in June 1916, that "we Americans have got to ... hang our Irish agitators and shoot our hyphenates and bring up our children with reverence for English history and in the awe of English literature."[1] Severe cultural conflict was inevitable so long as such attitudes persisted.

Similarly, German-Americans continued through 1916 to offend native Americans with their rallies and demonstrations, their fund-raising bazaars for the German Red Cross, their intemperate editorials and speeches against loans to the Allies, trade in war goods, and travel by American citizens on the vessels of belligerent nations. They continued to shower Congress and the White House with petitions, letters, and telegrams. Some were capable of astounding naïveté as they ignored the effect of their tactics on nativistic Americans. The presidential election of 1916 provided a focus for this mutual lack of understanding as German-Americans seized the opportunity to pursue their group interests and to involve themselves in electioneering as never before.

Speculation about Woodrow Wilson's chances for another term began a year before the election. He was only the second Democrat to be chief executive in more than half a century, and had won in 1912 because Republican voters had split between Theodore Roosevelt and William Howard Taft. To overcome a reunited GOP in 1916 would be much more difficult; no major bloc of voters could be ignored in the strategy of reelection. During the first year of the European war the President had had some significant support among vocal German-Americans. That changed, however, in the fall of 1915 when Wilson joined in the assault on hyphenated Americans. He assumed, probably mistakenly, that his *Lusitania* policy had already alienated the bulk of German Democratic voters. His espousal of antihyphenism was expected to lose far fewer votes than it would gain among old-stock Americans, especially since he usually linked his attacks with strong support for increased defense appropriations. Moreover, the most conspicuous national figure to champion "preparedness" and condemn "hyphenated Americanism" was Theodore Roosevelt, whose expected return to the Republican fold would enhance his potential as a rival candidate for the presidency. When public sentiment shifted in favor of an enlarged army and navy, Wilson appealed to patriotism as he moved to occupy Roosevelt's ground. The President insisted, with all the moral authority of his office, that military power was necessary to preserve peace with honor or to defend the cause of righteousness if war should come.

There was no German-American consensus on preparedness. Claiming to be strictly neutral on the war issue and totally pro-American in their politics, German ethnic spokesmen did not object to American military strength per se, and some warmly supported preparedness. But others who resisted the movement did so chiefly because Wilson and Roosevelt favored it; besides, they were sure that American guns would eventually be aimed at Germany. Equally important, however, was the fact that from the beginning the preparedness movement was led by such fervent advocates of immigration restriction as Senator Henry Cabot Lodge and Representative Augustus P. Gardner. The preparedness organizations, principally the National Security League and the American Defense Society, were notoriously pro-Ally. One could readily sense an aversion for things German in their propaganda, which was widely disseminated in 1915 and 1916. Inevitably, many German-Americans interpreted the ascendancy of the movement to imply a lowering of their own status in American society. Preparedness was thus another cloud in the gathering storm of intolerance.

Fear and resentment of intolerance stimulated German-American opposition to Wilson in other ways. While the speech makers and the editors of the German-American press continued to attack him on the issues—the embargo, loans, travel, the submarine—lesser voices, probably more representative of ordinary American citizens of German origin, were offended by the President's insinuations that they were disloyal or unpatriotic if they disagreed with him or that they placed the interests of Germany ahead of those of their adopted homeland. Despite the bravado of the chauvinists ("The hyphen is for us an honor and we carry it as a distinction," declared one), rank-and-file German-Americans longed for an acceptance denied them by established society; a deep sense of inferiority (naturally shared by most immigrant peoples) made them unusually vulnerable to criticism. And when the criticism came from the President of the United States, the insult was sometimes more than they would bear.

Throughout 1916 German-Americans spoke out against Wilson for having fomented ethnic antipathies. In February, for example, the directors of the Northeastern Sängerbund advised their constituents to oppose Wilson because he "had insinuated that German-Americans were traitors." Several weeks later the Iowa German-American Alliance bewailed the "hatred against everything that is German" and expressed contempt for Wilson's innuendoes that they were "miserable illoyal creatures."[2] The German-American indignation is epitomized in a letter written two weeks before the November election by a Lutheran clergyman in Minnesota:

If ever I have been sorry for a deed, it is that I helped elect Wilson [in 1912]. I am a born American, . . . I have been as good an American as ever any of the Wilsons were. Yea a better American, because none of my ancestors raised a hand against the Stars and Stripes, like Wilsons ancestors, but some had an opportunity to fight for it. And to be called an undesirable citizen by a man, who's [sic] only boast is, that he is a fine breed Englishman, who feels at home in English surroundings, is indeed strong! . . . He deliberately insulted us! He knew better, he knew that he wronged us, but purposely he did do it, because he hated us, since we had not his English blood in our veins.[3]

To persons of such sentiments the $500 million loan to the Allies, for example, was far less important than the stirring of ethnic animosities at home. They intended to retaliate against Wilson's insults with political blows.

Activists in the National German-American Alliance had begun to discuss possible strategies in the fall of 1915. Dr. Leo Stern, president of the Wisconsin Alliance, was an early advocate of a plan to guarantee the nomination of a Republican presidential candidate who shared their understanding of neutrality or, at least, one from whom they could expect fair treatment. They proposed that German-American leaders in each state negotiate an arrangement with Republican party managers whereby they would promise to deliver a practically unanimous "German vote" in favor of Republican candidates in return for the selection of approved, distinguished German-Americans for one-fourth to one-third of the seats in the state's delegation to the Republican national convention. With such a bloc of delegates, the German-Americans assumed that they would be able to control the Republican nomination.[4]

The importance of the plan lies in the naïveté it exposed. Its proponents were remarkably ignorant of the practice, if not the theory, of American politics. Experienced German-American politicians such as Richard Bartholdt warned that no party leaders could ever be expected to cater to ethnic voters in a time of international crisis. Moreover, German-Americans were not noted for fixed and uniform loyalty to either party, and few had achieved sufficient distinction within the party structure to warrant their being chosen as delegates. The strategy was so unrealistic that no attempt was ever made to implement it, save in Wisconsin, where roughly one-third of the Republican delegation happened to be German-Americans. Even Stern, allegedly the chief advocate of the idea, abandoned it long before the convention met.

Hugo Muensterberg, the Harvard psychologist, offered a different plan. Late in December 1915, he made the astounding suggestion in the *Fatherland* that German-Americans should support Theodore Roosevelt for the Republican nomination. TR's personality, he wrote, "makes him a pro-German in all that is best in him." German-Americans should keep his insults in perspective and "not stumble over adjectives." Although Muensterberg's article evoked widespread comment in the English-language press, most newspapers refused to take it seriously.[5] Its significance lay in the willingness of German ethnics to consider anything that promised to beat Wilson. Few voters, however, would have preferred Roosevelt's devil to Wilson's deep blue sea.

More important than Muensterberg's ineptitude was the actual planning which took place at the organizational meeting of the National Association of German Newspaper Publishers, held in Chicago on 27 February 1916. Although opposition to Wilson was the recurring theme at the meeting, practical politics also received much attention. Besides editors and publishers, several prominent German-American militants, such as Hexamer and Bartholdt, were present. The sessions were closed to the public but the main points of their discussions leaked out: since all efforts to modify the administration's foreign policy had failed, political action was necessary; neither political party could afford to ignore the German-Americans if they presented a united front; the larger German-language newspapers must assist the smaller in the effort to mobilize and guide ethnic voters; although Wilson deserved steadfast opposition, he would be the preferred candidate if Roosevelt won the Republican nomination. There was also much talk of political cooperation with Irish-American organizations.[6]

The publishers meeting was held at the same time that Congress was debating the Gore-McLemore resolutions. These measures were designed to prohibit American citizens from taking passage on armed belligerent merchantmen. After Britain had authorized the arming of its merchant vessels, the Germans announced that their submarine commanders would be ordered to sink them on the grounds that they were actually warships. The German statement precipitated the Gore-McLemore resolutions, which had the active support of some distinguished and influential politicians, including William J. Stone of Missouri, the chairman of the Senate Foreign Relations Committee, Robert M. LaFollette of Wisconsin, and George W. Norris of Nebraska. Stone, for example, questioned the moral right of American citizens to endanger the nation's peace by the exercise of what was admittedly a legal right. But President Wilson, whose *Lusitania* policy permitted him no other course, opposed the resolutions as abridgments of American rights. National honor and self-respect were at stake, in Wilson's view. "To forbid our people to exercise their rights for fear we might be called upon to vindicate them," he asserted, "would be humiliation, indeed."[7] Not unexpectedly, both houses tabled the resolutions in a vote which revealed deep sectional and partisan differences, with midwestern Republican congressmen in the minority.

The fight over the Gore-McLemore resolutions led to much adverse publicity for the lobbying efforts of certain German-Americans. The *New York World,* the unofficial voice of the administration and an inveterate antagonist of the German ethnic community, published a series of articles exposing the political activities of the National German-American Alliance. Several purloined documents were published as evidence of a German plot to control the United States Congress through the Alliance. At the head of the conspiracy, the *World* alleged, was the prominent New York German-American, Alphonse Koelble. Although the documents revealed nothing incriminatory and little that was not already public knowledge, the exposé caused much concern among members of the House of Representatives, who voted down the McLemore resolve on 7 March 1916, several hours after the first *World* article appeared. Editor Frank Cobb, who saw the debate as a struggle between the President and the Kaiser, continued his attack on the Alliance during the weeks that followed and published regular reports on the activities of its leaders. The exposures failed to modify the behavior of the Alliance leaders and added to the hatred and suspicion that was beginning to infect American public opinion.[8]

Less than three weeks later, on 24 March, the submarine controversy flared up again when the unarmed French steamer *Sussex* was torpedoed in the English Channel. Eighty casualties were sustained, including injury to sev-

eral Americans. Wilson and his advisers, after careful de-
liberation, decided to submit an ultimatum to Germany
announcing that the United States would sever diplomatic
relations if it persisted in its unrestricted submarine warfare.

The new, grave threat of war with the old Fatherland was
like adrenalin in the veins of German-Americans. Individuals and organizations, both secular and religious, flooded
Washington with form letters and petitions—including as
many as 150,000 telegrams—frantically demanding peace
at any price. Editorials in the German-language press insisted that no discernible national interest could be served
by war with Germany. Mass meetings were organized to
protest "the ruinous policy of the President." But after several weeks, on 4 May, the German government succumbed
to the pressure of the Wilson Administration and promised
that henceforth it would observe the rules of visit and
search before sinking merchant vessels.

The "Sussex Pledge" relieved the German-American
community of a great emotional strain. War with Germany,
it appeared, would be avoided after all, and during the summer and fall of 1916 United States relations with Germany
gradually improved. But even before the Sussex crisis was
resolved, German-American militants returned to problems of the election. State and local branches of the National German-American Alliance were especially active.
(Unlike the National Alliance, few of the branches were
forbidden from participating in politics, as they were le-
gally independent of the parent organization). Several state
alliances passed resolutions to campaign actively and expressed opposition to the candidacies of both Wilson and
Roosevelt. "We are against Wilson and Roosevelt," announced the Illinois Alliance, "because in their whole conduct they have proved themselves to be so un-American.
We wish an American President, no tool of perfidious English politics." The New Jersey Alliance resolved to take
political action against all candidates "who represent the

interests of foreign governments who are at war against our old Fatherland." In Milwaukee the city alliance sought to bolster its strength by urging German aliens to seek citizenship so that they could vote. In Pennsylvania the state alliance undertook a drive to register voters of German origin, and in Oregon an Alliance speaker urged German-American Democrats to vote Republican as the best way to destroy President Wilson.[9]

Other voices joined in the clamor. In Chicago the Teutonic Sons of America declared Wilson to be "utterly unfit" to govern a society "composed in the main of people of hyphenated origin." In Cincinnati the *Volksblatt* denounced Roosevelt as an "utterly deteriorated specimen of mankind"—invective worthy of the Rough Rider himself.[10]

During April and May, German-American leaders evaluated other possible Republican candidates. Former Senator Elihu Root, who had served both as secretary of war and of state in Roosevelt's administration, was frequently identified as a German-hater as reprehensible as his erstwhile chief. But several other senators were mentioned favorably in the German-language press, including Lawrence Y. Sherman of Illinois, Albert Cummins of Iowa, and Robert LaFollette of Wisconsin. When the industrialist Henry Ford did well in the Michigan and Nebraska primaries, the *Boston Transcript* attributed his success to a cynical German ethnic vote. Associate Justice Charles Evans Hughes, a former governor of New York with a moderately progressive record, was cited by several German-language papers as worthy of support. The Chicago Alliance came out for Hughes as early as 24 April, and as he gradually emerged as the front-runner for the Republican nomination, German-American militants settled on him as a satisfactory alternative to Roosevelt. Hughes was essentially an unknown quantity but at least he did not have a reputation as a German hater, probably because his position as justice had removed him from rough-and-tumble political debate.

By the end of May so many German-language newspapers had endorsed Hughes that the *New York Times* dubbed him the "German favorite son."[11]

A final step toward influencing the Republican nomination was taken a few days before the GOP convention. The Central Alliance of Pennsylvania (under whose auspices the National Alliance had been organized in 1901) issued an invitation to German ethnic organizations of all kinds— the churches and their auxiliary societies, city and state alliances, lodges, turnvereins, choral groups, gun clubs, as well as representatives of the German-language press— to meet in a national German-American conference in Chicago at the Kaiserhof Hotel, 28 and 29 May 1916. The announced purpose was "to give expression to the united opinion of the American citizens of German descent and birth with reference to certain presidential candidates." The letter of invitation also proposed the selection of a conference committee which would be charged with the responsibility of conveying German-American attitudes, wishes, and intentions to the party leaders.[12]

The sponsors of the Chicago conference were almost exclusively militants associated with the National Alliance and naturally their point of view pervaded the gathering. They were most anxious to convey the impression that the Germans would vote as a bloc. Hence, cooperation between club Germans and church Germans was essential. Although substantial efforts were made to bridge the gap between these two main divisions and to play down the role of the Alliance leaders in staging the conference, the church Germans remained aloof. Several prominent churchmen attended the meeting, but they acted as private individuals rather than as official representatives of their church bodies. The selection of the members of the committee that was to pilot the German-American political effort also showed meticulous care for balance and cooperation. The chairman, John B. Mayer of Pennsylvania, and two members, Adolph Timm and Ferdinand Walther, were officers in Alliance organizations. The others were supposed to represent churches: a Lutheran clergyman active in his state alliance, the Reverend Siegmund von Bosse of Wilmington, Delaware, was secretary; Professor Friedrich Bente was to represent the Missouri Synod and other orthodox German Lutheran bodies; Joseph Frey, president of the Central-Verein, was to be the German Catholic member.

The ethnic press meanwhile trumpeted the alleged solidarity of the Germans in America. The *New Yorker Staats-Zeitung* declared the Chicago Conference to be an unparalleled expression of German ethnic harmony. But it was hardly so. For example, Joseph Keller, the president of the Indiana Alliance, considered the venture unwise and refused to attend. Henry Weismann of the New York Alliance consistently warned against hasty political decisions. The North American Turnerbund refused to send delegates, and Roman Catholic clergy were notably absent. In general, the religious press gave the affair scant notice.[13]

The Chicago conference adopted a series of resolutions which illustrate the shift away from specific issues to concerns stimulated by the antihyphen movement. They condemned "all demogogues who seek to profit by national antipathies, and who try to extol their own loyalty by impugning that of others." As a counterattack to Wilson's charge that ethnic politics caused dissension, the conference deplored "those speeches, made by public officials, or former public officials, which are intended to—or which serve to—produce a division among the American people on grounds of nationality." The resolutions supported "adequate preparedness" and demanded an even-handed foreign policy which would defend American interests vigorously and impartially. They called for both political parties to nominate men who were in harmony with these views. While no party or no candidate was endorsed, it was understood by Germans and non-Germans alike that the consensus of the Chicago meeting favored Hughes.[14]

A few days later the Conference Committee, headed by John B. Mayer, interviewed the chairman of the Republican National Committee to notify him that German-Ameri-

Rehse in *New York World*

CROWNING HIM

A sharp attack on Hughes as the German-American candidate.

---

can voters would support neither Roosevelt nor Root. Meanwhile, in New York, Alphonse Koelble announced his belief that Hughes was the German-American choice. Viereck also came out for Hughes in the *Fatherland* just as the Republican party convened in Chicago.[15] Then, on 10 June, Justice Hughes won the prize. German-Americans who had worked diligently for his nomination convinced themselves, like the rooster who believed that his crowing brought forth the rising sun each day, that Hughes owed his nomination to their efforts.

The majority of German-language newspapers and dozens of state and local German-American alliances endorsed Hughes during the summer months. Prominent persons such as Henry Weismann and Charles Hexamer also gave him public support, although the latter took special care to speak as a private citizen rather than as president of the National German-American Alliance. The press lavished many columns on Hughes's campaign, printing his speeches, praising his political wisdom, and reporting his many endorsements.[16] The misgivings of the editors, which were considerable, were not revealed until late in the campaign.

Antihyphenism became an essential element in the Democratic party strategy. Eager to upstage Roosevelt and Republican warhawks, Wilson and the national Democratic party leaders used every opportunity to denounce all persons whose understanding of Americanism differed from their own. If "hyphenates" could be made to appear disloyal, the candidate they supported must be equally undesirable. The German-American vote was loudly repudiated and Hughes was smeared as the Kaiser's candidate in innumerable cartoons, speeches, and editorials.

The Democrats gathered in Chicago for their national convention on Flag Day, 14 June 1916. Mammoth preparedness parades were organized in the great cities, as in New York, where 125,000 persons marched past a huge electric sign which proclaimed "Absolute and Unqualified Loyalty to our Country." As historian John Higham has described it, "monolithic adjectives ... summoned Americans to a concept of national unity surpassing any they had known."[17] The city of Washington conducted a similar pageant and provided Wilson with an unusual opportunity to dramatize himself as the premier patriot, as the champion of national defense, and as the relentless foe of citizens with divided allegiances. Shouldering a child's flag, the President placed himself at the head of the parade and marched the long mile down Pennsylvania Avenue and from thence to the

Kirby in *New York World*

BERLIN'S CANDIDATE

Democratic cartoonists smeared Republican Hughes as the Kaiser's favorite.

base of the Washington Monument, where he delivered a Flag Day address to the multitude and the nation.

The President spoke briefly and eloquently, stressing the importance of the Stars and Stripes as a symbol of national unity and loyalty. He affirmed his confidence in the patriotism of the "vast majority of those men whose lineage is directly derived from the nations now at war." With this statement on record, he launched another sharp attack

on unnamed citizens who "were doing their best to undermine the influence of the Government of the United
States." Wilson's charges were based on nothing more substantial than rumor and suspicion, but his words were
harsh. He continued:

There is disloyalty in the United States, and it must be absolutely
crushed. It proceeds from a minority, a very small minority, but a
very active and subtle minority. It works underground, but it also
shows its ugly head where we can see it; and there are those at this
moment who are trying to levy a species of blackmail, saying, "Do
what we wish in the interest of a foreign sentiment or we will
wreak our vengeance at the polls."

Wilson was right, of course, when he accused the allegedly
disloyal minority of planning political action against him,
but he seems never to have reflected dispassionately
enough to recognize that when a democracy denies the
right of a minority to act politically it is no democracy at all.
While neglecting to define loyalty, Wilson implied that political opposition to his administration by immigrant citizens was tantamount to disloyalty. He predicted that the
American nation would "turn with a might and triumph of
sentiment" against ethnic political action and would "teach
these gentlemen once for all that loyalty to this flag is the
first test of tolerance in the United States." Finally, he unin-
tentionally encouraged acts of bigotry when he asked his
audience, "Are you going yourselves, individually and collectively, to see to it that no man is tolerated who does not
do honor to that flag?"[18]

The same day, President Charles J. Hexamer of the National Alliance delivered a Flag Day speech at the Betsy
Ross house in Philadelphia, where the first national banner
presumably was sewn. Hexamer's rhetorical devices were
much like Wilson's. First he stressed his great pride in his
American citizenship and elaborated upon the rights and
responsibilities attached to it. "Our Constitution grants us,"
he asserted somewhat inaccurately, "and our flag stands
for, the inalienable right of every American, regardless of

racial derivation, creed or color, to life, liberty, and the pursuit of happiness." Without referring directly to Wilson and certainly without knowledge of the President's address, Hexamer attacked the civic righteousness of the superpatriots, charging that when they impugned the loyalty of immigrant citizens they were "committing a crime against the life of our body politic and are shaking the very foundation upon which our republic rests." In contrast to Wilson, Hexamer predicted that the "good sense of the American people" would extinguish "the embers of mistrust and hate" which bigots "knowingly or ignorantly, tried to blow into flames."[19]

Despite a heavy schedule of public appearances, President Wilson kept in close touch with Democratic party leaders in Saint Louis, where the national convention began its quadrennial session, also on 14 June. Wilson had communicated frequently by letter and telephone with members of the resolution committee, as they prepared the party platform in the days before the convention opened. Even though the Democratic party had traditionally been identified as the friend of immigrant voters, Wilson was determined to have a strongly worded plank denouncing the hyphenates, and in order to quash suspected opposition within the resolutions committee, he exercised bald power to get his way. But Wilson was not alone. His influential secretary, Joseph Tumulty, was especially eager to "swat the hyphen," possibly because of a desire to repudiate the stand taken by his fellow Irish Catholics, many of whom were infuriated by Wilson's policies which favored Britain and the anticlerical regime in Mexico. Other advisers simply insisted that the German-Americans would vote Republican in any case and hence every effort should be made to identify the Democratic party with patriotism. Senator Paul O. Husting of Wisconsin also urged that the platform denounce ethnic politics, but for different reasons. He was certain that the ability of the National Alliance to control German-American voters was more apparent than real. If the Democratic party would challenge the Alliance openly, the ordinary German-American voter could have a clear choice between Wilsonian patriotism and the self-serving chauvinism of the Alliance leaders. Believing that this tactic would save many Democratic votes among German-American citizens, Husting introduced an uncompromising statement that was eventually adopted substantially as he had recommended:

We condemn all alliances and combinations of individuals in this country, of whatever nationality, who agree and conspire together for the purpose of embarrassing or weakening our Government or of improperly influencing or coercing our public representatives in dealing or in negotiating with foreign powers. We charge that such conspiracies among a limited number exist and have been instigated for the purpose of advancing the interests of foreign countries to the prejudice and detriment of our country.[20]

Husting's plank was partially successful. Unquestionably it alienated the National German-American Alliance and its adherents; they could only seek still closer ties with Hughes and the Republicans. Alphonse Koelble, for example, severed his connection with Tammany Hall, announcing that he could not hold office in an organization which was working for Wilson's reelection.[21] Other defections occurred elsewhere and no doubt some wavering German-language newspapers were driven to endorse Hughes. Yet Husting, whose father was an immigrant, underestimated the sensitivity of the rank-and-file German-Americans to his charges. Like Wilson, the Wisconsin senator seemed unaware of the intolerance he was encouraging.

The Democratic antihyphen plank aroused great editorial interest across the land. The *Saint Louis Post-Dispatch* called it the most important in the platform; to the *New York Times* it was the "backbone of Americanism"; and the *Louisville Courier-Journal* touched the absurd when it asked, "Shall the voters of the United States elect their own President, or shall William of Hohenzollern, working through the Kaiser Alliance and the Reservists educated by Dernburg and organized by Bartholdt, appoint one for them?"[22] German-language newspapers inevitably took the Democratic platform as an insult directed against all German-American citizens rather than against National Alliance leadership.

The nearly defunct Progressive party, still struggling for its life after four years, convened in Chicago as the Republicans were choosing Hughes as their standard-bearer. In a final, futile gesture, the Progressives again nominated their rambunctious Bull Moose, Theodore Roosevelt, who declined the honor in a formal statement to the Progressive national committee. He also used the occasion to endorse Hughes and to express again his obsessive hatred of the hyphenates:

No good American, whatever his ancestry or creed, can have any feeling except scorn and detestation for those professional German-Americans who seek to make the American President in effect a viceroy of the German Emperor. The professional German-Americans of this type are acting purely in the sinister interest of Germany. They have shown their eager readiness to sacrifice the interests of the United States whenever its interest conflicts with that of Germany. They represent that adherence to the politico-racial hyphen which is the badge and sign of moral treason.[23]

The GOP elephant was thus forced to perform a delicate balancing act. Somehow it had to retain the support of both the German ethnic voters and their most intransigent and irresponsible critics. The slightest bow toward the Germans would expose a perfect target for Democrats; the slightest approbation of Roosevelt's indiscretions would risk the loss of countless German-American ballots. The dilemma enhanced Hughes's natural disposition toward blandness. Though not lacking in courage, the bearded ex-justice was the embodiment of dignity and reserve. He tried through most of the campaign to appease both sides with carefully worded platitudes, sufficiently vague to satisfy his German supporters without alienating the superpatriots, no mean accomplishment.

Theodore Roosevelt was a constant embarrassment to the Republicans. Always the jingo, he bombarded his foes with invective. Self-righteousness had dulled his political acumen; he misread or ignored the pervasive public sentiment for peace and by his imprudent conduct greatly strengthened the image of Wilson as the man who "kept us out of war." At the end of summer Roosevelt toured the country on behalf of Hughes's candidacy. His immoderate rhetoric had so upset certain state and local Republican leaders that they informed him that he was not welcome to campaign in their districts. Others pleaded with him to tone down his utterances on the "hyphen" question. At the same time, however, Republican leaders did practically nothing to attract German-American voters. The National German-American Alliance and the editors of the German-language press were already so fervently in favor of Hughes that Democrats could easily smear him as the "Kaiser's Candidate." Thus, except for a few isolated instances, Republican campaigners neither encouraged nor discouraged German support.[24]

By the end of August, however, Hughes's image as the German-American favorite was becoming too strong. So he sent Roosevelt a congratulatory message, which was widely publicized, after TR had relieved himself of a typically abusive condemnation, at Lewiston, Maine, of the "professional German-Americans." Yet Hughes's statement was imprecise enough to permit his apologists to insist that he had meant to approve only those portions of Roosevelt's speech which denounced Wilson's Mexican policy.[25]

German-American leaders had never believed that Hughes was pro-German; they only trusted that he was not anti-German. His endorsement of TR's Lewiston speech shook their faith, and some of them, members of the American Independence Conference, met secretly with him in mid-September to get a better understanding of his position. A rapprochement of some sort was apparently reached, for in the weeks that followed Hughes made several statements that were critical of British violations of American neutrality. "We propose to protect American lives on land and sea," he pointedly announced in Philadelphia on 9 October; "we do not propose to tolerate any improper interference with American commerce or with American mails. We do not propose to tolerate that any American who is exercising any American rights shall be put on any blacklist by any foreign nation."[26] Hughes was taking advantage of a relaxation in tensions between the United States and Germany and of a widespread disgust with the British, who during the summer of 1916 had repeatedly violated American neutrality in minor but irritating ways.

Several days after this speech the Democratic national committee charged that Hughes had sold out to subversive elements in the United States, citing as evidence certain documents acquired from the American Independence Conference. These records were simultaneously published in the *New York Times* and in the *Herald.* Democratic pressures on Hughes to repudiate his German-American support became most intense, and although he insisted that he had done nothing amiss, he announced on 24 October, "I want the support of every true American who believes in the principles for which I stand, whatever his race. I don't want the support of anyone to whom the interest of this nation is not supreme." Intended as a mild rebuke of those, as he put it, "whose allegiance to our flag is not single and complete," the statement remained one to which German-Americans could subscribe. Their position, after all, was that Wilson, Roosevelt, and the warhawks were sacrificing American interests to those of Britain and her allies. However, Hughes was less equivocal in Columbus, Indiana, where he expressed his firm opposition to an embargo on munitions and to a revival of the Gore-McLemore resolutions. Finally, just days before the election, German-Americans were dismayed by the news that, at a Republican rally for Hughes in Madison Square Garden, Theodore Roosevelt had been boomed by the audience as the next secretary of

Cassel in *New York Evening World*

HOMELESS!

Both presidential candidates rejected the German-American vote.

state. When Hughes addressed the assembly he lauded Roosevelt for his excellent work in the campaign and said nothing to discount the probability of TR's appointment.[27]

In contrast to the Republican strategy of offending no major group of supporters, the Democrats both attacked and appeased German-Americans throughout the campaign. Wilson himself never altered his superpatriotic, antihyphenate line. His much-publicized speech of 2

September, in which he formally accepted the Democratic nomination, contained another simplistic, unsupported attack:

The passions and intrigues of certain active groups and combinations of men amongst us who were born under foreign flags injected the poison of disloyalty into our most critical affairs, laid violent hands upon many of our industries, and subjected us to the shame of divisions and sentiment and purpose in which America was contemned and forgotten. . . . I neither seek the favour nor fear the displeasure of that small alien element amongst us which puts loyalty to any foreign power before loyalty to the United States.[28]

Unlike Roosevelt, Wilson never specifically named the German-Americans, partly because he wanted his condemnation to apply with equal force to his Irish-American detractors, among whom Jeremiah O'Leary, the president of the rabidly anti-British American Truth Society, was the best known. When O'Leary sent Wilson an abusive telegram denouncing his foreign policies, the President countered on 29 September with a terse reply which he shrewdly released to the newspapers: "I would feel deeply mortified to have you or anybody like you to vote for me. Since you have access to many disloyal Americans and I have not, I will ask you convey this message to them."[29]

In the opinion of some observers, Wilson's squelch was the turning point of the campaign. O'Leary lashed back with a long, bitter reply, but Wilson's was the effective word. Meanwhile Democratic editorialists and cartoonists, especially in eastern states, continued to paint Hughes as one who had delivered himself, body and soul, to the German-Americans. But other party leaders, chiefly in midwestern regions, made a spirited effort to woo German-American voters. They argued that so long as Roosevelt and other ardent interventionists remained influential in the Republican party, the best hope for peace lay with Wilson. The President had kept the peace and would continue to do so, they said. (Ironically, this was precisely the view of the German ambassador. Wilson himself knew of Bernstorff's sentiments, though the rules governing the

Sykes in *Philadelphia Evening Ledger*

"Nobody Loves Me!"

There seemed to be no acceptance of organized political activity on an ethnic basis in the American system.

Montreal Daily Star

THE COMING PRESIDENTIAL RACE

A Canadian cartoonist observed that German-American support could injure the Republican party.

behavior of diplomats restrained the envoy from airing his preference publicly.) The peace issue was especially emphasized by the Bryanites in the Democratic party. Their devotion to the cause inspired them, in one instance, to picture the President on billboards as "the King of Peace."[30]

Indiana was one state in which Democrats worked especially hard to retain German votes. Charles Lieb, a German-born congressman from Evansville, Indiana, praised Wilson for his skilful management of diplomatic crises. The Democratic gubernatorial candidate frequently reminded German voters that Wilson's patience had saved them from having to fight with their old Fatherland. Democratic campaigners in Indiana, as elsewhere, played on German fears by asserting that if Hughes were elected, Roosevelt would become secretary of state.[31]

In neighboring Illinois it was rumored that Senator James Hamilton Lewis, who addressed himself in written and spoken words to German-Americans, had been especially asked by Wilson to develop arguments capable of inducing German-American Democrats to stay with the party. Another Illinois politician, a national committeeman of German extraction, followed the strategy of using Roosevelt to divide German-American voters from their chauvinistic leaders. Wilson, he said, represented acceptable middle ground between the Roosevelt extremists on one side and alliance extremists on the other. Illinois Democrats also publicized the views of prominent German-Americans, such as Paul Mueller of the *Chicago Abendpost,* who refused to endorse Hughes.[32]

Throughout the country Democrats pointed out that ever since the Sussex Pledge American relations with Germany had been good while relations with the Allies had deteriorated. They repeatedly charged that Anglophiles supported Hughes because, if elected, he would appoint Roosevelt to the Department of State and that war would soon follow. Paid advertisements to this effect appeared in the German-language newspapers, causing some editors to warn their readers to heed editorials rather than advertisements. In

Missouri, Democrats urged German-Americans to vote for Allen Benson, the Socialist candidate, assuming that in this way normally Republican votes could at least be siphoned off into a harmless third-party column. The German-language bureau of the national Democratic headquarters circulated huge quantities of campaign literature calling upon the Germans to vote as Americans and to spurn the leadership of the National Alliance.

Of the leading Democrats in the country, Senator William Stone of Missouri, the chairman of the Senate Foreign Relations Committee, made the most serious effort to salvage German-American support for the Democratic party. He conferred with individual German-American editors in Chicago and Saint Louis and prepared special appeals to ethnic voters, urging them not to separate themselves politically from the mass of their fellow citizens. On 16 September, about the same time that Hughes had met secretly with the representatives of the American Independence Conference, Stone arranged to meet with several influential German-Americans in New York. A dinner was planned at Terrace Gardens and was attended by Joseph Frey of the Catholic Central-Verein, President J. M. Kohlmeier of the national association of turnvereins, George Sylvester Viereck of the *Fatherland,* Victor Ridder of the *New Yorker Staats-Zeitung,* and several German-American businessmen and professional persons. Stone pleaded the Wilson case as earnestly as he could, stressing that the President had kept the peace and that relations with Germany were better than they had been at any time since the beginning of the war.[33]

A month went by before the Hughes and Stone meetings became the subject of a series of charges and countercharges splashed across the pages of America's major newspapers. Norman Hapgood, a well-known journalist working for Wilson's reelection, had alleged that Hughes had reached an understanding with German-American leaders on 16 September and that his Philadelphia speech denouncing British interference with American mails was the price for continued German-American support. In a desperate counterattack, Victor Ridder, who continued staunchly to support Hughes, denied any collusion with the Republican candidate and then accused the Democrats of the worst sort of duplicity. Senator Stone, he revealed, had indicated that Wilson's attacks on the German-Americans were intended for public consumption only and that privately the administration was prepared to cooperate with them. Ridder further asserted that Attorney General Albert S. Burleson had also tried to achieve accord with German-American leaders. Stone, of course, rejected Ridder's allegations as "utterly untrue." Burleson admitted to having met with Viereck for about five minutes on 24 September at the Democratic National Headquarters at the latter's request, but he cleverly added the entirely believable observation that the glib Viereck had done all the talking and he the listening.

In general, the Democratic strategy of depicting Hughes as the candidate of the German-American extremists was successful. Democratic newspapers effectively created the impression that, with the exception of an obscure weekly in Bismarck, North Dakota, the German-language newspapers were solidly against Wilson and that the National Alliance was politically impotent, a paper organization erected on duplicate memberships subscribed by ambitious men who used singing societies, rifle associations, veterans unions, and bowling and pinochle clubs to make new friends and customers cheaply and efficiently. The implication was clear. Ordinary German-American citizens without axes to grind could vote freely for Wilson; the mass of ethnic voters could not be delivered to one party or one candidate.

But German-American newspapers and organizations were by no means as unified or enthusiastic in their support of Hughes as the Democrats suggested. While it is true that few of them endorsed Wilson, several major German-language newspapers refused to come out in favor of Hughes. Moreover, this reluctance to endorse him increased as the

campaign wore on, especially after the public reconcilia-
tion of the Republican candidate with Roosevelt. Other
journals were sharply critical of Hughes's failure to grap-
ple with important issues, even though in the end they may
have urged his election because they disliked him less than
Wilson. Still others endorsed no candidate or criticized Wilson only, saying nothing about Hughes. At least one espoused blank ballots as an honorable alternative.
Nevertheless, most of the major journals, such as the *New
Yorker Staats-Zeitung* and the *Illinois Staats-Zeitung,*
were tightly bound to the Republican, believing that Wilson
had to be defeated because of his alleged enmity for the
German people in the United States. Indeed, the German-
American extremists applied intense pressure on those
who refused to conform. For example, when Paul Mueller
of the *Chicago Abendpost* concluded shortly before the
election that a speedy end to war was possible only if Wilson was reelected, he was denounced as a pro-British tool
and was threatened with a boycott.[34]

Just as the German-language press was not unanimous in
its support of Hughes, so the National Alliance and similar
organizations were less than monolithic. Charles J. Hexamer and most of the National Alliance leaders did indeed
support Hughes, as did many state and local officers. Hexamer himself distributed a memorandum at his own expense in which he wrote that "no self-respecting American
of German birth or extraction can vote for President Wilson." Various organizations prepared lists of approved candidates for various offices and some specifically requested
their members to vote for Hughes. But the Texas Alliance
remained loyal to Wilson and a surprisingly large group,
including the Ohio, Indiana, Illinois, Wisconsin, and Nebraska alliances, refused to endorse the Republican candidate, even though most of them adopted resolutions
criticizing the Wilson Administration. When the executive
committee of the Ohio Alliance resolved to support Hughes
in spite of the negative action taken by its members in
convention, it was met with loud protests and angry resig-
nations. One group of Ohio Germans responded by endors-

ing Wilson; another expressed its "measureless contempt
for those un-American schemers who have brought discredit upon the name of German-Americans" by attempting to deliver the German vote to Hughes.[35]

Neither did prominent individuals, including some
whom Theodore Roosevelt indiscriminately categorized
as "professional German-Americans," uniformly favor
Hughes. While most hoped to take their revenge on Wilson
for having branded them as disloyal, a few were more cau-
tious, fearing that active political opposition to Wilson
would spawn greater distress in the future. Professor Hugo
Muensterberg believed that the anti-Wilson stance of the
extremists was "suicidal" and wrote a letter to the President in which he promised that he would endeavor to counter their influence behind the scenes. Henry Weismann of
the New York State Alliance, though too deeply offended by
Wilson's antihyphenism to support him, was determined to
keep his organization out of the campaign. Unlike those
who saw Wilson as a threat to the status of Germans in
American society, other ethnic leaders continued to interpret events in terms of their impact on foreign affairs. Since
relations with Germany were much improved in the summer and fall of 1916, and since public attention had shifted
to British violations of American neutrality, their estimate
of Wilson's policies tended to improve. Former Congressman Henry Vollmer, who denied that Wilson ever intended
to insult the German-Americans, announced his intention
to vote for him. Even George Sylvester Viereck had so modified his attacks on the administration in the month before
the election that some critics suggested that the *Fatherland*
actually favored Wilson. German Ambassador Johann von
Bernstorff, who prudently denied any capacity to influence
German-American leaders, had urged Viereck to soften his
line on the ground that the diplomatic task of working with
the State Department had been vastly complicated by the
intransigence of the extremists.[36]

German-American Socialists, having their own candidate for the presidency, saw no virtue in either Hughes or
Wilson. In their view, both major parties were captives of

capitalism and were interested in promoting war for the prosperity of the exploiter class. Their German heritage was only incidental to the class struggle and they despised the ethnic culturemongers almost as heartily as did Theodore Roosevelt. Socialists remained firm in their devotion to working-class goals. They refused to exploit politically the heightened sense of ethnicity, just as they refused to quail before the new hostility to things German.[37]

Most German-American churches also remained loyal to their institutional goals. That usually meant avoiding political involvement, even though the German-American cultural militants were eager to enlist them in the warfare against Wilson, antihyphenism, and Anglo-Saxon culture. Before the campaign was over, both Archbishops Messmer of Milwaukee and Moeller of Cincinnati discouraged or forbade Catholic priests in their jurisdictions from engaging in political activity. The bishops were most anxious to counter the charges of anti-Catholic propagandists, common in such scurrilous sheets of the time as the *Menace,* that the Pope aimed to subvert the American government to his goals.[38]

Conservative Protestant churches such as the Lutheran and Mennonite bodies tended to ignore the election. Official publications of the Lutheran Church—Missouri Synod, for example, carried not a single line of comment. Indeed, they even refrained from reporting the activities of Professor Friedrich Bente, who, as a member of the Chicago conference committee, worked hard for Hughes. The official publication of the General Mennonite Conference warned that the national election was beset with dangers—enthusiasm for earthly affairs could overshadow the vision of the Heavenly Kingdom. Here and there local church organizations or conferences abandoned their reserve and joined hands with the secular societies. In Nebraska, for example, the Evangelical Synod of North America and the Iowa Lutheran Synod sent official delegations to the annual convention of the state alliance in September 1916. Individual pastors also accepted special invitations to attend and were granted rights of speech and voting.

Generally, however, the suspicions between church and club Germans were too deeply rooted for anything more than superficial cooperation. The Catholic Central-Verein, for example, continued to resent the efforts of the National Alliance to dictate to it in ethnocultural affairs. Alliance principles were not Catholic principles. Concerted action could be taken only when special circumstances revealed a common interest.[39] To conservative German-American Catholics the election of 1916 was not such a case. Leaders of the Central-Verein, especially Friedrich Kenkel and Joseph Matt, were upset by the ease with which Joseph Frey, the national president of the organization, had been enmeshed in Republican campaigning. Much like Charles Hexamer of the National Alliance, Frey had distributed a printed letter in October (allegedly at his own expense but mailed in the envelopes of the National Republican Committee) in which he urged "the decisive defeat" of Wilson.[40]

Almost all German Catholic newspapers were critical of Wilson. But few were as pro-Hughes as the Saint Louis *Herold des Glaubens,* which insisted that the only way German-Americans could retaliate against Wilson for his having stamped on their toes was to vote as a bloc for the Republican candidate. Both Irish and German Catholics expressed displeasure with the President's lack of genuine neutrality and Catholics of all origins were embittered by his support of the anticlerical Carranza regime in Mexico. But the Catholic tradition of voting Democratic was deeply engrained, and urban workers, among whom Catholics were strong, readily detected an antilabor bias in many of Hughes's speeches. Thus, German Catholic journalists such as Kenkel and Matt did nothing to encourage Hughes's election, even though they regularly attacked Wilson and his policies.[41]

German-language publications catering to Protestant subscribers were more solidly in the Republican camp. *Die Abendschule* of Saint Louis, to cite one example, was solidly committed to Hughes. However, papers published in certain Mennonite communities provided interesting exceptions to the rule. The *Hillsboro* [Kansas] *Vorwaerts* really preferred the Socialist candidate, but sensing that the nonresisting, apolitical Mennonites would scarcely be attracted to socialism even in wartime, it shifted to Wilson as the peace and prosperity candidate. Other Kansas Mennonite editors tended to be indifferent to the outcome of the election or only mildly supportive of Wilson's candidacy.[42]

As the campaign drew to a close, the ethnic militants made a last great effort to proselytize the church Germans for the Republican gospel. Hoping to counteract the ill will engendered by the Rooseveltian interventionists, the German-dominated American Independence Conference, working in collusion with the Republican party, arranged a series of meetings with German Protestant and German Catholic clergymen and laymen. At each of these gatherings, held in Detroit, Cincinnati, Chicago, and Milwaukee, the importance of electing the GOP candidate was stressed. The participants were told, allegedly on the authority of Hughes himself, that under no conditions would Theodore Roosevelt be appointed to the cabinet.[43]

The Milwaukee meetings received the most attention in the nation's press. Two sessions were planned, one for the Protestants on 25 October and one for the Catholics the following day. The letter of invitation to the Protestants, which promised that all expenses would be paid, carried an addendum signed by self-appointed representatives of several German church bodies. The names reveal denominational attitudes toward political involvement. While clergymen of the more pietistic bodies—the Evangelical Synod, the Evangelical Association, the German Reformed church, and a Methodist conference—affixed their signatures, no pastor of either the Wisconsin or Missouri Lutheran synods (the two most numerous German Protestant church bodies in the state) would so violate the orthodox principle of noninvolvement in partisan politics. Instead, Louis Lange, the publisher of *Die Abendschule,* was enlisted to encourage Lutheran and Evangelical clergymen to attend.[44]

Approximately 250 persons appeared at the Protestant gathering. They were amply supplied with pamphlets, buttons, and other accoutrements of political warfare by the state Republican headquarters, which was located on the same floor of the building in which they met. At the close of the session, the participants were reimbursed for their expenses and sent home by their hosts, who expected that on the last Sunday before the election, pulpits would ring with Republican oratory. Indeed, the Reverend Henry C. Niefer, president of the Wisconsin district of the Evangelical Synod, advised the assembly that it was their Christian duty to defeat Wilson.[45]

The meeting for German Catholics was a fiasco. Archbishop Messmer revealed his keen displeasure with the proceedings and only about fifty persons showed up. Refusing to become missionaries for a political party, the few participants passed a resolution declaring that they could not and would not take a stand in party politics.

At various times in the campaign, political observers, especially those in Wilson's camp, had declared the German vote to be a myth.[46] They concluded that the German-American community was in fact many communities and that in the end the Germans would divide much as they had divided politically in the past. There were other issues, they said, besides those related to ethnicity and they would cause German-Americans to vote much like other citizens. They were sure Wilson would get his share, the incessant claims of the cultural militants notwithstanding. However, this prediction ignored the subtle shift that had occurred in German-American perceptions of the issues. Whereas in 1914 and 1915 the debate had been cast in terms of neutrality, the arms traffic, loans, and travel on belligerent ships, in 1916 the importance of these issues had been overshadowed by status anxieties. The *New Yorker Herold* expressed the attitude succinctly:

We German-Americans wish to play no racial politics. We do not wish to separate ourselves from other citizens for selfish aims or separate goals. We wish to work for the progress and development of the country like every other American. But if we are insulted, if men in public life turn against what is German and if they scorn and revile it—then German blood flames up, then the "furor teutonicus" appears, then there are "German blows."[47]

It is impossible to determine the extent to which resentment stimulated German-American citizens to oppose the President's reelection. Voting is an individual act and personal motivations can never be revealed by election statistics. The number of citizens who despised Wilson for having stirred up ethnic hatred was offset by others who wanted to reward him for having kept America out of war. For those German voters who were convinced that their ethnic group would fare better with Hughes in the White House there were others who were horrified by the possibility of Theodore Roosevelt becoming secretary of state. Statistically, one kind of response could cancel the other and obscure the more important fact that there continued to be large numbers of American citizens whose political behavior was rooted in their ethnocultural heritage. Many individual German-American citizens felt keen pressures working at cross purposes; some, no doubt, resolved the tension by not voting at all.

Yet it appears that Americans of German birth did in fact vote proportionately more Republican than the rest of the population in 1916. In general, Hughes received a larger share of the votes cast in districts where German-Americans lived than he did in the states, counties, or cities of which these units formed parts. In other words, as the proportion of German-born persons increased there was a corresponding increase in the percentages of votes cast for Hughes.[48] By contrast, contemporary observers, whose analytical devices were rarely systematic, concluded that the "hyphen" vote was either nonexistent or, with more accuracy, that it was canceled in its own territory by antihyphen votes.[49] The election results in Milwaukee, the most German of America's major cities, were frequently cited as proof of this interpretation, since Wilson won a plurality of its votes while losing the state. Yet, as Table I

TABLE I

Percentage of Votes Cast for Presidential Candidates in Milwaukee by Wards Grouped According to Percentage of German-Born Residents in the Election of 1916

% German- Born	N	*Wilson* *Democratic*	*Hughes* *Republican*	*Benson* *Socialist*
14 and over	2	26.8	39.4	33.5
11–13.9	4	37.0	34.1	28.6
8–10.9	6	40.7	34.3	24.3
5– 7.9	8	46.8	33.5	19.2
0– 4.9	5	60.3	30.2	9.1
City (8.7%)		45.2	33.8	21.9

SOURCE: U.S., Bureau of the Census, *Fourteenth Census of the United States: 1920. Population* (1922), 3: 1137–38; *Wisconsin Blue Book, 1917* (Madison: Industrial Commission of Wisconsin, 1917), p. 218.

shows, Milwaukee Germans were strongly opposed to Wilson, mildly in favor of Hughes, and uncommonly disposed to vote for Allen Benson, the Socialist party candidate for president.

The tendency of German-American voters to reject Wilson in favor of his rivals represented a change over their behavior in 1912, when their preference for Wilson was apparent in many districts. One historian identified 108 strongly German counties throughout the Midwest and analyzed their behavior in 1916 in comparison to the elections of 1908 and 1912. He concluded that in the great majority of cases Wilson either lost support or failed to gain votes at the same rate that he had in other counties.[50] Similarly, another study has shown that the mild relationship of the

German-born by counties in Wisconsin with the 1912 Wilson vote (as indicated by a Pearsonian coefficient of correlation of .36) virtually disappeared in 1916 (.02). In Nebraska, the shift away from Wilson was rather more dramatic (.52 calculated for 1912 in contrast to −.44 for 1916).[51] Turnout was significantly higher in 1916 than it had been in 1912, but it does not seem to have been associated with voters of German birth.[52]

Many German-Americans, especially in the cities, turned to the Socialist candidate, Allen Benson, as an alternative preferable to either Wilson or Hughes. The Socialist party had been a major political force for a decade among the foreign-born in many industrial cities of the East and Midwest. In 1916 its appeal to labor combined with its vigorous antiwar stance to make it unusually attractive to German-born workers, as the Milwaukee data reveal. Saint Louis, Missouri and Davenport, Iowa also show unusually high levels of association between the German-born and Socialist votes in 1916.[53]

Traditional patterns of voting associated with religious belief continued in a modified form. German Protestants of the pietistic denominations registered their customary Republican preferences. German Lutheran districts tended to increase their Republican percentages over 1912. Incidence of Democratic voting was still most common among German Catholics, yet in many of their communities the proportion of Republican votes increased dramatically over earlier elections.

A few examples illustrate these trends. In the twenty-one counties of the United States in which German Evangelicals constituted more than 5% of the population, a moderate preference for Hughes was shown at 52% compared to 45% for Wilson. When the German Evangelical population exceeded 10%, the Republican proportion increased to 62%. In Warren and Gasconade counties in Missouri, where both German Evangelicals and German Methodists were concentrated, the Hughes vote registered 77% and 82%, normal Republican margins for these units. A study of fourteen

Mennonite townships in Kansas reveals 59% for Hughes, compared to 50% for the state as a whole. Wilson received 6% fewer votes in these townships than he had in 1912.[54] In sixty-five counties from Ohio to the Great Plains in which German Lutherans constituted more than 10% of the total population, Hughes won 52% of the votes compared to 44% for Wilson. Five Wisconsin counties in which the German Lutheran membership exceeded 20% of the population cast 58% for Hughes compared to 49% for Hughes in the state as a whole. In thirteen German Lutheran townships in Wisconsin Hughes outpolled Wilson 67% to 31%. Wilson took a similar drubbing in German Lutheran townships in Nebraska, where he averaged 38%, a drop of 25 to 30% from normal Democratic proportions. Similarly, a sample of eight German Catholic townships in Nebraska shows a Wilson vote of 46%, a startling shift away from the 80 to 85% that these precincts had ordinarily given Democratic candidates.[55] In Wisconsin, twenty-two German Catholic rural and small-town precincts gave Hughes 59% and Wilson 38%, a dramatic drop compared to previous elections.

The variations in German-American voting behavior in 1916 are also closely related to state and local political circumstances, especially as they involved other ethnic groups and other ethno-cultural issues, most notably prohibition. In Hoboken, New Jersey, for example, the German predisposition to vote Republican was matched by a strong tendency on the part of equally numerous Italians to vote Democratic, a phenomenon which suggests a rivalry between the two ethnic groups. In Iowa, the Democratic candidate for governor was intimately associated with the prohibition movement, while his Republican rival openly opposed it. This relationship strengthened the tendency of Iowa Germans to vote for Hughes. The reverse circumstances prevailed in neighboring Nebraska, where the Republican gubernatorial candidate was "dry," and the Democratic party retained its historical "wet" image, even though it had been weakened by the strenuous efforts of William Jennings Bryan and his allies to convert the party into an agency of moralistic reform. At the same time, Nebraska's Democratic Senator Hitchcock, a "wet" whose excellent reputation among German-American voters was enhanced by his fight for the embargo, was seeking reelection. These facts help to explain why Wilson, who won the state impressively with 55.3%, managed also to eke out a few more votes than Hughes in the ten most German counties of the state. Ohio and Michigan Republicans also projected a "dry" image, while in Wisconsin, the Republican gubernatorial candidate, Emanuel Philipp, was a wealthy conservative, a self-made man of German origins who opposed prohibition, woman suffrage, and interventionism. In North Dakota, the strong German-American vote for Hughes may be partially explained by the fact that the Non-Partisan League, which had virtually taken over the Republican party in 1916, was unusually attractive to German-American farmers for economic reasons.

In sum, the Germans had not voted solidly as a bloc, even though they had generally displayed a moderate preference for the Republican Hughes and favored Wilson less than they had in 1912. Contemporary analysts, who were chiefly interested in whether the German-Americans had had decisive influence in the election of 1916, concluded that they had not determined the partisan character of a single electoral vote. While this contention was by no means proved, it tended to obscure the more important fact that countless Americans had gone to the polls in a vengeful spirit or with troubled hearts. Political leaders had discovered that a narrow concept of patriotism, proclaimed loudly and fervently, could be a powerful political weapon. Loyalty to the flag, a hazy notion most potent when ill-defined, could be used with impunity against one's enemies. As the year 1916 drew to a close, some German-born citizens were more determined than ever to assert their freedoms of speech, press, and assembly and to preach their perceptions of what was best for America. Others shrank in fear before the unmasked face of intolerance and hatred, hoping that somehow war with Germany could be avoided.

Notes

1. Walter Hines Pages to Edwin A. Alderman, London, 22 June 1916, Burton J. Hendrick, *The Life and Letters of Walter H. Page,* 3 vols. (Garden City, N.Y.: Doubleday, Page, & Co., 1922), 2:144.
2. Carl Wittke, *German-Americans and the World War* (Columbus: Ohio State Archaeological and Historical Society, 1936), p. 87; U.S., Congress, Senate, Committee on Judiciary, *Hearings on the National German-American Alliance,* 65th Cong., 2d sess., 1918, p. 369f.
3. The Reverend Henry Boettcher to the Democratic National Committee, 22 October 1916, quoted in Meyer J. Nathan, "The Presidential Election of 1916 in the Middle West" (Ph.D. diss., Princeton University, 1966), p. 250.
4. Clifton J. Child, *The German-Americans in Politics, 1914–1917* (Madison: University of Wisconsin Press, 1939), p. 115f.; *Hearings on the National German-American Alliance,* p. 121 and *passim.*
5. *Fatherland,* 22 December 1915; *Literary Digest,* 52 (1 January 1916): 3.
6. Heinz Kloss, *Um die Einigung des Deutschamerikanertums: Die Geschichte einer unvollendeten Volksgruppe* (Berlin: Volk und Reich Verlag, 1937), pp. 276–78; Michael Singer, "Deutschamerika in den Kriegsjahren," *Jahrbuch der Deutschamerikaner für das Jahr 1918* (Chicago: German Yearbook Publishing Co., 1917), pp. 190–93; Frederic L. Paxson, *American Democracy and the World War: Pre-War Years, 1913–1917* (Boston: Houghton Mifflin, 1936), p. 336; Wittke, *German-Americans and the World War,* p. 90.

7. Woodrow Wilson to William Stone, 25 February 1916, quoted in Joseph P. Tumulty, *Woodrow Wilson as I Know Him* (Garden City, N.Y.: Doubleday, Page, & Co., 1921), p. 206f.

8. Child, *German-Americans in Politics,* pp. 90–98.

9. *Hearings on the National German-American Alliance,* p. 65f.; Wittke, *German-Americans and the World War,* pp. 79–81; Child, *German-Americans in Politics,* p. 117.

10. Andrew J. Townsend, "The Germans of Chicago" (Ph.D. diss., University of Chicago, 1927), p. 144; Guido Andre Dobbert, "The Disintegration of an Immigrant Community: The Cincinnati Germans, 1870–1920" (Ph.D. diss., University of Chicago, 1965), p. 214.

11. *Literary Digest,* 52 (6 May 1916): 1267; Ibid. (3 June 1916): 1620; Townsend, "Germans of Chicago," p. 147.

12. *Hearings on the National German-American Alliance,* pp. 63, 415, and *passim;* Kloss, *Um die Einigung,* pp. 278–84; Child, *German-Americans in Politics,* pp. 122–24; Singer, "Deutsch-amerika," pp. 194–97.

13. *Hearings on the National German-American Alliance,* pp. 121, 289; Wittke, *German-Americans and the World War,* pp. 90–91.

14. Child, *German-Americans in Politics,* pp. 125–26.

15. *New York Times,* 30,31 May 1916, 7, 9 June 1916; *Hearings on the National German-American Alliance,* pp. 100, 415.

16. Ibid., p. 98; Child, *German-Americans in Politics,* pp. 132–35; Wittke, *German-Americans and the World War,* p. 94.

17. John Higham, *Strangers in the Land: Patterns of American Nativism, 1860–1925* (New Brunswick: Rutgers University Press, 1955), p. 200.

18. Woodrow Wilson, *The Public Papers of Woodrow Wilson,* ed. Ray Stannard Baker and William E. Dodd, 6 vols. (New York: Harper & Brothers, 1925–1927), 4:207ff.

19. *Hearings on the National German-American Alliance,* p. 368.

20. Quoted in Child, *German-Americans in Politics,* p. 145f.; see also Tumulty, *Wilson,* p. 188; Louis L. Gerson, *The Hyphenate in Recent American Politics and Diplomacy* (Lawrence: University of Kansas Press, 1964), p. 64; Thomas J. Kerr IV, "German-Americans and Neutrality in the 1916 Election," *Mid-America,* 43 (April 1961): 99.

21. Child, *German-Americans in Politics,* p. 146.

22. *Literary Digest,* 53 (1 July 1916): 4.

23. *New York Times,* 27 June 1916.

24. Nathan, "Presidential Election of 1916," pp. 43, 76, 237, and *passim.* For a scathing denunciation of the effort to smear Hughes as the Kaiser's candidate, see *Nation,* 103 (6 July 1916); 6f.

25. *New York Times,* 3 September 1916; see also *Outlook,* 114 (13 September 1916): 63.
26. Quoted in Arthur S. Link, *Wilson,* vol. 5: *Campaigns for Progressivism and Peace, 1916–1917* (Princeton: Princeton University Press, 1965), p. 137; see also Kerr, "German-Americans and Neutrality," p. 102.
27. *New York Times,* 25 October 1916, 2, 5 November 1916. For a version that appeared in a strongly German city, see *Fort Wayne* (Indiana) *Journal Gazette,* 6 November 1916.
28. *New York Times,* 3 September 1916; Wilson, *Public Papers* 2:282–83.
29. *New York Times,* 30 September 1916; *Literary Digest,* 53 (14 October 1916): 935.
30. *New York Times,* 21 October 1916.
31. Cedric C. Cummins, *Indiana Public Opinion and World War, 1914–1917* (Indianapolis: Indiana Historical Bureau, 1945), p. 231; Wittke, *German-Americans and the World War,* p. 99; Nathan, "Presidential Election of 1916," p. 65.
32. Wittke, *German-Americans and the World War,* p. 98; Nathan, "Presidential Election of 1916, p. 234.
33. *New York Times,* 11, 12, 13, 14 October 1916.
34. Wittke, *German-Americans and the World War,* pp. 104–7.
35. *Hearings on the National German-American Alliance,* pp. 98, 189; Nathan, "Presidential Election of 1916," pp. 243, 251.
36. *New York Times,* 8 August 1916; Phyllis Keller, "German-America and the First World War" (Ph.D. diss., University of Pennsylvania, 1969), pp. 147–48, 280, 347; Child, *German-Americans in Politics,* pp. 120, 139, 152; Wittke, *German-Americans and the World War,* pp. 100–101; Johann Bernstorff, *My Three Years in America* (New York: Charles Scribner's Sons, 1920), p. 256; Charles Seymour, ed., *The Intimate Papers of Colonel House,* 2 vols. (Boston: Houghton Mifflin, 1926), 2: 372.
37. *New York Times,* 27 August 1916.
38. Philip Gleason, *The Conservative Reformers: German-American Catholics and the Social Order* (Notre Dame: University of Notre Dame Press, 1968), p. 169; Dean R. Esslinger, "American German and Irish Attitudes toward Neutrality, 1914–1917: A Study of Catholic Minorities," *Catholic Historical Review,* 53 (July 1967): 206; Nathan, "Presidential Election of 1916," p. 135.
39. See quotation from the *Saint Louis Amerika,* 8 August 1915, in John C. Crighton, *Missouri and the World War, 1914–1917: A Study in Public Opinion* (Columbia: University of Missouri, 1947), p. 151 n.
40. Gleason, *Conservative Reformers,* p. 169f.

41. Ibid., p. 170; *New York Times,* 3 October 1916.
42. James C. Juhnke, "The Political Acculturation of the Kansas Mennonites, 1870–1940" (Ph.D. diss., Indiana University, 1966), pp. 140ff.
43. Wittke, *German-Americans in World War,* pp. 107–8.
44. *New York Times,* 24, 25, 26 October 1916; *Milwaukee Journal,* 24 October 1916; *Milwaukee Sentinel,* 25 October 1916.
45. *New York Times,* 25 October 1916.
46. For example, see *New York Times,* 2 October 1916.
47. Quoted in *New York Times,* 8 November 1916.
48. For example, the six Iowa counties having 8% or more German-born residents cast 62% of their votes for Hughes, while forty-three counties with less than 2% German-born voted 51.5% compared to 54% for the entire state. In Saint Louis the association of percentages of German-born residents by wards according to the census of 1920 with percentages of votes cast for Hughes produces a Pearson product-moment coefficient of correlation of .52, indicating a moderately strong relationship. Unless otherwise noted, these data and those which follow are based upon U.S., Bureau of the Census, *Fourteenth Census of the United States: 1920. Population* (1922), 3; U.S., Bureau of the Census, *Religious Bodies, 1916* (1919); Edgar E. Robinson, *The Presidential Vote, 1896–1932* (Stanford: Stanford University Press, 1947); and a variety of state blue books, legislative manuals, etc., containing election data for wards and townships.
49. *New York Times,* 8, 9, 12, 19 November 1916; *Literary Digest,* 53 (25 November 1916): 1394. *Milwaukee Journal,* 8 November 1916.
50. Nathan, "Presidential Election of 1916," pp. 258ff.
51. Clifford L. Nelson, *German-American Political Behavior in Nebraska and Wisconsin, 1916–1920,* University of Nebraska-Lincoln Publication no. 217 (Lincoln, 1972), p. 20.
52. In Wisconsin, for example, the percentage of increase in turnout in 1916 over 1912 associated with German-born inhabitants by counties produces a product-moment coefficient of correlation of .02.
53. Both cities register coefficients above .8.
54. Juhnke, "Kansas Mennonites," p. 140–47.
55. Burton W. Folsom II, "Ethnoreligious Response to Progressivism and War: German-Americans and Nebraska Politics, 1908–1924" (M.A. thesis, University of Nebraska-Lincoln, 1973), p. 57.

CHAPTER SEVEN

Patriots or Traitors

WINTER AND SPRING 1917

For three months following the election of 1916 ethnic tension eased. The self-appointed spokesmen of *das Deutschtum* in America were widely discredited and their dreams of unity dissolved by the realities of electoral politics. Naturally, attacks on German-American leaders and organizations, their politics and patriotism, tended to subside. At the same time, German-Americans were encouraged by international developments. Prospects for keeping the peace with Germany seemed better than they had for months. In December the Kaiser's government, confident after military victories in Rumania, launched a peace offensive and proposed that negotiations be undertaken immediately without reference to terms. Meanwhile, relations with Britain had continued to deteriorate, as many Americans became exasperated with the British for their violations of American neutrality, tightening of economic controls, and refusal to consider seriously German peace overtures.

President Wilson, who knew that Germany had for some time been interested in the possibilities of a negotiated peace, feared that failure of the German effort would mean a resumption of unrestricted submarine warfare. American intervention would be almost impossible to prevent, it appeared, if Germany would make so desperate a bid for military victory. Wilson thereupon publicly supported the

German peace move on 18 December by urging both sides to define their war goals, and he negotiated secretly with the belligerent governments to end the carnage. When the latter tactic proved fruitless, he went to Congress on 22 January 1917, with his famous "Peace without Victory" address, in which he called for a negotiated settlement among equals without indemnities and annexations.

But it was too late. There had been a shift in the locus of power within the German government to those who advocated military rather than diplomatic means to achieve peace. Germany replied to Wilson's appeal with an announcement on 31 January that beginning the next day it would sink without warning ships of all nations headed for Allied ports. The German war lords understood that the United States would probably declare war, but it was worth the gamble, they believed, because submarine warfare could cut off American supplies to the Allied armies and starve them into submission before a military force of importance from the United States could be fielded in France. Three days later, on 3 February, the Wilson government broke off diplomatic relations with Germany.

For the ordinary German-American citizen it was a stunning shift of events. Almost overnight, it seemed, hopeful prospects had been transformed into a near certainty of war. There was panic in some quarters. A few German-Americans, fearing that their property would be confiscated in the event of war, hurried to withdraw their bank deposits. In New York and elsewhere, many German aliens who considered America their home rushed to acquire the protective coloring provided by first citizenship papers. At the opposite extreme, diehard chauvinists continued to grind out defenses of German actions and to attack the administration for its policies. Convinced that justice and right were on their side, they often posed as martyrs victimized by public prejudice fed by the Anglo-American press.[1]

But most German-American leaders were temperate in their reactions to the new circumstances. They understood that their task was to prepare their constituencies for the likelihood of war and to urge them to appropriate behavior. War would mean many difficulties for German-speaking citizens. The only way to combat intolerance and suspicion, moderate voices cautioned, was for German-Americans to avoid anything that could cause the least offense, and at the same time, they should perform willingly every duty imposed by citizenship. Their dread of war with Germany was conditioned by fear for their own status in America, not by solicitude for the Kaiser and his government.

Advocates of moderation also included some spokesmen of the German-American churches. While there were still a few ignorant, if not arrogant, displays of German partisanship among the church Germans, protestations of loyalty were more often heard. The *Lutheran Witness,* for example, was most charitable to "those whom God has placed at the head to guide this country of ours through these perilous days." New and unheard-of conditions, the *Witness* observed, complicated their tasks. "No Christian citizen of this country wishes to see it made a door mat for the feet of other nations." "We cannot stand silently and idly by to see our country become a mere dog's tail to wag according to the humor of some other country."[2]

Much publicity attended the actions taken by the National German-American Alliance. Following a special meeting of state and national officials early in February, the National Alliance pursued a course that was entirely consonant with its origins and history. It promoted every effort to avert war—mass meetings, peace resolutions, popular referenda—while proclaiming total and explicit loyalty to the United States. President Charles J. Hexamer personally endorsed the dismissal of German Ambassador Bernstorff, proposed a loyalty pledge for German-Americans, and announced that relief funds collected for the Central Powers would go to the American Red Cross, should war come. He even suggested the possibility of forming volunteer regiments of German-American soldiers, presumably on the Civil War pattern. Similarly, Julius Moersch, president of the Minnesota Alliance, wrote to his affiliated societies that there was little hope for peace and that German-Americans "will ever remain unwaveringly loyal . . . to the land we now call home, the birthplace of our children."[3]

The majority of the German-language newspapers adopted the same position—hoping that war could be averted, but pledging loyalty to America. They continued to argue that neither principles of international law nor national interest demanded American entry. It appeared to them that the United States was motivated chiefly by the financial advantages gained by the munitions trade and was influenced by a press prejudiced in favor of the Allies. Recognizing the imminence of war, they frequently pleaded with their readers to flood their congressmen with messages opposing American intervention.[4]

President Wilson still hoped that war could be avoided and that Germany would alter its course under the pressure of a diplomatic rupture. Meanwhile, voices demanding the arming of American merchant vessels grew louder and more insistent. Wilson considered plans for armed neutrality as a middle course between submission to the Germans and a declaration of war. On 25 February, he learned of the notorious Zimmermann note, which had been intercepted, deciphered, and released to the American government by the British. The telegram, dispatched by the German Foreign Secretary Arthur Zimmermann to the German minister to Mexico, proposed that, in the event of war between Germany and the United States, Mexico should attack her northern neighbor with the expectation of regaining her "lost territories" of Texas, New Mexico, and Arizona. Wilson now lost all faith in the German government and decided to go ahead with his plans to meet the threat head on. He immediately asked Congress for authority to arm merchantmen and to wage what his enemies called an undeclared naval war against the submarine. Legislative opposition to the armed ships bill was sharp, and in order to win popular support for what he knew was a risky policy, Wilson released the Zimmermann note to the press.

Public indignation was immediately aroused. The note excited more consternation than any event since the sinking of the *Lusitania*. Many editors who had formerly resisted intervention now joined in urging Congress to declare war. One of the most egregious blunders in the history of modern diplomacy, the Zimmermann note was so inept that its authenticity was widely questioned. A few German-Americans were especially quick to declare it to be forgery—an "impudent hoax," George Sylvester Viereck called it, concocted by British propagandists. They simply could not believe that the Germans could be capable of such stupidity. Other German-American commentators, less hasty in their judgments, saw the scheme as a genuine act of unfriendliness and concluded that if the telegram proved to be authentic Germany was indeed guilty of an unpardonable offense. Those who tried to interpret the intrigue favorably were even more cruelly cut when on 3 March Zimmermann blandly admitted that he had dispatched the note and that its contents were substantially correct as published. Even Viereck agreed that the mere proposal of an alliance with Mexico against the United States was "a cruel blow to Americans of German descent."[5]

In the midst of this furor Congress debated armed neutrality. A clear majority in both houses supported the armed ships bill and it was passed, 403 to 14, in the House of Representatives. In the Senate, however, a small group of antiwar legislators headed by Robert M. LaFollette of Wisconsin defiantly filibustered the bill to death until the session was terminated on 4 March, as specified by the Constitution. Although the German-American press hailed these senators as courageous men of conviction, Wilson castigated them as "a little group of willful men, representing no opinion but their own." LaFollette was subjected to much abuse and a resolution censuring him was introduced in the Wisconsin state legislature. Yet virtually all congressmen had agreed that armed neutrality would lead to war. As historian Arthur S. Link has pointed out, the antiwar senators "thought they were being true to their country's traditions in refusing to permit the President to wage undeclared war without the express knowledge and consent of Congress."[6] Then, several days after Wilson took the oath of office for his second term as President, he acted on his executive authority to order the arming of American merchantmen, without the benefit of legislative approval.

The events of March demonstrated unmistakably that the German government had no intention of altering its course. Unrestricted submarine warfare was expected to produce victory; American entry was part of the risk. Hence, German assaults on American shipping continued. The *Algonquin* was sunk without warning on 12 March; four days later the *Vigilancia* was torpedoed with the loss of fifteen lives; the *City of Memphis* went down off the Irish coast on 17 March, followed by the *Illinois* the next day. On 20 March, the President received the unanimous advice of his cabinet that he should summon Congress to a special session for the purpose of declaring war against Germany. Wilson, who had wanted very much to avoid war, could find no honorable alternative to full-fledged belligerency, trapped as he was by the logic of events and by his own policies since 1915. On 21 March, as noisy interventionists were clamoring for a swift declaration, Wilson issued the call for Congress to assembly on 2 April.

In the interim, peace advocates intensified their efforts to halt or hinder the formal entry of the United States into the holocaust. Mass rallies were staged in major cities. Countless letters and telegrams were dispatched to Washington from all parts of the country. The most active and widely publicized pacifist organization was the Emergency Peace Federation, which had sponsored a national conference attended by 2,000 delegates in Chicago at the end of February. The movement attracted a distinguished leadership: Jane Addams served as chairman of the executive committee, and other prominent participants included Amos Pinchot, Oswald Garrison Villard, and David Starr Jordan. Although most of these persons adhered to pacifist principles, some explained their opposition to American entry in nationalist terms. They believed that the United States could be more influential in world affairs if it remained neutral; Wilson, they argued, could more easily translate his ideals into practical reality if America was not a party to the dispute. Others, such as Jordan, used Socialist rhetoric to denounce war as a capitalist conspiracy. Wall Street, according to many peace advocates, was eager for American involvement in order to protect its vast investments in war. Another peace organization publicized the collosal expenditures of tax moneys that would be required; a third warned that participation would destroy democracy at home. Still other pacifist groups called for a national referendum to demonstrate that the great mass of common people was much opposed to American entry.

The Socialist party leadership was badly split by the prospect of war. Several nationally prominent party figures, including John Spargo, Upton Sinclair, Algie M. Simons, and Allan Benson, now publicly favored American intervention. Most rank-and-file members and most Socialist editors, however, remained loyal to their antiwar dogma, and thousands attended peace rallies conducted in cities having Socialist mayors, notably Milwaukee and Minneapolis. Eugene V. Debs, the perennial Socialist candidate for president, declared that he preferred being shot as a traitor to going to war for Wall Street. Socialists of German ethnic origin, of whom Victor Berger of Milwaukee was the best known, sustained their undaunted opposition to American entry.[7]

Although discretion required German-Americans to remain silent during those critical days, not all were capable of it. Some German-language papers printed fervent editorials pleading for peace and supplied form letters and telegrams in English for readers to copy and send to their congressmen. A few of the extreme chauvinists took to criticizing Hexamer for his effort, as they saw it, to convert the National Alliance into a patriotic organization. They particularly despised his proposed loyalty pledge, which they considered insulting. Others frantically organized last-minute peace rallies. The German-Americans of New Ulm, Minnesota, sent a peace delegation to Washington; Professor Edmund von Mach, well known for his pro-German sympathies, distributed antiwar propaganda to congressmen. A group of Lutheran clergymen of the Missouri Synod hurried to the national capital to lobby against American entry.[8]

A few German-American communities responded to the call for popular referenda. Although the wording of the referendum statements was often loaded, these devices nonetheless reflected genuine sentiment against war. Voters in Monroe, Wisconsin, a strongly German-Swiss community which placed a war referendum on the official ballot of its 3 April election, recorded a ten to one ratio against American entry. In New Ulm a similar ballot registered 23 to 1. Unofficial voting in the very German cities of Manitowoc and Sheboygan, Wisconsin, ran as high as 100 and 200 to 1 against the declaration of war Congress was then considering.[9]

But most German-Americans were at once less publicity-conscious and more judicious in their behavior as war became imminent. If they wished to demonstrate, they usually did so at meetings sponsored by Socialists or pacifists, groups for whom opposition to war was ideological. Many willingly signed loyalty pledges. The many vereins were generally more interested in declaring their loyalty to the United States than in acting politically to prevent American involvement. For them German culture had served social and economic rather than ideological purposes; they had no desire to jeopardize further their status in American society by stressing identity with Germany. The church Germans had even less reason to agitate against American entry. For them German culture had been chiefly a means to enhance their capacity to perform their religious functions. They agreed that the state had the God-given authority to wage war and the right to demand the loyalty of its citizens. Mennonite church bodies, to be sure, were totally committed to doctrines of pacifism and non-resistance, but members of most other German churches were unhesitating in their willingness to bear arms, pay taxes, and support the government. Indeed, Lutherans were sometimes criticized in other contexts for their slavish adherence to the Pauline injunction, "Let every soul be subject unto the higher powers ... [for] the powers that be are ordained of God."[10] The same conservatism that prompted the doctrinally orthodox Lutheran synods to cherish their German language and culture also fixed their loyalty to governmental authority. There were a few instances of peace rallies sponsored by one German church or another, but they were not common.

When Congress assembled on 2 April 1917, in response to the President's call, the American people expected a declaration of war. This is not to say that they wanted it or welcomed it. Probably a majority of America's politicians, journalists, clergymen, educators, financiers, industrialists, and businessmen—the elite whose pronouncements were commonly mistaken for popular opinion—shared Wilson's assessment of affairs and supported his request with enthusiasm. But it is less likely that the majority of the citizens—taxpayers and prospective soldiers—perceived war and its necessity in Wilsonian terms, willing though most were to defer to his judgment.

Wilson was eloquent as he addressed Congress, his audience attentive and receptive. War, the President assured the lawmakers, had been thrust upon this country by the German government which by its submarine policy had thrown "to the winds all scruples of humanity." Germany was waging war against mankind, against all nations. The United States had tried armed neutrality as a means to meet the lawless and indiscriminate challenge but that proved to be ineffectual. The choice now was either war or submission to Germany's violation of "the most sacred rights of our nation and our people." America must fight, not for selfish ends, for conquest, dominion, or material compensation, but for "the peace of the world and for the liberation of its peoples ... and [for] the privilege of men everywhere to choose their way of life." "The world," Wilson said, "must be made safe for democracy."[11]

The President emphasized that America's quarrel was with the Imperial German Government, and not with the German people, whose "sincere friends . . . we are." Linking the German people of Europe with those in the United States, Wilson continued with an effort to forestall domestic intimidation:

We shall, happily, still have an opportunity to prove that friendship in our daily attitude and actions toward the millions of men and women of German birth and native sympathy who live among us and share our life, and we shall be proud to prove it toward all who are in fact loyal to their neighbors and to the Government in the hour of test. They are, most of them, as true and loyal Americans as if they had never known any other fealty or allegiance. They will be prompt to stand with us in rebuking and restraining the few who may be of a different mind and purpose.[12]

Wilson went on to warn that "if there should be disloyalty, it will be dealt with a firm hand of stern repression." The tenor of his remarks reveals no change from his demand of December 1915, reiterated in his 1916 Flag Day address, that creatures of disloyalty be "crushed out." Like the earlier pronouncements, this one also failed utterly to define loyalty and disloyalty. In the past Wilson had seemed reluctant to attribute patriotic motives to persons whose perceptions of the national interest were at variance with his own, and it mattered not if those who disagreed were ethnic leaders such as Charles Hexamer or political figures such as Senator LaFollette. In Wilson's view they contributed to national discord at a time of crisis; they were therefore open to charges of pro-Germanism. The President, a distinguished historian of our political institutions, was sensitive to the ethnic heterogeneity of American society, and like his old foes Theodore Roosevelt and Henry Cabot Lodge, he believed that immigrant assimilation occurred when the newcomers conformed progressively to the established norms of the society. In normal times, they assumed, America could afford to be warm, tolerant, and generous to her immigrants, but in times of crisis, and certainly in 1917 when, as Wilson put it, "civilization itself seems to be in the balance," national unity and security had to be given priority over libertarian concerns.

There is evidence, some of it of dubious quality, that Wilson anguished over his decision for war, being fearful of the damage civil rights would suffer because of domestic hatred, brutality, intolerance, and the insistence on a needless conformity generated by the spirit of war.[13] It is not unreasonable to believe that he harbored such fears, although a less intelligent and perceptive man than Wilson might have ignored these children of Mars. He abhorred war and its use as an instrument of national policy. "It is a fearful thing," he said as he addressed Congress, "to lead this great peaceful people into war"; he was mindful of "the solemn and even tragical character of the step." Nevertheless, Wilson chose to use his powerful rhetoric (as he had in the past and as he would again during the war) to encourage the repression of the "disloyal," a category of citizens so ill-defined that anyone who dissented from official opinions could be swept into it. Instead of dissipating popular fears of German-American subversion, he encouraged it asserting that "Prussian autocracy" had filled "our unsuspecting communities and even our offices of government and set criminal intrigues" against national unity, industry, and commerce. Instead of voicing concern over attacks on innocent persons, he called attention to the danger of spies and, indeed, partly justified American entry on the threat they allegedly posed to American security.[14]

A resolution declaring war against Germany was introduced in the Senate on the next day. Advocates of intervention delivered lengthy speeches in support of the President's recommendation. However, a small group of opponents, including LaFollette of Wisconsin, George Norris of Nebraska, and William Stone of Missouri, spoke bitterly against the resolution. Nevertheless, on 4 April the Senate passed the measure, 82 to 6, and sent it to the House of Representatives, where it was debated until the early morning hours of 6 April. Fifty-four votes were registered in the House against war, 373 in favor. The representatives in opposition tended to be progressive Republicans or Bryanite Democrats from midwestern and southern states. While some had strongly German constituencies, others, principally from the South, did not. Shortly after 1 P.M. President Wilson signed the resolution in the lobby of the White House and the nation was officially at war.

Opposition to the declaration was deeper and more widespread than the congressional vote suggests. Some congressmen received immense quantities of mail opposing American entry.[15] A few of them decided that they heard the voice of the people and voted accordingly, and others acted on the basis of their own idealism, but most, it appears, were willing to accept Wilson's decision as their own. By acceding to his leadership, they freed themselves from the unpleasant responsibility of choosing between repugnant alternatives. Thus they plunged the nation into war. Very quickly devotion to the flag became the symbol of a new harsh and unyielding patriotism. Patience and prudence were trampled underfoot during the months that followed as well-intentioned citizens rushed to "stand by the President."

But superpatriotism did not flower in a single day nor did it thrive without cultivation. It was fed, in the first place, by fear. New rumors of German-American subversion had been flitting about since the diplomatic break with Germany in February. Suspicious persons seemed to discover evidence of sabotage everywhere. Some spoke of the possibilities of domestic disturbances resembling civil war, as though upon the declaration of war German reservists would rise up to form an enemy army in the heart of America. Others urged the indiscriminate internment of German aliens on the assumption that they were all likely to be spies in the service of the Kaiser. Government agents began investigations of German aliens and German-Americans employed in munition factories and shipyards.

The President and his cabinet discussed the problem of German-American subversion in a meeting held 30 March 1917, and even though Wilson exercised a moderating influence, some of his advisers had succumbed to the fear that America was swarming with spies. Attorney General Thomas Gregory, who had earlier objected to Secret Service surveillance of German aliens, now believed that the country had "a very large number of German citizens" from whom the government "must necessarily expect trouble of a sinister sort."[16] Influenced by his assistant, Charles Warren, Gregory won tacit endorsement from the cabinet for a plan to use an organization of volunteers to gather information for the Department of Justice on suspected aliens and disloyal citizens. The attorney general was anxious to consolidate counterespionage activities under his supervision and away from the Secret Service, which was administered by the Department of the Treasury. By relying on the assistance of civilians he could accomplish this purpose and cope with the vast increase of cases requiring investigation; at the same time, he would channel the enthusiasm of patriots eager to ferret out all evidences of Teutonic conspiracy.

Gregory's corps of amateur sleuths was the American Protective League. Organized in March 1917 by a Chicago businessman, the league mushroomed into a vast network of more than 200,000 untrained, volunteer detectives, whose enterprise was nationalized and bureaucratized. Divisions and subdivisions were created and captains, lieutenants, and operatives were appointed. As a semi-official auxiliary of the Bureau of Investigation, the league supplied its members with oaths of office, badges, and imposing certificates. Its agents conducted many hundreds of thousands of investigations during the course of the war. First they spied on enemy aliens, but soon the web spread to entrap any citizen who held dissenting views. Inquiries were extended to cases of suspected sedition and disloyalty. Operatives probed the private affairs of foreign-born applicants for government positions, of candidates for commissions in the armed forces, and especially of alleged slackers, hoarders, and deserters. Even though the American Protective League failed to catch a single bona fide German spy, it succeeded in creating a climate in which persons with German names or accent or of German birth were objects of suspicion and alarm. Since the APL was founded on fears of German conspiracies, it sought to justify its continued existence by systematically publicizing the threat of internal subversion throughout the war period.[17]

There were many other agencies of superpatriotism dedicated to the task of mobilizing national resources and individual talents. If America was saving the world for democracy and if it was defending civilization against Teutonic barbarism, nothing could be left to chance. Every technique had to be used to stimulate the loyalty of a diverse people insufficiently instructed in patriotism. Several organizations were created by law or executive order, such as the Committee on Public Information and the many state councils of defense, while others were private structures with no direct ties to the government.

The Committee on Public Information had been created by Wilson's executive order early in April 1917, to coordinate the national government's domestic propaganda effort. Its basic objective, simply put, was to sell the war aims of the United States to the people. As chairman of the committee the President chose George Creel, a young, flamboyant journalist with boundless imagination and prodigious energy. Creel organized an enormous advertising agency to harness public opinion behind Wilsonian idealism and wartime notions of patriotism. The CPI published scores of pamphlets in millions of copies, produced dozens of short movies, distributed thousands of posters and photographs, prepared war exhibits, and staged patriotic pageants and loyalty days for ethnic groups. Seventy-five thousand citizens were enlisted as Four Minute Men, who delivered brief, canned addresses to more than seven million audiences in theaters, concert halls, churches, and meeting places of fraternal orders and labor unions. It was an astounding feat of organization, and it did much to create the mood for patriotic sacrifice.[18]

The major task, as the administration saw it, was to win the support and cooperation of America's numerous and varied immigrant population. Creel was positive in his approach. Rather than trying to force poorly assimilated ethnic groups to submit to the national will, he relied on persuasion and explanation. Instead of attacking ethnic institutions as subversive and un-American, he sought to use them as channels for patriotic propaganda.[19]

The Creel Committee, as it was commonly called, gave special attention to the German-Americans. Staff members systematically monitored the German-language press, but they did so for the purpose of working with it rather than destroying it. A group of historians under the leadership of Professor Guy Stanton Ford of Minnesota wrote and translated into German a series of patriotic tracts and urged their use in German-language classes in the place of textbooks, which they believed were infected with German propaganda. One pamphlet, entitled "American Loyalty by Citizens of German Descent," was circulated in well over a million copies, nearly half in the German language. It consisted of several short contributions by prominent German-Americans, including Franz Sigel, Jr. and Otto Kahn.[20]

Despite the sensible efforts of the Creel Committee to encourage and counsel rather than to command and threaten, it also contributed immeasurably to the climate of intolerance. It suppressed dissent as disloyalty; it defined patriotism as conformity to a preconceived, idealized pattern of thought; it abetted the oppression of innocent citizens as it agitated against an imagined German spy system. In the name of national unity it extolled English culture and condemned anything derogatory of Great Britain. By its calculated manipulation of public opinion, the CPI cultivated a hatred for everything German, even though it gave lip service to Wilson's assertion that the country was at war with the German government, not the German people.

State councils of defense were frequently the direct agents of superpatriotism. Shortly after war had been declared, President Wilson dispatched a letter to each state government, urging the formation of state commissions on the pattern of the Council of National Defense, which had been created by Congress in 1916 during the preparedness debates to coordinate production of food and munitions. Most states responded quickly to the President's request. The resulting state councils of defense were strikingly varied in function and authority. In some states the governor simply appointed a panel of prominent citizens but gave them no authority commensurate with their assignment. In other states, especially in the Midwest where the German population was frequently perceived as a genuine threat to national unity, legislatures enacted statutes creating the councils and granted them sweeping legal powers, including the authority to subpoena witnesses and to punish for contempt. In most instances, comprehensive structures of subordinate county and local councils of defense were also instituted, and the various functions were farmed out to appropriate committees of unpaid civilian appointees. Council activity was frequently centered in food and fuel production and conservation, in the mobilization of labor, and in sanitation and public health problems. The network of local councils was usually employed to promote the sale of government war bonds, to collect contributions to the Red Cross, and to coordinate the activities of the Committee on Public Information on that level.[21]

But public attention was most often attracted to the zealous manner in which subcommittees on patriotism, Americanization, or disloyal activities performed their duties. In several states the councils of defense were easily the most important persecutors of allegedly disloyal German-American citizens. These guardians of democracy were notoriously willing to use vigilante methods in their pursuit of "slackers" and "Kaiserism"; thousands of Americans learned firsthand the meaning of guilt by association, accusation by secret informers, the loss of free speech, terrorism, and violence.

The most powerful of the independent superpatriotic organizations were the National Security League and its offshoot, the American Defense Society. The NSL was organized in December 1914 to promote military preparedness and universal military training. It attracted the support of prominent pro-Ally politicians, military figures, and wealthy industrialists and financiers. Ostensibly nonpartisan, the league failed to satisfy the political appetites of some of its frankly anti-Wilson members, who withdrew in August 1915 to form the American Defense Society. The new organization became a more tightly Republican, though less influential, version of the NSL.[22]

After the United States declared war, the National Security League turned its energies to forging national unity through systematic propaganda efforts of its own. By sending speakers to local chambers of commerce, schools, and service organizations, it attracted a membership estimated at nearly 100,000 persons. The league explicitly defined patriotism in conformist terms; no one was deemed loyal who failed to support the aims for which the United States entered the war. Naturally, German-Americans were subjected to special scrutiny. Shortly after war was declared, the league asked German-American societies of all kinds to demonstrate their loyalty to America by gathering in public meetings to adopt declarations against the goals and behavior of the German Imperial Government. Few vereins were prepared at that time to succumb to such pressure from self-appointed censors on the ground that genuine loyalty did not require public display. Not surprisingly, the NSL equated German-American silence with giving aid and encouragement to the enemy.[23]

The National Security League engaged the services of Princeton history Professor Robert M. McElroy as its educational director, whose job it was to coordinate a group of historians in speaking tours, in investigations of disloyal literature, and in pamphleteering. The latter included the publication of a series entitled "Patriotism Through Education." One tract in this series, "The Tentacles of the German Octopus in America," authored by Professor Earl F. Sperry of Syracuse University, was a direct assault on *das Deutschtum*. Sperry repeated all the standard misrepresentations found in Allied propaganda about Pan-Germanism. He attacked German-American churches, schools, societies, and newspapers indiscriminantly as inhibitors of assimilation and as agents of a world-wide Teutonic conspiracy. Sperry called for an angered public opinion to exert its forces against German-American institutions, as he noted their failure to declare their loyalty when asked to do so by the NSL. Widely distributed and often quoted, Sperry's propaganda raised the pitch of anti-German hysteria and deepened the ugly mood of intolerance.[24]

The splinter American Defense Society, which claimed Theodore Roosevelt as its honorary president and the racist Madison Grant as one of its trustees, pursued many of the same activities as the National Security League, although it made special war on the German language. By eliminating German-language instruction from elementary and secondary school curricula, the ADS proclaimed, the nation could destroy the means by which the Kaiser and his henchmen were seeking to pervert American youth. One of its publications, "Throw Out the German Language and All Disloyal Teachers," illustrates the logic of its superpatriotism: "Any language which produces a people of ruthless conquestadors [*sic*] such as now exists in Germany, is not a fit language to teach clean and pure American boys and girls." The Germans, according to this tract, were "the most treacherous, brutal and loathsome nation on earth . . . The sound of the German language . . . reminds us of the murder of a million helpless old men, unarmed men, women, and children; [and] the driving of about 100,000 young French, Belgian, and Polish women into compulsory prostitution."[25] True to these sentiments, the society also encouraged the public burning of German-language books and campaigned to change the names of cities, streets, parks, and schools in America to the names of Belgian and French communities destroyed in the war.

Partisan politics was often just below the surface of organized patriotic activity. Politicians coveted the publicity that normally attended involvement and they welcomed invitations to serve in volunteer capacities, hoping thereby to be identified as staunch defenders of "Old Glory." Governors, mayors, and others in executive positions could devastate their opposition by the astute exercise of their powers of appointment. Rivals could be excluded from participating prominently in patriotic rallies, Liberty bond drives, and speaking programs. Indeed, politics sometimes conditioned the creation of patriotic organizations at the state and local level. According to his Democratic enemies, Republican Governor Emanuel Philipp of Wisconsin had packed the membership of the Wisconsin State Council of Defense with his friends and supporters, presumably with an eye on the 1918 elections. Democrats tended therefore to concentrate in the Wisconsin Loyalty Legion, which in many ways paralleled and competed with the State Council of Defense. When informed of this state of affairs, President Wilson instructed George Creel's Committee on Public Information to coordinate publicity and propaganda through the Loyalty Legion rather than the official but Republican-dominated State Council of Defense.[26]

Patriotic organizations also lent themselves to political causes which were in the interest of their members, especially if they could be justified as part of the war effort. The National Security League, with its ultraconservative, business-oriented constituency, became notoriously antilabor. Socialists and Industrial Workers of the World (Wobblies) could be denounced as inhibitors of the war effort, as well as purveyors of dangerously radical ideologies. The cause of prohibition was similarly advanced under the aegis of patriotism. Restraint of intoxicants would improve national efficiency, it was alleged. Besides, alcohol was needed in the manufacture of explosives. The Wisconsin

Loyalty Legion thus clamored for prohibition as it attacked Governor Philipp for his connections with the Milwaukee brewing industry and the beer-loving German-American voters of the state.[27]

There were other organizations that took advantage of the war to further their long-range goals. Militantly patriotic social workers led by Frances Kellor discovered that the Americanization programs for immigrant workers sponsored by their social action groups seemed congruent with the wartime national interest. Doubting that America could survive a prolonged war because of its many races and divided allegiances, they, like George Creel, believed that positive or affirmative methods were needed, even though they were unrelenting in their demands for conformity to preconceived notions of patriotic behavior. As advocates of New Nationalist doctrines of efficiency and central planning, Kellor and her Committee for Immigrants in America sought to convince industrialists that the social welfare programs in their factories should include instruction in citizenship and the English language. Agitation of this kind led to extensive Americanization programs in many plants. But coercive measures were also introduced. Pay increases and promotions for immigrant workers were sometimes tied to progress in learning English; employment was made conditional on attendance at night classes; company foremen assisted workers in acquiring citizenship; and factory newspapers dispensed superpatriotic propaganda.[28]

Clergymen, journalists, college professors, and other conditioners of public opinion assumed personal responsibility for developing a national spirit of conformity. Countless editorials, lectures, and sermons were dedicated to the exegesis of 100 percent Americanism. Flattered by the attention government officials gave them, many preachers willingly encouraged hate. These veterans in the war against sin found it easy enough to transfigure Kaiser Wilhelm into the Prince of Evil. Thousands participated in atrocity mongering, but few clergymen exceeded the limits of credibility as frequently as the Reverend Doctor Newell Dwight Hillis of the Plymouth Congregational church of Brooklyn, New York.[29]

Hillis addressed hundreds of audiences in the several Liberty Loan drives. His lectures, published in two volumes in 1918, recounted the crimes of bloodthirsty German fiends who murdered for pleasure and who specialized in assaulting and mutilating women. In one lurid tale, Hillis implicitly exonerated a Belgian woman, endowed "with the dignity and beauty of the Lady of Sorrow," who strangled her child by a German soldier-rapist. "German blood is poisoned blood," Hillis had her scream; "German blood is like putrefaction and decay, soiling my innermost life." The Germans were genetically defective in Hillis's view, basically unchanged since Tacitus's descriptions of Teutonic brutality nineteen hundred years ago. Hillis also spoke approvingly of a plan to exterminate the German people by sterilizing ten million German men. Audiences stimulated by this kind of pornography were not likely to heed Wilson's distinctions between the German people and their government. If German blood was tainted, it could not be altered by residence or citizenship in the United States. Hence, Hillis often made references to German-American ingratitude, stupidity, treason, and malignity. One description of a series of alleged German-American offenses repeats the refrain, "That man should have been arrested at dark, tried at midnight, and shot at daybreak." No man, declared Hillis, "can serve God and the Allies, Germany and the devil, at one and the same time."[30]

The campaign to enforce uniformity among America's diverse people gathered momentum during the first several months of the war, as the President, government agencies, private groups, and individuals instructed them in the meaning of patriotism. Few persons were interested in definitions finer than one offered by the Minnesota Commission of Public Safety: "The test of loyalty in war times is whether a man is wholeheartedly for the war and subordinates everything else to its successful prosecution."[31] Dissenting idealists—pacifists, socialists, Quakers, Mennonites —and realists who believed that the best interests of the United States were not being served by involvement in the European war were rendered vulnerable to sweeping charges of pro-Germanism, cowardice, and treason. Citizens were thrust into one of two categories—patriots or traitors. There was no middle ground.

Presumably one could measure the loyalty of German-Americans by their willingness to participate in the rituals of patriotism, to venerate its saints and symbols, and to respect its priesthood. Loyalty meant singing patriotic anthems, listening to speeches, reciting pledges of allegiance. Patriots willingly contributed to the Red Cross, purchased Liberty bonds, and, if called, served in the armed forces. They renounced the Kaiser and all his works; they kept eternal vigilance against his evil agents who lurked everywhere, conspiring, tempting, and perverting innocent America. One-hundred percent Americans did not insist on using the German language, reading German-language newspapers, or supporting societies that perpetuated alien cultures. Above all, loyal German-Americans did not criticize the President of the United States.

Notes

1. Carl Wittke, *German-Americans and the World War* (Columbus: Ohio State Archaeological and Historical Society, 1936), pp. 120–24; Clifton J. Child, *The German-Americans in Politics, 1914–1917* (Madison: University of Wisconsin Press, 1939), p. 157; *New York Times,* 4 February 1917.
2. *Lutheran Witness,* 36 (20 February 1917): 47.
3. *New York Times,* 10 February 1917; Child, *German-Americans in Politics,* p. 157f.; Franklin F. Holbrook and Livia Appel, *Minnesota in the War with Germany,* 2 vols. (Saint Paul: Minnesota Historical Society, 1928, 1932), 1: 49.
4. See, for example, *Milwaukee Germania-Herold,* 7 February to 2 April 1917; *Literary Digest,* 54 (17 February 1917): 388.
5. *Literary Digest,* 54 (17 March 1917): 687; U.S., Congress, Senate, Committee on the Judiciary, *Hearings on Brewing and Liquor Interests and German Propaganda,* 65th Cong., 2d sess., 1918, vol. 2, p. 1611; *American Weekly,* 14 March 1917. As war approached in February 1917, Viereck changed the name of his paper from the *Fatherland* to the *American Weekly.*
6. Arthur S. Link, *Wilson,* vol. 5: *Campaigns for Progressivism and Peace, 1916–1917* (Princeton: Princeton University Press, 1965), p. 363f.
7. Willis Raff, "Coercion and Freedom in a War Situation: A Critical Analysis of Minnesota Culture during World War I" (Ph.D. diss., University of Minnesota, 1957), p. 48; Mary Henke, "World War I: Dissent and Discord in Milwaukee" (M.A. thesis, Loyola University of Chicago, 1966), p. 84; Lorin Lee Cary, "Wisconsin Patriots Combat Disloyalty: The Wisconsin Loyalty Legion and Politics, 1917–18" (M.A. thesis, University of Wisconsin, 1965), pp. 34, 37.

8. *Literary Digest,* 54 (7 April 1917): 968; Wittke, *German-Americans and World War,* pp. 124–28; Child, *German-Americans in Politics,* p. 157f.; *Hearings on the Brewing and Liquor Interests,* 2: 1532–35.

9. Karen Falk, "Public Opinion in Wisconsin during World War I," *Wisconsin Magazine of History,* 25 (June 1942): 394; Holbrook and Appel, *Minnesota in the War,* 2: 40.

10. Romans 13: 1.

11. Woodrow Wilson, *The Public Papers of Woodrow Wilson,* ed. Ray Stannard Baker and William E. Dodd, 6 vols. (New York: Harpers & Brothers, 1925–1927), 5: 6–16.

12. Ibid., p. 15.

13. For a lively debate concerning Wilson's alleged concern for the fate of civil rights in war, see Jerald S. Auerbach, "Woodrow Wilson's Prediction to Frank Cobb: Words Historians Should Doubt Ever Got Spoken," *Journal of American History,* 54 (December 1967): 608–17. Arthur S. Link defended Wilson, and Auerbach rebutted in *Journal of American History,* 55 (June 1968): 231–38. The most searching analysis of the evidence is provided by Brian J. Dalton, "Wilson's Prediction to Cobb: Notes on the Auerbach-Link Debate," *Historian,* 32 (August 1970): 545–63.

14. Wilson, *Public Papers,* p. 13.

15. See the example of Representative Claude Kitchin of North Carolina, Link, *Wilson,* 5: 429 n.

16. Joan M. Jensen, *The Price of Vigilance* (Chicago: Rand McNally, 1968), p. 30.

17. Ibid., p. 25 and *passim.*

18. George Creel, *How We Advertised America* (New York: Harper & Brothers, 1920); James R. Mock and Cedric Larson, *Words that Won the War: The Story of the Committee on Public Information* (Princeton: Princeton University Press, 1939), p. 42 and *passim.*

19. Creel, *How We Advertised,* p. 184; and Robert E. Park, *Immigrant Press and Its Control* (New York: Harper & Brothers, 1922); pp. 444–47.

20. Blakey, George T., *Historians on the Homefront; American Propagandists for the Great War* (Lexington: University Press of Kentucky, 1970), p. 86; Mock and Larson, *Words,* p. 164.

21. Frederick Lewis Allen, "The 48 Defenders," *Century,* 95 (December 1917): 261–66; for individual state organizations see, for example, Missouri Council of Defense, *Final Report* (n.p., 1919); *Report of the Wisconsin State Council of Defense* (n.p., 1919); Robert N. Manley, "The Nebraska State Council of Defense: Loyalty Programs and Policies during World War I"

(M.A. thesis, University of Nebraska, 1959); Carl H. Chrislock, *The Progressive Era in Minnesota, 1899–1918* (St. Paul: Minnesota Historial Society, 1971), p. 131f.; Marguerite E. Jenison, *The War-Time Organization of Illinois* (Springfield: Illinois State Historical Library, 1923), p. 29f.; Cary, "Wisconsin Patriots," p. 63.

22. Robert D. Ward, "The Origin and Activities of the National Security League, 1914–1919," *Mississippi Valley Historical Review,* 47 (June 1960): 51–65; Horace C. Peterson and Gilbert C. Fite, *Opponents of War, 1917–1918* (Madison: University of Wisconsin Press, 1957), p. 18.

23. Michael Singer, "Kämpft Amerika gegen Deutschamerika?" *Jahrbuch der Deutschamerikaner für das Jahr 1918* (Chicago: German Yearbook Publishing Co., 1917), pp. 14–15; *New York Times,* 12, 17 July 1917, 6, 12 August 1917.

24. Blakey, *Historians on the Homefront,* pp. 47, 59, 85; *New York Times,* 6 September 1917. Earl Sperry, *Tentacles of the German Octopus,* Patriotism through Education Series, no. 21 (New York: National Security League, n.d.).

25. Quoted in Wallace Henry Moore, "The Conflict Concerning the German Language and German Propaganda in the Public Secondary Schools of the United States" (Ph.D. diss., Stanford University, 1937), pp. 33–34; *The American Defense Society: History, Purposes and Accomplishments* (New York, 1918); *Literary Digest,* 56 (30 March 1918): 29–31.

26. Seward W. Livermore, *Woodrow Wilson and the War Congress, 1916–1918* (Seattle: University of Washington Press, 1968), pp. 42ff.; Cary, "Wisconsin Patriots," p. 63.

27. *Literary Digest,* 54 (26 May 1917): 1574; Cary, "Wisconsin Patriots," p. 67.

28. Gerd Korman, *Industrialization, Immigrants, and Americanizers: The View From Milwaukee, 1866–1921* (Madison: State Historical Society of Wisconsin, 1967), pp. 136, 158, 161.

29. Ray H. Abrams, *Preachers Present Arms* (New York: Round Table Press, 1933), pp. 79, 95–124.

30. Newell Dwight Hillis, *The Blot on the Kaiser's 'Scutcheon* (New York: Fleming H. Revell, 1918), pp. 56–59, 93–97, 140–45, 173–77. See also Hillis's *German Atrocities: Their Nature and Philosophy* (New York: Fleming H. Revell, 1918).

31. Chrislock, *Progressive Era in Minnesota,* p. 139.

CHAPTER EIGHT

Superpatriotism in Action

1917

"Those were the sweetless, wheatless, meatless, heatless, and perfectly brainless days when your fathers broke Beethoven's records, boycotted Wagner's music, burned German books, painted German Lutheran churches and Goethe's monument in Chicago the color of Shell filling stations today; strung up a Mennonite preacher in Collinsville, Oklahoma, by his neck until he fainted, repeated the process until he fainted again, and graciously relented; hanged another to a limb of a tree in Collinsville, Illinois, until he was dead."[1] So mused Oscar Ameringer, a German-born American Socialist, as he recalled the enthusiasm with which Americans fought World War I at home. He was describing the fruit of a trend, rooted in the prewar decade, which grew vigorously during the neutrality period and ripened after the declaration of war.

By no means were all Americans caught up in the hysteria of superpatriotism. Many were ambivalent in their own feelings about American involvement and could sympathize with the German-American in his predicament. During the first four or five months of the war a number of prominent public officials and journalists were explicit about their confidence in the loyalty of the Germans. Even President Wilson, for example, wrote in August 1917:

I have been made aware from various sources of the unfortunate position in which a very large number of our loyal fellow-citizens are placed because of their German origin or affiliations. I am sure that they need no further assurance from me of my confidence in the entire integrity and loyalty of the great body of our citizens of German blood.[2]

Meanwhile the public and private agencies of propaganda delineated the new patriotism and noisy bigots increasingly baited German-Americans. But most citizens, preferring to accept ethnic protestations of loyalty at face value, adopted a wait-and-see attitude.

The millions of Americans of German birth or descent were anything but uniform in their response to war. The most obstinate among them insisted on displaying pictures of Kaiser Wilhelm as they had in the neutrality period, or refused to rise and sing the "Star-Spangled Banner" in public gatherings. Some were perhaps stupid; certainly they were indiscreet. A German farmer in Kansas flew the German flag above his home; an Indiana man muttered insults as he ripped a likeness of President Wilson from the wall. Others were merely tactless or naïve. In Chicago, a city where sixty alleged leaders of pro-German propaganda had been arrested almost simultaneously with the declaration of war, a group of German Lutheran clergymen met to make plans for serving the young men from their churches who would soon be drafted into the armed forces. They conducted their sessions in the German language and called themselves the Evangelische Lutherische Missionsbehoerde fuer Heer und Flotte, as they prepared to deal with the national government. Fortunately, a fellow pastor in Washington, D.C., convinced them of the need to translate the name to the Lutheran Army and Navy Board.[3]

At the opposite end of the spectrum were German-Americans who embraced all the tenets of superpatriotism. They hoped to shed all marks of German ethnicity and were severely critical of persons and institutions that, in their opinion, inhibited assimilation. A variety of associations were organized to accomplish the conformists' goals. In

New York, for example, a group founded a society to implement an advertiser's boycott of German-language newspapers. Other similar organizations sprang up across the country to establish the absolute loyalty of the Germans in America. In Chicago a group of German Lutheran laymen formed the American Lutheran Patriotic League. On a broader scale there was the National Patriotic Council of Americans of German Origin, a large association that was backed by Secretary of the Interior Franklin K. Lane. The most highly publicized organization was the Friends of German Democracy. Really a propaganda agency sponsored by the Committee on Public Information, it distributed much literature denouncing the Hohenzollern autocracy and calling for the creation of a German republic. Its founders, who hoped to tap the old tradition of German liberalism, included such prominent persons as Mayor Rudolph Blankenburg of Philadelphia, Franz Sigel, Jr., Otto Kahn, Jacob Schiff, and the aged Forty-eighter, Dr. Abraham Jacobi.[4]

Most Germans in America held attitudes somewhere between the pro-German and superloyalist extremes. Like most Americans they regretted that war had to come but there was no question in their minds about meeting their responsibilities as citizens. Although they were fearful of the domestic consequences of war, they were psychologically unprepared to cope with the myriad ways in which superpatriotism effected mundane aspects of their lives. Most experienced feelings akin to those described by Theodore Ladenburger, a German Jewish merchant of New York who had emigrated from Germany twenty-five years earlier. Ladenburger had exulted in his success in America and although he retained an emotional attachment for Germany, he had agreed strongly that American entry into the European conflict was appropriate and just. Yet, he wrote,

from the moment that the United States had declared war on Germany, I was made to feel the pinpricks of an invisible but so much more hurtful and pernicious ostracism as a traitor to my adopted country. I had never looked for sympathy in my bewildering dilemma. But in view of my record as a citizen I did expect from my neighbors and fellow citizens a fair estimate and appreciation of my honesty and trustworthiness. It had all vanished. Outstanding was only the fact, of which I was never ashamed—nor did I ever make a secret of it—that I had been born in Germany.[5]

Thus Ladenburger and innumerable other German-Americans tended to perceive themselves as objects of suspicion, innocent victims of whispered lies, citizens whose distinguished records of civic virtue were ignored or forgotten, whose private lives were subjected to unfair investigation, and whose deeds were condemned without a hearing or judged disloyal unless proven otherwise. They were sensitive, as never before, to the slightest slur, the knowing glance, the condescending remark. But native-born, established Americans regarded the status of German-born citizens in a society at war with Germany rather differently. They considered themselves to be tolerant of German-Americans and understanding of the emotional stress imposed by the war. They agreed that the great majority were firmly loyal, but that it was only fair to judge the German-Americans by their deeds, especially because of their apparently pro-German behavior during the neutrality period. Americans naturally wanted to analyze every word uttered by their German-born neighbors and scrutinize every action taken by ethnic organizations for evidence of disloyalty, sedition, and treason.

From the first days of the war, most German-language newspapers gave the superpatriots little cause for alarm. In general, they closed ranks quickly behind President Wilson, declaring their unequivocal loyalty and printing editorials counseling subscribers to do their patriotic duty and to avoid giving offense. There was also much superficial display of patriotism. Front pages were splashed with American flags, national anthems, and patriotic poetry; editors gave advertising space to war bond drives, patriotic meetings, and appeals for contributions to the Red Cross and the YMCA. This was more than cynical or expedient submission to popular demands for conformity. During the neutrality period, they, like many other Americans, had insisted that the United States would best be served by avoiding war; but now they saw no alternative to working for the speedy victory of American arms over Germany.[6]

A few German-American editors, however, found the transition painful. A Seattle paper, for example, denounced the declaration of war as a national catastrophe brought about by "British gold, Wall Street, ammunition makers, and the indifference of the people." More caustically, the *New Haven Anzeiger* observed that everything in this world has an end; bologna even has two ends, but "stupidity alone is without end and without limit." Some papers cast their patriotism in terms that permitted them to nourish hatred for England. According to the *Cincinnati Volksblatt*, "To support the United States is a duty. To support the President as the representative of the United States is no less a duty; but to have to support England, that hypocritical robber nation, that hereditary enemy of our country, that's what makes one heartsick." Others hoped that somehow the war might end before the United States became fully engaged in the fighting. Still others tried to avoid editorial comment on the questions raised by American involvement and limited themselves to straight reporting of war news. Not a few German-American editors believed that Germany would win in any case. Hence, they liked to give reports of German victories prominent placement on their front pages. By the end of summer, however, most German-American intransigents had so modified their stance that their publications had become vehicles of patriotic propaganda, as George Creel and his agency had hoped.[7]

A few die-hards anguished over conscription. George Sylvester Viereck, for example, contended that draftees of German origin should be excused from fighting in France. There were many other avenues of service, he argued, without being forced to fire upon one's kinsmen. A few papers repeated Viereck's arguments and a number of pe-

South Bend (Indiana) *Tribune*

It Wouldn't Grow in America!
A stereotyped pacifist and German-American share
disappointment over the failure of draft riots to develop.

titions were sent to Congress urging amendments to the
draft law which would favor German-Americans. Basically, however, this seems to have been an elitist concern
not founded on widespread sentiment. Except for Socialists
and those who objected for religious reasons, German-
Americans responded to the draft as willingly as any group
in America. Only in New Ulm, Minnesota, where antiwar
feelings were nourished by a few intransigent leaders, was
there a major ethnic demonstration against conscription. It
was obvious to almost all other German-American spokesmen that such behavior gave substance to charges of ethnic

disloyalty. Hence, nearly all German-language newspapers urged full compliance with the law and explained its detailed requirements for the benefit of readers whose comprehension of English was limited.[8]

The advent of war presented insuperable difficulties for the thousands of organizations whose objectives were closely related to the maintenance of German culture. In general, they sought to remain as inconspicuous as possible and refrained from drawing attention to themselves by formal declarations or public activities. The National German-American Alliance, however, because of its prominence, followed an explicitly patriotic course. It issued a call to all members to meet every responsibility imposed by citizenship. Although it was subsequently accused of dilatory patriotism, the alliance took much pride in its participation in the several Liberty bond drives. Absolute loyalty to the United States was a constant theme in its literature, as was the requirement of proper conduct. But the various alliances understandably hesitated to display sympathy for America's allies and they were less than eager to publicly condemn Germany's war aims or to blame the war on the Kaiser, as the superpatriots demanded.[9]

A few local German-American organizations responded to the declaration of war with dramatic gestures. An association of New York societies offered its shooting range and park in New Jersey to the War Department. The Germania Club of Jacksonville, Florida, offered the facilities of its new $100,000 clubhouse to the Red Cross free of charge. But these were exceptions. The behavior of the Cincinnati Alliance was typical of many more of the vereins. Like the national organization, it quickly declared its loyalty, organized itself for the sale of war bonds, and supported Red Cross activities. Its officers exhorted members to destroy German flags, to remove pictures of the Kaiser and his generals, and to stop trying to send money and gifts to relatives in Germany. Its members scrupulously avoided discussing the war as the organization returned to its traditional interest in state and local issues—prohibition, woman suffrage, and school affairs.[10]

Ethnic organizations whose purposes were ideological, unlike the social and cultural vereins, resisted pressure to conform to wartime standards of patriotic behavior. This was especially true of the Socialists. Their newspapers, both in the English and German languages, boldly attacked the declaration of war as a crime against the American people, intended to safeguard Wall Street investments and disguised in lofty but hypocritical rhetoric. Shortly before American entry, the executive committee of the Socialist party called for an emergency convention in Saint Louis on 7 April 1917, to forge a wartime program. Reaffirming their allegiance to international working class solidarity against capitalist exploitation, the Socialists resolved to stand firm in their opposition to the war, conscription, press censorship, and all restrictions of free speech. The Saint Louis manifesto aroused the apostles of conformity to storms of denunciation. Except for a splinter group of Anglo-Americans who endorsed the war, most Socialists were then excoriated as pro-German traitors. The *New York World,* for example, declared that there was no longer any room for the Socialist party in the United States because it was almost wholly a German product working for a German victory. Before long Socialist newspapers were subjected to much harassment and many fell under the ban of censorship.[11]

American entry into the war created a problem of peculiar dimensions for the German-American churches. None of them had had formal or institutional ties with Germany, much less the German government; indeed, many church Germans had emigrated in protest to the religious policies of German states. They took their own allegiance to the United States for granted, something above question. While they continued to place high value on their ethnocultural heritage, they believed it to be unrelated to the war and devoid of genuine political implications. Hence, they could make declarations of loyalty freely and without reservation, unnecessary though they seemed. During April and May the leaders of nearly all German-American denominations contributed to the flood of loyalty pledges. They said that the citizen who had once pleaded for peace would now render faithful service, as befits a Christian. Willingness to work and fight, however, was not tantamount to approval of war in general as a means of national policy, or of this war in particular as being in the best interest of the United States. Nor were they willing to equate patriotic service with modifying their use of German language and culture. They believed that they had every right to continue using German in their worship services, schools, business meetings, and publications. Naturally, this stance made the German churches easy targets of war-born chauvinism. Unlike most of the vereins, which readily faded under superpatriotic pressure, the churches tried in 1917 to maintain a "business-as-usual" policy.[12]

Some German-American churchmen quickly recognized that the times demanded positive action in order to prevent further erosion of their status in American society. In contrast to those who remained aloof, they sought appointments to local councils of defense, to Red Cross and Liberty bond drive committees, or as Four Minute speakers. Others freely violated their liturgical sensibilities by displaying the American flag in their sanctuaries and by having their congregations sing the "Star-Spangled Banner."

Advocates of such measures were usually assimilationists who were seeking to Americanize their churches. Often identified as theological liberals, they believed that the church's mission demanded a rapid transition to the English language, that the church should become thoroughly involved in patriotic activities, and that this involvement should be widely publicized, thereby defending the church against unfounded charges of disloyalty. Conservatives, by contrast, tended to ignore the demands made upon them by the superpatriots. The church was apolitical, they insisted; to abandon the German language would inhibit the church's responsibility to preach the Gospel; to permit patriotic speechmaking in the church would dilute its message; to indulge in patriotic display would violate the boundary between church and state and cheapen both in the process. Confident in their loyalty, conservatives hoped to weather the storm by retreating still further into their ethnic shells.

In general, German-Americans of all kinds were bewildered by the onset of war. Since the test of loyalty rested in superficial behavior, they were expected to declare their allegiance with great fervor, to work vigorously and sacrificially for victory over Germany, and to reject German ethnocultural elements of their identity. If they remained silent on the subject of the war or assented passively to it, as most of them did, they were likely to be charged with lukewarm patriotism. If they conformed enthusiastically to the new standards, they could be charged, as some were, with making a show of patriotism to mask their essential disloyalty.

By June 1917, hostility toward German-Americans had begun to mushroom. This was due in part to the frustration government leaders and superpatriots felt against what they thought was a lack of enthusiasm for the war. From their point of view, popular attitudes were being poisoned by disloyalists of all kinds, chief of whom were the publishers of foreign-language newspapers, German-American clergymen, pacifists, socialists, and politicians of the LaFollette stripe, who, they said, spoke English words conceived in alien thought.

President Wilson set the tone in his Flag Day speech of 14 June 1917. "The military masters of Germany," he assured the nation, have "filled our unsuspecting communities with vicious spies and conspirators and [have] sought to corrupt the opinion of our people." German agents, he charged, have "diligently spread sedition among us and sought to draw our own citizens from their allegiance." Spokesmen for Germany "in high places and low" in the United States continue their "sinister intrigue" as they declare that the European war has posed no dangers for America and claim that England seeks world economic domination. Moreover, the President continued, these persons "seek to undermine the Government with false professions of loyalty to its principles."[13] It was inevitable that Wilson's address, of which the Committee on Public Information distributed nearly seven million copies, should intensify the spy hysteria and weaken concern for civil liberties.

Flag Day, 1917, also marked the end of the first Liberty Loan drive, which brought more than $3 billion to the United States Treasury. Its success was due to effective organization coupled with skillful advertising. Much of the work had been directed by local councils of defense, which sent out workers to every door and stationed solicitors on street corners and in lobbies of hotels and business buildings. Quotas were assigned to every state and county. In many places committees designated specific amounts for individual citizens to subscribe. Extraordinary social pressure was often applied which literally forced persons to supply the required sums. Yet the fervent nationalists were disappointed with the results. Although Americans had purchased bonds in unprecedented quantities, devious means had too often been necessary to persuade reluctant buyers. German-Americans in particular were singled out for their apathy. The German-language press had often withheld editorial endorsements. Solicitors took special note each time a German-American refused or was hesitant to buy. Reports from several states alleged that counties with large proportions of foreign-born persons had fallen short of their quotas.

Shortly thereafter a series of intemperate attacks on German-language newspapers appeared nationally. In July, the *Atlantic Monthly* published an article by Frank Perry Olds that flatly accused the entire German-language press of disloyalty. Instead of supporting the United States in the war against Germany, Olds charged, it merely revised its propaganda to fit present needs; it had spread "anti-government lies, anti-Ally calumnies, and anti-war agitations"; its aim was to defeat America by "discrediting our motives, by

CAMOUFLAGE

A German-American makes public display of patriotism but privately hopes for a German victory.

preventing assistance to the Allies, and by causing discontent and opposition in our own country." Writing in *Outlook,* Hermann Hagedorn parroted Olds. He insisted that the German-language papers were Germany's strongest ally. "Atmosphere is an illusive peg to hang an indictment onto. But it is the German atmosphere that makes them the menace they are." He dismissed their protestations of loyalty as mere pretense. "Beward of the German-American," agreed a New York weekly, "who wraps the Stars and Stripes around his German body." The *Topeka* [Kansas] *Capital* meanwhile demanded the suppression of every German-language publication because each was disloyal and desired a victory for the Kaiser. Though less sweeping in its judgments, the *New York Times* agreed that the German-American press sought to bolster Germany by indirection, innuendo, and the suppression of the truth. Soon an aroused citizenry was demanding to know why such seditious sheets should be granted the protection of law and enjoy the privilege of the mails. One person revealed his ignorance of the niceties of democracy in a letter to the editor of the *Chicago Tribune:* "Let us hope that before long our government will stop dilly-dallying with these so-called German-Americans and put them into concentration camps until the end of the war, which end would be materially hastened by such action, especially if coupled with the entire suppression of the German-American press." Rather more imaginatively, Rear Admiral Cooper Goodrich proposed that the German-language newspapers be put out of business by levying a license fee of one to ten cents on each copy, depending on frequency of issue.[14]

The alleged failure of the American people to respond with enthusiasm to war also prompted the Nebraska State Council of Defense, newly appointed and eager to perform its duties, to conduct an investigation into the loyalty of the numerous German people of the state in general and "conspicuous leaders" of the Lutheran church in particular. Unimpeachable testimony from responsible and discreet men, announced the council on 10 July 1917, revealed

offenses ranging "from utterances of a treasonable character to direct acts and words of disloyalty." The sale of war
bonds had been opposed, the council continued, and Red
Cross work had met with alarming antagonism; the Lutheran church had failed to organize for war relief work
and certain clergymen had shown partiality for the German cause. The *Lincoln Star,* whose publisher was a member of the council, followed with an editorial indicating
that the charges were intended as a "timely warning" because the Lutheran church had become a medium for poi-
sonous German propaganda. Whatever its purposes, the
council contributed mightily to the growing anti-German
hysteria and to the identification of German-American
churches as agents of German imperialism when references to its charges appeared in papers across the land.[15]

Representatives of the several Lutheran synods appeared
before the Nebraska State Council of Defense to defend
their churches and to clarify the Lutheran doctrine of submission to civil authority. A major source of misunderstanding arose from the government's request that
clergymen "preach up" Liberty bond sales, Red Cross activities, and food and fuel conservation, all of which were
unrelated to the church's preaching function. To the liturgical, orthodox German Lutheran mind, compliance would
be a violation of conscience and the principle of absolute
separation of church and state. The church "is here to pro-
claim the glad tidings of salvation," chimed in *The Lutheran* of Philadelphia, "and not to foster the spirit of
hatred with which the nations now seek to encompass each
other's ruin."[16] Some months later several Nebraska pastors of the Missouri Synod were severely criticized for
refusing to participate with clergymen of other denominations in a patriotic rally in Lincoln. But what appeared to
superpatriots as apathy was in reality adherence to this
church's firm opposition to "unionism," that is, public worship and prayer with persons whose religious beliefs were
not identical with its own.[17]

Like the attacks on German Lutherans in Nebraska, the antidraft rally held in New Ulm, Minnesota, on 25 July 1917, was extensively reported in the national press. Ten thousand persons heard City Attorney Albert Pfaender, a prominent member of the city's large and powerful German community, challenge the constitutionality of conscription for overseas service. He advocated compliance with the law but argued that Congress be petitioned to amend it. Questioning whether the declaration of war would have been approved by a majority of voters, he demanded that future declarations be submitted to popular referenda.[18]

The New Ulm demonstration could scarcely be termed seditious, yet it evoked stern responses and greatly strengthened the disposition of chauvinists to destroy German language and culture in the name of national unity. Governor Joseph A. A. Burnquist, an ex officio member of the Minnesota Commission of Public Safety, suspended Pfaender and two other city dignitaries from office for their parts in the meeting. The Commission followed with an investigation and a brainwashing program. It staged a patriotic rally for the good burghers on 4 September 1917, at which they dutifully passed resolutions pledging unconditional submission to the draft law.[19]

Much more publicity attended the escapades of the People's Council of America for Peace and Democracy, which had been a quiet co-sponsor of the New Ulm rally. The People's Council was a group of pacifists and Socialists sparked by Louis Lochner, a Milwaukee journalist of German-American origin. During July and August the council sought to hold a national convention to publicize their demands for a negotiated peace without forced annexations and indemnities. After Governor Emanuel Philipp of Wisconsin stopped a Milwaukee meeting in response to the objections of hysteriacs, the council moved to Minneapolis, where Socialist Mayor Thomas Van Lear was sympathetic. But Governor Burnquist forbade their assembling anywhere in Minnesota. Recessing across the state boundary to Hudson, Wisconsin, the pacifists were then menaced by a Minneapolis mob which, it was said, came equipped with heavy ropes. The People's Council thereupon fled to Chicago, where it convened on 1 September under the aegis of Mayor William Hale Thompson. Illinois Governor Frank O. Lowden meanwhile dispatched four companies of National Guard infantry to save Chicago from the pacifists. Thompson was furious over the governor's interference, but by the time the militia arrived from Springfield the convention was over and the troops descended upon a Polish wedding festival which had taken over the hall.[20]

While Lochner's peace doves fluttered about looking for a place to roost, the National Security League released its evidence of German-American disloyalty. Seditious replies to its request for German-American endorsements of American war aims, the league reported, had been received from several organizations. One respondent, for example, wrote, "I believe that President Wilson is not fighting for humanity, for civilization, against barbarism, militarism, or autocracy, but for J. P. Morgan's money." More rashly, another replied, "I believe that Woodrow Wilson is at present the greatest autocrat in the World; that the Representatives at Washington are cowards, and did not represent our people by voting for war."[21]

Other incidents served to convince many government officials and legislators that steps had to be taken to ensure greater national unity and to curb German-American disloyalty. On several university campuses, including Minnesota and Nebraska, professors were charged with having made unpatriotic utterances. At Columbia University two professors were dismissed and three more resigned in protest. The air was filled, it seemed, with socialist propaganda against the war. Labor radicals in the Industrial Workers of the World, according to one oft-repeated rumor, were heavily subsidized by the Germans to cripple the American war effort by striking and instigating other disturbances. When

Frank Little, an IWW leader of Butte, Montana, was lynched in August, many clucked about the illegality of mob murder while hailing his death as a warning to all disloyalists. The distinguished statesman Elihu Root tossed fuel on the flames when, upon his return from a trip to Russia, he remarked that there were men walking our streets "who ought to be taken out at sunrise and shot for treason." In Chicago, Germanophobes conducted an investigation that same month into a spelling textbook used in the city's public schools. An insipid tale about the honesty of Kaiser Wilhelm as a school boy was decried as insidious propaganda. By the end of the month, *Literary Digest* reported that editors in all parts of the country were demanding the suppression of all "treasonable, seditious, and disloyal" activity and some suggested that the People's Council, the IWW, and the Socialist party would have to be destroyed.[22]

Congress responded to the rising fever by imposing new restrictions on the German-language press. The Espionage Act, passed in June, included among its provisions a section which closed the mail system to any materials "advocating or urging treason, insurrection, or forcible resistance to any law of the United States." Its effect was to give postal inspectors the authority to determine what printed matter was seditious or treasonable and to revoke second-class mailing privileges from offending publishers, a responsibility for which they had few qualifications.[23]

In September, at the behest of Senator William H. King of Utah, Congress attached a rider to the Trading-with-the-Enemy Act which greatly enlarged the authority of the government to control the expression of opinion. The law, signed by Wilson on 6 October required German-language newspapers to supply English translations of "any comments respecting the Government of the United States, ... its policies, international relations, the state or conduct of war, or of any other matter relating thereto." The local postmaster was to receive and review translations. If the material was offensive, mailing privileges were to be withdrawn; if, over a period of time, a postmaster was satisfied that a paper was loyal, he could issue a waiver of the translation requirement.[24]

This legislation sounded the death knell for scores of German-language papers operating on a marginal budget. *Unsere Zeit* of Chillicothe, Ohio, for example, made no effort to comply. On the day the law went into effect it simply announced in a front-page, English-language editorial that it was ceasing publication. Others like the *New Haven Anzeiger* hung on for a time. Because much time and energy of its tiny staff was consumed in translating, the paper became increasingly trite and war news gradually disappeared from its pages. For the papers that continued to be published, the law forced support for the Wilson Administration and its war program. Moreover, the law was sometimes capriciously enforced. Some papers readily obtained waivers while others never received them.[25]

Given the state of public opinion in the fall of 1917, the Post Office Department exercised its censorial authority with discretion. It freed most German-language newspapers from the translation requirement, and only a few were denied the use of the mails. Usually the papers that experienced difficulties with the federal government were Socialist. Their troubles are properly ascribed to the war on radicalism rather than on German language and culture. This was most clearly the case when Victor Berger's *Milwaukee Leader,* an English-language daily, and the *Philadelphia Tageblatt,* another Socialist paper, lost their second-class mailing privileges in October. Violations of the Espionage Act were charged in both cases; the ensuing litigation was publicized widely, serving to polarize attitudes still further. To many German-Americans, the accused journalists were symbolic victims of Wilsonian persecution. They also won the sympathy of many persons who ordinarily abhorred their political doctrines.[26]

German-language newspapers suffered many other forms of harassment from both official and private sources.

Several offices were raided in September and October in connection with the Justice Department's campaign against the Industrial Workers of the World. Operatives of the American Protective League and agents of the Bureau of Investigation zeroed in on the *Chicago Arbeiter-Zeitung* and the *Sozial Demokraten,* as well as the *Philadelphia Tageblatt.* Files were seized, literature confiscated, and editors arrested. If the editors were German aliens, they were often interned. Fritz Bergmeier of the *Saint Paul Volkszeitung,* for instance, was arrested as early as August 1917, and sent to the internment camp at Fort McPherson, Georgia. Advertising boycotts were more subtle in operation. According to Oscar Ameringer, the United States Food Administration hinted to breweries that, unless they ceased advertising in the *Milwaukee Leader,* they could expect difficulties in securing malt, hops, and sugar. Similar pressure was allegedly applied by the Fuel Administration. In other instances, trainmen threw off bundles of German-language newspapers at wrong stations; Boy Scouts burned stolen bundles; and school teachers discouraged their pupils from delivering "disloyal" newspapers. In some communities the German-language papers were attacked in the English-language press and at patriotic rallies.[27]

By October, the German spy hysteria had spread from the superpatriots to affect the entire country. People believed and repeated absurd stories of German espionage. Their most notorious disseminator was John Rathom, the Australian-born editor of the *Providence* [Rhode Island] *Journal,* whose liberties with the truth earned him much censure long before the end of the war. His "pure and unadulterated fabrications," as Attorney General Thomas Gregory later called them, were reprinted with all gravity in scores of newspapers. Rathom regularly warned that all German and Austrian aliens should be considered spies unless proved otherwise. Soon this nonsense was transformed into a working assumption. The *New York Tribune* asserted that spies were "everywhere"—in the army and navy, in factories producing war materials, and in laboratories. The *New York Times* was certain—"the thing needs no proof"—that Germany was giving financial support to pacifists and other "pro-German" organizations. Senator Ben Tillman of the Naval Affairs Committee demanded that "the German devils" infesting the Navy Department be "ferreted out and hanged." The omnipresent spies were plotting sabotage of all kinds: destroying or poisoning water supplies, freeing interned German sailors, hampering the production of guns and ammunition, and contaminating food supplies destined for American soldiers. Diabolical ingenuity was ascribed to the Kaiser's minions and dupes, who allegedly deposited ground up glass in bandages, sugar, and flour.[28]

A fierce hatred for everything German pervaded the country by the fall of 1917. Nurtured on the belief that Americans had to loathe Germany in order for the nation to be fully mobilized, the feeling had been fostered more or less unconsciously by government policies, but intentionally by many private persons and organizations. Utterly ridiculous things were printed, as this quotation from the *Liberty Bell:* "The Satanic Kaiser stalks gloomily among his hordes of Satan-whelps, calls upon God to help him in his nameless crimes, and urges his faithful imps to still greater deeds of brutality.... Bill the Butcher should be handed to his mother on the point of a red-hot bayonet."[29] Milder versions of the same idea were advanced in many sermons, speeches, and editorials. Some commentators attacked the Wilsonian distinction between the Kaiser's government and his people. Samuel P. Orth, a respected student of American immigration, called it a "fatal delusion." Evangelist Billy Sunday agreed: "All this talk about not fighting the German people is a lot of bunk." In Sunday's view the fight was simply "Bill against Woodrow, Germany against America, Hell against Heaven." "Either you are loyal or you are not," he cried, "you are either a patriot or a blackhearted traitor."[30]

The persecution of Germans in America that flowed from such patriotism far exceeded the "pinpricks of ostracism" described by Theodore Ladenburger. Petty harassment was

SMASH IT!

Richards in *Philadelphia North American*

common. Employers of German-Americans would receive
telephone calls asking if they still had "that German spy"
on the payroll. Persons reading German-language newspapers on public conveyances were verbally abused and spat
upon. Promotions in the business world, government, and
armed forces were denied to persons bearing German
names. A German name was sometimes sufficient evidence
for the American Protective League to launch an investigation into the private affairs of a person, regardless of his
citizenship. Suspicion was heightened by the fact that German spies and disloyal German-Americans were believed
to be everywhere but could not, in fact, be found anywhere.[31]

The mildest expression could cause offense. Jacob Best, a
prominent Milwaukee brewer, had subscribed generously

A SWEETHEART IN EVERY PORT

German-Americans were explicitly attacked as conspirators
with German spies in the United States.

to the Liberty Loan drive. But when he dismissed an impor-
tunate bond salesman with an impatient "To hell with Liberty bonds," he was charged with disorderly conduct and
fined. When a northerner with a German name, caught
unprepared by a cold snap in Florida, disgustedly exclaimed, "Damn such a country as this," he was arrested for
having violated the Espionage Act.[32] Gradually suspicion
escalated to threats of violence, to forced Liberty bond sales,
to yellow paint applied liberally to monuments, churches,
parochial schools, and homes, to minor acts of vandalism,
to tar-and-feather ceremonies, to forced marches, anthem
singing, and flag kissing, and finally to the murder of Robert Prager in April 1918. While there is no other authen-
ticated instance of another German having been lynched,
the mob spirit had become so common by November 1917,
that President Wilson felt constrained to condemn it force-
fully in a speech to the American Federation of Labor in
Buffalo. A man who takes the law into his own hands by
joining a mob, the President warned, is not "worthy of the
free institutions of the United States."[33] Yet, as one historian has observed, "It was not so much the acts of physical
violence [that tormented the German-Americans] but the
dread thereof and the knowledge that the public at large
would stand idly by, either approving or indifferent, in the
presence of misdeeds perpetrated by a small group of deranged fanatics."[34]

Names were the most obvious evidence of German ethnicity and soon a name-changing campaign swept the land.
Demands were registered with the Treasury Department
that all banks with "German-American" in their titles be
renamed. Responding to the agitation of groups like the
American Defense Society, city fathers altered the names
of towns, villages, streets, parks, and schools to suit the
temper of the times. Germantown, Nebraska, was renamed
Garland after a local soldier who died in service; East Germantown, Indiana, was changed to Pershing; Berlin, Iowa,
became Lincoln. In Chicago, Bismarck School was renamed General Frederick Funston School. Among the

scores of changes in street names, Cincinnati's German Street was transformed to English Street. German dishes were expurgated from menus; sauerkraut became liberty cabbage, hamburger became liberty steak, and Bismarck pastries became American beauties. Even German measles were cleansed of disloyalty by a patriotic physician in Attleboro, Massachusetts, who renamed the disease liberty measles, an unimaginative choice at best.[35]

By November Beethoven had been banned in Pittsburgh. German music performed by German musicians was an easy target. Although there had been some minor complaints in spring, 1917, it was not until the fall concert season was under way that this exotic variety of fanaticism flowered. The famous violinist Fritz Kreisler, who had served briefly in the Austrian army in 1914, was scheduled to concertize in Pittsburgh on 8 November. Trouble began as several worthy Daughters of the American Revolution appealed to the director of public safety to cancel the concert as a threat to the peace. Kreisler was not permitted to perform and he escaped the city's wrath under police escort. After several other cities, including Baltimore, Cleveland, and Washington, canceled scheduled appearances, Kreisler retired from the concert hall for the remainder of the war period.[36]

Other musicians endured the rigors of alien detention camps. The most famous case was that of Dr. Karl Muck, conductor of the Boston Symphony Orchestra. Though German by birth and sympathy, Muck was technically a citizen of Switzerland. His entanglements with nationalistic fervor started with his reluctance, on grounds of taste, to perform the "Star-Spangled Banner" at the beginning of concerts. He withstood much chauvinist abuse but finally succumbed to it by agreeing to conduct the anthem as a friendly courtesy and offering at the same time to resign as conductor. The management, headed by the railroad financier Henry Higginson, insisted that he stay on. Meanwhile clamors for his dismissal intensified and guest appearances of the Boston Symphony in other cities were canceled. In December, former President Charles W. Eliot of Harvard, himself intensely pro-Ally in sentiment, analyzed the opposition: "Several excellent women have said to me that they cannot stand seeing that hateful Dr. Muck leading admirably an orchestra composed of Germans and demonstrating the superiority of Germany in music during the last hundred years. . . . They cannot bear to admit that Germany has any merits whatever, or ever had."[37] Finally, near the end of the season in March 1918, federal agents arrested Muck as a threat to the safety of the country and he was interned, despite his Swiss nationality. His arrest prevented him from conducting a scheduled performance of the *Passion According to Saint Matthew* by Johann Sebastian Bach.[38]

Many other incidents occurred in which superpatriots attempted to protect American audiences from the contamination of disloyal music. The Philadelphia orchestra, for example, announced on 10 November 1917, that no German music would be included in its programs. The Metropolitan Opera Company of New York forbade the production of German works. The conductor of the Cincinnati Symphony Orchestra, Dr. Kunwald, suffered a fate remarkably like Dr. Muck's. In New Jersey, the superintendent of schools announced that he would forbid the performance of German music in schools under his supervision. In California, the state board of education directed that all pages in music textbooks that contained German folk songs were to be cut out. According to the American Defense Society, German music was "one of the most dangerous forms of German propaganda, because it appeals to the emotions and has power to sway an audience as nothing else can."[39]

German theater was especially vulnerable to chauvinist attacks. Unlike German music, it had few patrons and fewer defenders outside the German ethnic community. Even in the best of times the production of German-language plays was a shaky enterprise, and now such efforts virtually ceased. German theaters in Milwaukee and Saint Louis, for example, closed their doors. Companies lacking their own buildings found it impossible to rent suitable facilities. Early in the war period, Milwaukee defenders of democracy felt so strongly about the disloyalty of German theater that they mounted a machine gun outside the Pabst Theater to prevent the staging of Schiller's *Wilhelm Tell,* which ironically is one of the most eloquent of protests against the kind of tyranny Kaiser Wilhelm was supposed to represent. With similar thoughtlessness, statues of German cultural and political figures, including Goethe, Schiller, Frederick the Great, and Bismarck, were vandalized, splashed with yellow paint, or removed from public display.[40]

But there were voices raised against such idiocies. The *Chicago Tribune* ridiculed the campaign:

We think the German state is a menace to our safety or its policy to our interests.... Therefore we are to penalize ourselves by refusing to take advantage of the vast wealth of thought and feeling and beauty the genius of a race had produced. We disapprove of the kaiser and his projects. Therefore we punish him by snubbing Beethoven. We do not like Von Tirpitz. Therefore we refuse to listen to Bach, or read Goethe and Heine.... We shall keep as clear-headed as we please and we shall not sink into the spiritual waste and folly of boche [German] hating.[41]

Few persons had the courage to point out that the war on German culture left the enemy untouched and that instead of uniting the American people in a time of crisis, it forced an ethnic cleavage between worthy citizens of German origin and the rest of American society.

The gravest danger to America, according to the superpatriots, was posed by the continued use of the German language. It was not merely a matter of newspapers, church services, and meetings of vereins. More seriously, they thought, was the potential perversion of America's youth by German-language instruction in schools and by German-language textbooks and library books. How could a child learn to hate the Kaiser, as proper patriotism required, when he was daily confronted with laudatory references to him, his people, and their language and culture? Clearly, the German language had to be banished from the elementary school curriculum, students in high schools had to be encouraged to reject German as a language for study, and textbooks, magazines, and newspapers had to be censored or removed from schools and libraries, lest these institutions serve the insidious purposes of German propaganda.[42]

Incessant agitation against the German language was under way by the autumn of 1917. The National Security League and the American Defense Society clamored loudly against the sentiment, still common at the end of summer, that the study of language would not affect loyalty. The Nebraska State Council of Defense, after its indiscriminate attack on the Lutheran churches in July, focused on the Lutheran Church—Missouri Synod for its use of German in worship services and parochial schools. The council also took steps to cleanse the Nebraska state traveling library of German-language books. Other states and cities took up the challenge to unmask kaiserite propaganda in the guise of language instruction. The movement was especially strong in New York, where by December the city board of education banned all textbooks containing favorable comments on the German emperor.[43]

The hysteria over the "Hun" language, stimulated by the continued agitation of the National Security League, reached its highest pitch during the spring months of 1918. A score of articles advocating the abolition of the German language in America appeared in periodicals with national circulation. Repression was repeatedly justified on the grounds that the German churches and schools, as well as the German-language press, were intent upon retarding the assimilation process, thereby making 100 percent Americanism impossible. Retention of the German language was described as the key to the Pan-German conspiracy.[44] In this view, the German war lords were using language to retain the allegiance of former subjects of the Kaiser, holding them in bonds of loyalty.

Dozens of cities, large and small, decided to remove German from the curricula of their school systems. State governments followed suit. Censorship committees to ferret out German propaganda in textbooks were created in Connecticut, Minnesota, and California. In February, the South Dakota State Council of Defense, acting on authority granted by the legislature, ordered the abandonment of German-language instruction in all public schools from the elementary to the collegiate levels. The Montana State Council of Defense extended the ban to apply to private and parochial schools as well. Its order also abolished German in the pulpits of the state and specified that all German-language textbooks be removed from schools and libraries. "There shall be no temporizing with treason in Montana," proclaimed the governor.[45]

The most drastic measure was enacted by the Louisiana legislature. It totally prohibited the use of the "enemy language" in the public and private elementary and secondary schools of the state. A similar bill was vetoed by Kentucky's governor. In July 1918, the South Dakota council extended its restrictions by prohibiting the use of the German language over the telephone and in assemblies of three or more persons in any public or semi-public place whatever, except in cases of extreme emergency. Iowa Governor William Harding issued a proclamation instituting the same kinds of regulation. "If their language is disloyal, they should be imprisoned," declared the secretary of the Iowa State Council of Defense. "If their acts are disloyal, they should be shot." By summer of 1918, approximately half of all the states had curtailed or abolished instruction in the German language, and several, along with dozens of counties, cities, and villages, had restricted the freedom of citizens to speak German in public.[46]

Some prominent educators counseled moderation. Among the most eloquent was United States Commissioner of Education Philander P. Claxton, who expressed the hope that the nation could establish the safety of democracy without learning to chant a hymn of hate. Several well-known presidents of prestigious universities also objected to the ban, but rarely did they oppose its abolition on the elementary school level. Yet for every prominent person who espoused moderation there was another, such as the superintendent of education in Illinois, who declared that "this intense and widespread hatred against everything and anyone who manifests the slightest pro-German tendency" was "altogether desirable."[47]

Perhaps the most frightening form which the war on language took was book burning. German-language textbooks most often provided the fuel for these chauvinist fires, but library and literary materials were not exempt. Usually the books were burned in association with patriotic rituals. Ceremonies were conducted in widely scattered communities from the East Coast to the Great Plains. Historian Carl Wittke discovered nineteen instances in Ohio alone.[48]

Teachers of the German language found themselves in unenviable circumstances. Where legislative or administrative action had not eliminated their jobs, plummeting enrollments had. Some teachers were reassigned to other duties, but most received no such consideration. A few were simply fired for having instructed their charges in the principles of disloyalty. Soon the expression of unpopular opinions on any subject could arouse suspicion. The *New York Times,* for example, noting that the majority of students in the city's high schools were of foreign stock, charged that "in the very places where Americanization, the teaching and learning of democratic ideals are most needed, instruction has been given far too often by half-baked disciples of socialism, internationalists, [and] pro-Germanists." The *Times* further urged the dismissal of teachers who opposed the war and who did not "believe in Liberty Bonds."[49]

Lutheran parochial schools were singled out for special condemnation as nurseries of kaiserism. In contrast to the more numerous Catholic schools, the Lutheran institutions served a constituency that was exclusively German in origin. Most teachers in these schools were either pastors or persons specially trained in Lutheran teachers colleges. By the time of World War I, the language of instruction was normally English, although German was commonly used in religion classes. As the attack mounted in the fall of 1917, a startling amount of misinformation was disseminated about the purposes, practices, and patriotism of these schools. It was frequently charged that the national anthem was neglected, that the American flag was rarely on display, and that German cultural heroes displaced Washington, Franklin, and Lincoln. Other reports asserted that the teachers were born and trained in Germany and that they lacked proper certification. School days were allegedly shorter than those of the public schools and terms were abbreviated.[50]

Quickly the stories attained mythic proportions. The *New York Sun,* for example, declared that "in Nebraska the Herr Professors ... whip children who speak English in German schools." Former Senator Lafayette Young of Iowa demanded in April 1918 that the federal government take steps to protect the innocent children enrolled in these schools from the malignant effects of German propaganda. In the Midwest alone, he charged, there were more than a thousand such schools that closed each day's session by singing *"Deutschland über Alles"* or *"Die Wacht am Rhein."* In his opinion, 90 percent of the teachers in these schools were traitors and deserved to be treated accordingly. Meanwhile several state councils of defense, acting with doubtful legality, banned the use of the German language in Lutheran schools. The Missouri State Council of Defense tried a more positive approach by establishing an honor roll for every school, church, and organization that eliminated the instruction and use of the German language. But other superpatriots harassed the so-called German schools by urging the enactment of legislation, as in Nebraska, which would require the certification of teachers in all nonpublic schools.[51]

State legislatures responded to the presumed threat posed by German-Americans, Socialists, and other allegedly dissident persons with a variety of other laws. Some were duplicative of federal espionage legislation, but others placed unusual restrictions on the liberty of citizens. It was unlawful in Iowa, for example, to "incite or abet, promote or encourage hostility or opposition to the Government of the United States or the State of Iowa." Minnesota and Nebraska made it illegal to discourage enlistments in the armed forces. In New Hampshire, Montana, and Nebraska, it was unlawful to encourage strikes or lockouts in any factory producing war materiel. In at least four states it was a misdemeanor merely to possess an enemy flag. And the Indiana legislature unwittingly rewarded the display of loyalty with cruel and unusual punishment when it decreed that school children must sing the "Star-Spangled Banner" "in its entirety" on all patriotic occasions.[52]

Some legislative actions affected aliens only. The most important of these were amendments to the state constitutions of Kansas, Nebraska, and South Dakota that withdrew voting rights from aliens not naturalized. During the nineteenth century several midwestern states had granted suffrage to persons who had taken out their first citizenship papers. This had been done to encourage European immigrants to settle in those states. The last of these laws were wiped from the books when citizens contemplated the anomaly of the Kaiser's subjects voting in American elections in time of war.[53]

Generally, however, German aliens were touched more directly by federal regulations. At the beginning of the war, the President had acted under the ancient Alien and Sedition Act of 1798 to restrict their activities. Later, as the spy hysteria intensified in the fall of 1917, Wilson issued new orders requiring all German aliens fourteen years of age and older to register with the government. On the assumption that all were potential enemy agents, they were barred from the vicinity of places deemed to have military importance, such as wharves, canals, and railroad depots. Moreover, they were expelled from the District of Columbia, required to get permission to travel within the country or to change their place of residence, and forbidden access to all ships and boats except public ferries.[54] These regulations, necessary as some of them were, affected as many as 600,000 persons. The American Protective League was given the responsibility of screening all applicants for the required permits and over 200,000 were then investigated. Subsequently several thousand were interned in concentration camps as minor infractions of the rules were exaggerated into major offenses.[55]

Property owned by German aliens was also subjected to governmental control. Aliens were required by law to surrender records of their businesses to the custodian of alien property, who was then to determine if the United States was endangered by continued management of the property by enemy aliens, in which case it was to be surrendered to his care for the duration of hostilities. A reasonable law, it became the vehicle for superpatriotic sentiment when Wilson appointed A. Mitchell Palmer as custodian. Although Palmer did not have the power of confiscation, he adopted aggressive policies designed to eliminate German-owned businesses in the United States. He was especially determined to use his authority against German-owned breweries that had been, in his words, a "vicious interest"—unpatriotic and pro-German in conduct because they had obstructed the prohibition movement.[56]

Of course, not all these laws were passed in order to curb the alleged threat to national security posed by persons of German ethnicity. Similar legislation would have been necessary in any case in wartime. The problem for German-Americans lay in the insensitive administration of the laws. Of them all, none impinged more directly on the interests of a German-speaking group than the draft law as it touched the pacifistic Mennonites.

Early in the war it became apparent that conscription of some sort would be necessary. Congress quickly debated and passed the Selective Service Act, which became law on 18 May 1917. Political radicals, anarchists, certain socialists, and IWW members registered bitter opposition, but the majority of Americans acquiesced to the law as necessary and fair. It was the patriotic duty of young citizens to serve, they believed, and unwillingness was cowardly and un-American. But none of the Mennonites saw it that way. For four centuries they had held that bearing arms in warfare was contrary to God's commandments. Indeed, many had immigrated to the United States precisely in order to escape service in European armies. They believed that conscription was a deviation from historic American ideals.

Many, perhaps most, Mennonite young men were willing to accept some sort of noncombatant service, although they would have preferred agricultural or Red Cross work in lieu of duty within the army itself. The most conservative Mennonites, however, were intransigent. They refused to serve in any way. Any service as a soldier—medical assistance, repair work, cleaning garbage cans, scrubbing latrines—was to aid the war machine.[57] They viewed wearing a military uniform with revulsion; it was an abomination akin to forcing an orthodox Jew to eat pork.

Registration for the draft began on 5 June 1917, and the first call to service came in August. Meanwhile officials of Mennonite conferences met to prepare a statement explaining their doctrine of nonresistance to the government. They pointed out that the exemption of members of churches whose creeds and convictions forbade participation in war, a provision of the Selective Service Act, was nullified by another which empowered the government to draft nonresistors into noncombatant service. Yet noncombatant service remained undefined, awaiting explication by the President. In September, several Mennonite delegations secured interviews with Secretary of War Newton D. Baker in order to clarify their status. Baker assured them that their religious beliefs would be respected. He strongly urged young Mennonite men to register for service, report for duty when called, request noncombatant service, and wait for the presidential clarification. Many Mennonite draftees complied, trusting the secretary's assurance that they would not be drilled or uniformed and that some form of service not in violation of their consciences would be found.[58]

But Baker was deliberately deceptive. On 10 October 1917, he dispatched a confidential memorandum to the commandants of army camps that efforts should be made to get conscientious objectors to renounce their convictions and accept regular service. He directed that nonresistors were to participate in training activity until their pleas for noncombatant service could be heard. Baker believed that extensive interpersonal relationships with non-Mennonites would erode their attitudes. Social pressure, he hoped, would gradually transform conscientious objectors into soldiers. The secretary of war further directed that if pacifistic draftees refused to drill, they were to be segregated in order to quarantine their unpatriotic ideas, but that efforts to make soldiers of them were to be continued. All the while the President postponed defining noncombatant service until 20 March 1918.[59]

Baker's memorandum failed to describe the methods by which conscientious scruples were to be weakened. In most cases, Mennonite draftees were treated with at least a modicum of propriety, though nearly all were reviled as yellow, cowards, Huns, and pro-Germans. But in some camps they were systematically abused. Some were denied adequate food, others were beaten, a few tortured. At Camp Funston guards on motorcycles chased them across fields, presumably to provide them with exercise, until they dropped from exhaustion. At Camp Lee, one was scrubbed with brushes dipped in lye. At Camp Taylor, another was forced to stand at attention in the blazing sun with his head back against a plank until he fainted. A more subtle brutality was exercised at the same camp, according to one witness, when Mennonite objectors were isolated with soldiers suffering from venereal disease. Terrified by the mistaken belief that they would be infected, the Mennonites thought that later, when they returned home, they would contaminate their families and fellow believers.[60]

Eventually, on 1 June 1918, Secretary of War Baker appointed a board of inquiry to determine the sincerity of individual conscientious objectors and to recommend action ranging from indictments before court-martial to extended furloughs to perform agricultural or industrial work. Although the farm furlough plan was tardy and inconsistently administered, it solved the problem for many Mennonite objectors. A few, however, were persecuted by spiteful officers who created situations designed to end in court-martial proceedings for disobeying orders. Ultimately, 130 Mennonites were convicted and sentenced to prison terms ranging from ten to thirty years. Incarcerated at the military prison at Fort Leavenworth, Kansas, these obdurate souls suffered much for their beliefs.[61]

Perhaps none were more brutally treated than four Hutterites from South Dakota. First they were placed in solitary confinement in the prison on Alcatraz; they were beaten, denied adequate food and drink, and required to stand all day with their arms chained to bars above their heads. Denied cots and blankets, they were forced to sleep on damp, stone floors. After four months of this, they were transferred to Fort Leavenworth, where two of the four, Michael and Joseph Hofer, died of pneumonia a few days later.[62]

The Mennonites and to a lesser extent the much more numerous Lutherans were easily victimized by the superpatriotic hysteria generated by the war. Often at no fault of their own, they were snared in traps unwittingly fashioned by the German-American cultural chauvinists. At first they were frightened and confused, but gradually, as the months rolled by, they regained their footing. They were determined to demonstrate by their actions that they were as patriotic in their own ways as anyone in the country and began to defend themselves against the superpatriots.

Notes

1. Oscar Ameringer, *If You Don't Weaken* (New York: Henry Holt, 1940), p. 323.
2. Woodrow Wilson to Representative L. C. Dyer of Missouri, quoted in *New York Times,* 4 August 1917.
3. Carl Wittke, *German-Americans and the World War* (Columbus: Ohio State Archaeological and Historical Society, 1936), pp. 144–45; Alan N. Graebner, "World War I and Lutheran Union: Documents from the Army and Navy Board, 1917 and 1918," *Concordia Historical Institute Quarterly,* 41 (May 1968): 51. See also Clifton J. Child, *The German-Americans in Politics, 1914–1917* (Madison: University of Wisconsin Press, 1939), pp. 164–65.
4. Wittke, *German-Americans and the World War,* pp. 137, 141; *New York Times,* 19 January 1918, 8 February 1918, 10 June 1918; *Lutheran Witness,* 37 (8 January 1918): 34; James R. Mock and Cedric Larson, *Words that Won the War: The Story of the Committee on Public Information* (Princeton: Princeton University Press, 1939), pp. 216–19; *Outlook,* 118 (24 April 1918): 658.
5. Theodore Laer [pseud.], *Forty Years of the Most Phenomenal Progress . . .* (New York: Putnam, 1936), p. 170.
6. *Literary Digest,* 54 (14 April 1917): 1051; Wittke, *German-Americans and the World War,* pp. 128–30; Franklin F. Holbrook, *Saint Paul and Ramsey County in the War of 1917–1918* (Saint Paul: Ramsey County War Records Commission, 1929), p. 12; Guido A. Dobbert, "The Disintegration of an Immigrant Community: The Cincinnati Germans, 1870–1920" (Ph.D. diss., University of Chicago, 1965), p. 331.
7. *Literary Digest,* 54 (14 April 1917): 1051; H. Wentworth Eldredge, "Enemy Aliens: New Haven Germans during the World

War," in *Studies in the Science of Society,* ed. George P. Murdock (New Haven: Yale University Press, 1937), p. 213; *Cincinnati Volksblatt,* 3 April 1917, quoted in Dobbert, "Cincinnati Germans," p. 323.

8. *American Weekly,* 18 May 1917; *Current Opinion,* 63 (July 1917): 2; Wittke, *German-Americans and the World War,* p. 161; Carl Chrislock, *The Progressive Era in Minnesota, 1899–1918* (Saint Paul: Minnesota Historical Society, 1971), p. 140.

9. U.S., Congress, Senate, Committee on the Judiciary, *Hearings on the National German-American Alliance,* 65th Cong., 2d sess., 1918, pp. 36, 74, 398, 450; Child, *German-Americans in Politics,* pp. 162–67; *Literary Digest,* 54 (5 May 1917): 1315.

10. *New York Times,* 10 April 1917; *Hearings on the National German-American Alliance,* p. 182; Wittke, *German-Americans and the World War,* p. 141, Dobbert, "Cincinnati Germans," pp. 344–45.

11. Robert E. Park, *The Immigrant Press and Its Control* (New York: Harper & Brothers, 1922), p. 347; John M. Work, "The First World War," *Wisconsin Magazine of History,* 41 (Autumn 1957): 36; *Literary Digest,* 55 (22 September 1917): 16; David A. Shannon, *The Socialist Party of America* (New York: Macmillan, 1955), pp. 93–98.

12. Philip Gleason, *The Conservative Reformers: German-American Catholics and the Social Order* (Notre Dame: Notre Dame University Press, 1968), p. 174; Ray H. Abrams, *Preachers Present Arms* (New York: Round Table Press, 1933), p. 51; Ralph Moellering, "Some Lutheran Reactions to War and Pacifism, 1914 to 1917," *Concordia Historical Institute Quarterly,* 41 (August 1968): 121–31.

13. Woodrow Wilson, *The Public Papers of Woodrow Wilson,* ed. Ray Stannard Baker and William E. Dodd, 6 vols. (New York: Harper & Brothers, 1926), 5:60–67.

14. Frank Perry Olds, "Disloyalty of the German-American Press," *Atlantic Monthly,* 120 (July 1917): 136–40; Hermann Hagedorn, "The Menace of the German-American Press," *Outlook,* 116 (August 1917): 579–81; "A Growing Demand for the Suppression of the German-American Press," *Current Opinion,* 63 (September 1917): 151–52; *Chicago Tribune,* 8 August 1917; *New York Times Magazine,* 24 June 1917, p. 14.

15. Robert Manley, "Language, Loyalty and Liberty: The Nebraska State Council of Defense and the Lutheran Churches, 1917–1918," *Concordia Historical Institute Quarterly,* 37 (April 1964): 1–16; *Lincoln Star,* 12 July 1917; *Literary Digest,* 55 (4 August 1917): 43–44.

16. Quoted in *Lutheran Witness,* 36 (7 August 1917): 237–40.

17. Alan N. Graebner, "The Acculturation of an Immigrant Lutheran Church: The Lutheran Church—Missouri Synod, 1917–1929" (Ph.D. diss., Columbia University, 1965), pp. 24–25.

18. Chrislock, *Progressive Era in Minnesota,* pp. 140–42; Franklin F. Holbrook and Livia Appel, *Minnesota in the War with Germany,* 2 vols., (Saint Paul: Minnesota Historical Society, 1928), 2:43.

19. Chrislock, *Progressive Era in Minnesota,* p. 142. See also the address of Julius Coller, "Loyalty of German-Americans to the United States Government," delivered at Jordan, Minnesota, 10 November 1917, U.S., Congress, Senate, 65th Cong., 2d sess., 1918, Document no. 164.

20. Louis P. Lochner, *Always the Unexpected* (New York: Macmillan, 1956), p. 68f.; R. B. Pixley, *Wisconsin in the World War* (Milwaukee: Wisconsin War History Co., 1919), p. 136; Mary Henke, "World War I: Dissent and Discord in Milwaukee" (M.A. thesis, Loyola University of Chicago, 1966), p. 107; Andrew J. Townsend, "The Germans of Chicago," (Ph.D. diss., University of Chicago, 1927), p. 171.

21. *Literary Digest,* 55 (1 September 1917): 10.

22. *Ibid.* (18 August 1917): 12; (25 August 1917): 26; (1 September 1917): 9; (20 October 1917): 10; *Current Opinion,* 63 (September 1917): 153; Horace C. Peterson and Gilbert C. Fite, *Opponents of War, 1917–1918* (Madison: University of Wisconsin Press, 1957), p. 102–9; Walter P. Metzger, *Academic Freedom in the Age of the University* (New York: Columbia University Press, 1955), p. 222–23.

23. Peterson and Fite, *Opponents of War,* pp. 15–17.

24. U.S., Congress, Senate, *Congressional Record,* 65th Cong., 1st sess., 1917, 55, pt. 7:7021–25; *Literary Digest,* 55 (September 1917): 16; Wittke, *German-Americans and the World War,* p. 173f.

25. LaVern J. Rippley, "Chillicothe Germans," *Ohio History,* 75 (Autumn 1966): 225; Eldredge, "New Haven Germans," p. 213; Wittke, *German-Americans in the World War,* p. 174.

26. *Literary Digest,* 55 (22 September 1917); Zechariah Chafee, Jr., *Free Speech in the United States* (Cambridge: Harvard University Press, 1954), pp. 86f., 298–305.

27. John Higham, *Strangers in the Land: Patterns of American Nativism, 1860–1925* (New Brunswick: Rutgers University Press, 1955), p. 220; Townsend, "Germans of Chicago," p. 174; Wittke, *German-Americans and the World War,* pp. 174–77; Joan M. Jensen, *The Price of Vigilance* (Chicago: Rand McNally, 1968), p. 161; Holbrook, *Saint Paul in the War,* p. 229; Ameringer, *If You Don't Weaken,* p. 315.

28. *Literary Digest,* 55 (6 October 1917): 9; Wittke, *German-Americans in the World War,* p. 146; Jensen, *Price of Vigilance,* p. 99.
29. Quoted in *Lutheran Witness,* 36 (7 August 1917): 239.
30. Samuel P. Orth, "Kaiser and Volk: An Autocratic Partnership," *Century,* 95 (November 1917): 100; *New York Times,* 19 February 1918.
31. Henke, "World War I in Milwaukee," p. 122; Dobbert, "Cincinnati Germans," p. 396; Holbrook and Appel, *Minnesota in the War* 1:195; Lochner, *Always the Unexpected,* p. 67.
32. Henke, "World War I in Milwaukee," p. 106; *Congressional Record,* 65th Cong., 2d sess., 1918, 56, pt. 5:4771.
33. Wilson, *Public Papers* 5:123. Wilson's Buffalo speech also reveals the extent to which he accepted the propaganda regarding Pan-Germanism.
34. Dobbert, "Cincinnati Germans," p. 395.
35. Wittke, *German-Americans and the World War,* p. 186; Dobbert, "Cincinnati Germans," p. 393; Wallace H. Moore, "The Conflict Concerning the German Language and German Propaganda in the Public Secondary Schools of the United States" (Ph.D. diss., Stanford University, 1937), p. 49.
36. *Literary Digest,* 55 (24 November 1917): 32; Louis P. Lochner, *Fritz Kreisler* (New York: Macmillan, 1951), pp. 161–67.
37. Bliss Perry, *Life and Letters of Henry Lee Higginson* (Boston: Atlantic Monthly Press, 1921), p. 493.
38. Ibid., pp. 484–97; *New York Times,* 12, 13, 15, 27, 31 March 1918.
39. *New York Times,* 10 November 1917; Wittke, *German-Americans and the World War,* p. 183; Dobbert, "Cincinnati Germans," p. 376; Wilhelm Mueller, *Die Deutschamerikaner und der Krieg* (Wiesbaden: Hofbuchhandlung Heinrich Staadt, 1921), p. 46; Moore, "German Language in the Public Schools," pp. 122ff.; *New York Tribune,* 3 March 1918.
40. Mueller, *Deutschamerikaner in der Krieg,* p. 56; Wittke, *German-Americans and the World War,* p. 184f.; Gerd Korman, *Industrialization, Immigrants, and Americanizers: The View From Milwaukee, 1866–1921* (Madison: State Historical Society of Wisconsin, 1967), p. 170.
41. Quoted in Michael Singer, "Deutschamerika in den Kriegsjahren," *Jahrbuch der Deutschamerikaner für das Jahr 1918* (Chicago: German Yearbook Publishing Co., 1917), p. 165.
42. *New York Times,* 26 January 1918, 25 February 1918. For a classic expression of the fear of German-language instruction, see a letter written by Will C. Wood, Commissioner of Secondary Schools in California, quoted in Moore, "German Language in the Public Schools," p. 161–63.

43. Wallace H. Moore, "German-Language Instruction during the War," *American-German Review,* 5 (April 1939): 14; Manley, "Language, Loyalty, and Liberty," p. 7; Frederick C. Luebke, "The German-American Alliance in Nebraska, 1910–1917," *Nebraska History,* 49 (Summer 1968): 183; *New York Times,* 6, 14 November 1917, 3, 5, 28 December 1917.

44. *Saint Louis Post-Dispatch,* 27 April 1918. As an example of the literature of suppression, see "Enemy Speech Must Go," *North American Review,* 102 (June 1918): 810–14; see also Andre Cheradame, *The United States and Pan-Germania* (New York: Scribners, 1918).

45. Moore, "German Language in the Public Schools," pp. 84, 89, 112, 125; Holbrook and Appel, *Minnesota in the War,* pp. 84–85; Joseph M. Hanson, *South Dakota in the World War, 1917–1919* (Pierre: State Historical Society, 1940), p. 61f.; *Saint Louis Post-Dispatch,* 2 May 1918.

46. U.S. Army, Office of the Judge Advocate General, *Compilation of War Laws of the Various State and Insular Possessions* (1919), p. 47; *New York Times,* 31 March 1918; Hanson, *South Dakota in the War,* p. 61; *A Proclamation to the People of Iowa* (Des Moines, 23 May 1918), quoted in Graebner, "Acculturation of an Immigrant Church," p. 27; Wittke, *German-Americans and the World War,* p. 156.

47. See Claxton's widely publicized letter to Robert Slagle, president of the University of South Dakota, 12 March 1918, *School and Society* 7 (30 March 1918): 374; Mueller, *Deutschamerikaner in der Krieg,* p. 53; Moore, "German Language in the Public Schools," pp. 36, 108.

48. Wittke, *German-Americans in the World War,* p. 190 n.

49. Wartime enrollments in high-school language classes are charted in Moore, "German Language in the Public Schools"; Wittke, *German-Americans and the World War,* p. 179; *Literary Digest,* 55 (8 December 1917): 32f.

50. Manley, "Language, Loyalty, and Liberty," p. 8; Graebner, "Acculturation of an Immigrant Church," pp. 21–23.

51. *New York Sun,* 20 February 1918, quoted in *Lutheran Witness,* 36 (16 April 1918). See also *Chicago Tribune,* 5 April 1918; *Washington Post,* 4 April 1918; *Lutheran Witness,* 36 (14 May 1918): 158.

52. *Compilation of War Laws,* pp. 34–43, 106.

53. Ibid., pp. 9–17.

54. Wilson's proclamation is reprinted in its entirety in *New York Times,* 20 November 1917.

55. *Literary Digest,* 55 (1 December 1917): 15; Jensen, *Price of Vigilance,* pp. 39, 161, 166.

56. U.S., Congress, Senate, Committee on the Judiciary, *Hearings on Brewing and Liquor Interests and German Propaganda,* 65th Cong., 2d sess., 1918, 1:1.
57. James C. Juhnke, "The Political Acculturation of the Kansas Mennonites, 1870–1940" (Ph.D. diss., Indiana University, 1966), p. 152; Arlyn John Parish, *Kansas Mennonites during World War I* (Fort Hays [Kansas State College] Studies, History Series, no. 4, May 1968), pp. 38–39; J. S. Hartzler, *Mennonites in the World War: Nonresistance under Test,* 2d ed. (Scottdale, Pa.: Mennonite Publishing House, 1922), pp. 49–54.
58. Parish, *Kansas Mennonites during World War I,* pp. 26–29; Hartzler, *Mennonites in the World War,* pp. 86–98.
59. Juhnke, "Kansas Mennonites," p. 157; Parish, *Kansas Mennonites during World War I,* 37; C. Henry Smith, *The Coming of the Russian Mennonites* (Berne, Ind.: Methodist Book Concern, 1927), p. 282.
60. Parish, *Kansas Mennonites during World War I,* p. 39; Smith, *Russian Mennonites,* p. 275; Hartzler, *Mennonites in the World War,* pp. 123–31; Ernest Louis Meyer, *"Hey! Yellowbacks!": The War Diary of a Conscientious Objector* (New York: John Day, 1930), pp. 45, 68.
61. Hartzler, *Mennonites in the World War,* pp. 103–21; Parish, *Kansas Mennonites during World War I,* pp. 40–45; Smith, *Russian Mennonites,* p. 274.
62. Smith, *Russian Mennonites,* p. 277f.; Hartzler, *Mennonites in the World War,* p. 146f.

CHAPTER NINE

Ethnic Reaction

1918

By 1918 a spirit of intolerance had filtered through all levels of American society. In the early stages of the war, many political leaders had felt that many citizens were apathetic in their patriotism. The people, they thought, were not enthusiastic enough about buying bonds, paying higher taxes, being drafted, or sending sons and husbands to European battlefields. Too many persons seemed willing to listen to demogogic politicians and unscrupulous newspaper publishers who disputed announced American war aims. Mobilization on the home front therefore had included a program to perfect the patriotism of America's heterogeneous population. Thousands of ordinary Americans were swept into the structures created by the Committee on Public Information, the American Protective League, the state and county councils of defense, and private patriotic organizations, and thus they too acquired an identity which bound them psychologically to the superficial display of loyalty.

At the same time, the American press continued to foster suspicion of Germans in America. *Everybody's Magazine,* for example, published a series of articles entitled "Invaded America" by Samuel Hopkins Adams, a respected journalist. Spread over a four-month period early in 1918, these pieces included bitter attacks on the German-language

press and on the Lutheran clergy as disloyal agents of kaiserite propaganda. *Atlantic Monthly* serialized Andre
Cheradame's frantic propaganda before his book on Pan-
Germanism was published in January 1918. Popular magazines such as *Life* carried dozens of cartoons that
threatened German-Americans and debased German culture. *New Republic,* among other journals, railed against
"the German spirit in America" as an ethnocentrism more
intense than that of other immigrant groups because it was
fostered consciously by the German government.[1]

The fine patriotic feeling that the Wilson Administration
had hoped to engender was easily transformed into rampant prejudice, even though the President and many other
prominent figures in national and state government asserted that the overwhelming majority of Germans in
America were absolutely loyal to their adopted country, its
ideals, and institutions. Only a tiny coterie of noisy pro-
German propagandists, they insisted, were to be chastised
as contemptible disloyalists. Yet ordinary citizens failed to
get the message: the administration told them to watch vig-
ilantly for spies, to be intolerant of "slackers," and to join
in the great moral struggle of democracy against evil Prussian autocracy and militarism. Their ears were attuned to
the inflammatory rhetoric of men such as John F. McGee,
head of the Minnesota Safety Commission, who on several
occasions urged the use of firing squads to dispatch "the
disloyal element" of his state; and Representative Julius
Kahn of California, who declared that the nation would
profit from "a few prompt hangings."[2] On every hand the
American people were encouraged to make war on German
language and culture and to watch persons and institutions
carefully for signs of subversion. The persecution of innocent American citizens was a natural and understandable
result. Hundreds of newspapers granted implicit approval
to violence. Samplings of small town newspapers reveal
anti-German allusions in almost every issue. More prestigious newspapers joined in: after the Prager murder in
April the *Washington Post,* for example, declared that the

people were not subverting law and order. "Enemy propaganda must be stopped," said the *Post,* "even if a few lynchings may occur."[3]

But nothing served to focus popular wrath against the Germans more than the United States Senate's investigation of the National German-American Alliance, beginning in February 1918. The hearings were conducted by a committee chaired by Senator William H. King of Utah, who had introduced a bill a month earlier to revoke the alliance's charter, granted by Congress in 1907. For a period of two months the investigation provided a steady supply of stories that served to confirm chauvinist fears. The principle witness against the alliance was Gustavus Ohlinger of Toledo, Ohio, whose attacks on the organization as part of a vast Pan-German conspiracy had already attracted national attention. The testimony revealed a startling amount of distortion and misunderstanding of the character and goals of the National Alliance and of the German ethnic group generally. German-Americans were perceived by their enemies as a monolithic body, united in purpose and action by the alliance. Efforts at language and culture maintenance were linked with anti-prohibitionist political activity as threats to national unity. The senatorial investigators rarely differentiated between prewar activities of the alliance and its policies after the declaration of war. Legitimate endeavors of the neutrality period were wrenched from their setting and condemned as disloyal and subversive. In essence, the chief offense of the alliance and its leaders was that their prewar vision of America had been at odds with the dominant notions of Anglo-conformity. They assumed the legitimacy of ethnic political interest; their detractors did not.[4]

The task of defending the alliance fell upon its youthful and inexperienced president, the Reverend Siegmund G. von Bosse of Wilmington, Delaware, who had succeeded to the leadership upon the resignation of Charles J. Hexamer in November 1917. The latter, suffering from ill health and wearied by abuse, found that his association with the alliance had become personally "distasteful."[5] He did not testify. But other longtime leaders appeared before the committee; a few succumbed to the air of intimidation and sought primarily to establish their own loyalty. Despite the creditable efforts of Von Bosse, the defense was ineffective. It could not have been otherwise, since Senator King and his colleagues never doubted that the alliance was pro-German and that it had to be destroyed.

On 11 April, two days before the committee concluded its investigation, the officers of the alliance dissolved the organization and turned its assets over to the American Red Cross. Meanwhile, most of the remaining state organizations quietly folded, usually by action of their executive committees, but in some instances by the revocation of charters by state legislatures. Many local alliances, having no legal foundation, simply withered and died. Others sought to survive by holding no meetings that would attract public attention. A few sought to divest themselves of ethnic identity. The Kansas City *Stadtverband,* for example, reorganized in January as the American Citizenship Association; the Cincinnati Alliance held on until April, when it emerged as the American Citizens League.[6]

Hundreds of secular ethnic organizations across the land suffered a similar fate. In New Haven, Connecticut, the German bicycle club, the shooting club, and several lodges disappeared, while three singing societies survived by merging into one. Many vereins attempted to halt dwindling memberships by erasing ethnic marks. Milwaukee's Deutscher Club renamed itself the Wisconsin Club. Chicago's Germania Sangerverein emerged as the Lincoln Club. Other societies publicized their extensive patriotic activities. In May the prestigious Liederkranz of Saint Louis, for example, proudly proclaimed that its members had subscribed $525,000 in Liberty bonds, equal to more than $1,000 per member, and that 101 of its members were serving in the armed forces.[7]

The survival of German ethnic businesses was virtually predicated upon name changes. To illustrate, the Germania

Bank of Milwaukee became the National Bank of Commerce; Buffalo's German-American Bank was changed to the Liberty Bank. The Germania Life Insurance Company of Saint Paul became the Guardian Life. In Saint Louis, the Kaiser-Kuhn wholesale grocery firm changed its name to Pioneer Grocery Company after its delivery wagons were regularly stoned by superpatriotic but semiliterate urchins. Proprietors also removed statutes and other evidences of Germanness from their buildings before trouble started. Heroic figures of Germania were displaced in Milwaukee and Saint Paul; she also fell in Cincinnati, in spite of the efforts of some Germans there to disguise her as Columbia.[8]

The German-language press, the glue which held the ethnic community together, was devastated by changed attitudes. Harassed by their enemies and abandoned by their friends, publishers tried hard in 1918 to mollify their critics, even to the extent of attacking the methods and goals of Imperial Germany. Editors sought to escape controversy by limiting their criticism of the government, the Allies, and the war effort to unembellished quotations from respected English-language publications. Some papers cast all war news in English in order to bypass the hobbling translation requirement. Others, especially in western states, changed their names and converted entirely to English. In spite of everything, scores of papers folded. The total number of German-language publications, including church, lodge, and trade periodicals, stood at 522 just before the war. Forty-seven percent had disappeared by the end of 1919. In the larger cities, as one paper would cease publication, another would survive by acquiring its subscription list. The number of German-language dailies dropped to twenty-six, less than half the prewar figure and their combined circulation was reduced by two-thirds to about 250,000 copies. Casualties among the small-town weeklies were especially severe. In Iowa, for example, where twenty-six papers (including one daily) had been published before the war, only eleven were in business two years later. In

This example of official United States government propaganda, produced by George Creel's Committee on Public Information, perpetuated the stereotype of the German soldier as a Hun who rapes women and bayonets children.

Indiana, only one of three dailies survived and all six weekly papers were discontinued. In states where the German ethnic population was small, the German-language press was usually wiped out entirely.[9]

The several Liberty Loan campaigns provided unlimited opportunities for action against German-Americans. It was true that many had not responded well to the first drive. But by the autumn of 1917, as the second campaign got underway, German-American spokesmen were strongly in support. Many organizations invested all their cash reserves in the government bonds to help their communities meet or even exceed their quotas.[10] Meanwhile the Treasury Department issued a stream of promotional materials which attacked the Kaiser personally and stressed "Hun" brutalities. The propaganda had the effect of stimulating superpatriots to add coercion to their sales techniques. Washington bureaucrats, of course, had not intended for terror to be used, yet they seriously underestimated the ease with which subtle social pressure could give way to raw violence.

Intimidation assumed various forms. Local Liberty Loan committees frequently apportioned their quotas to individuals on the basis of a crude estimate of a person's financial worth. Anyone who failed to comply could expect the application of intense pressure. In Iowa, several sales committees threatened to publish lists of "slackers" in local newspapers. In a few instances, names were posted on court house lawns. In one Iowa town, a yellow monument was erected which bore the names of a German farm family that had refused to subscribe. Recalcitrants sometimes found their property marked with large yellow signs announcing their imperfect patriotism. Uncooperative merchants were boycotted. In several midwestern communities, caravans of superpatriots, accompanied by photographers and stenographers, coerced allegedly disloyal citizens to buy. Protests of poverty or of earlier purchases were ignored. In some instances the mobs included a representative of a local bank who was authorized to arrange a loan on the spot, thereby enabling the alleged slacker to buy the prescribed bonds. Objections sometimes evoked higher assessments, as in the case of a Wisconsin victim, John Deml, who was attacked at midnight by seven carloads of patriotic hoodlums. A rope was cast about Deml's neck as he refused to succumb to terrorist tactics. Shrinking from the "ultimate solution," the mob satisfied itself by beating and bloodying its victim.[11]

No group of Germans in America suffered more because of the Liberty Loan campaigns than members of several Mennonite sects. Because of their firm adherence to pacifistic doctrines, most Mennonites refused to buy bonds on the grounds that such purchases were tantamount to participation in war activities. Their plight was made worse by their refusal to salute the flag, which they regarded as a form of idolatry. Inevitably, Mennonite names appeared on slacker lists and they became fair game for the one-hundred per-centers. In Ohio, a vigilance committee forced forty Amish families to purchase bonds by threatening them with eviction. In Kansas, several conservative Mennonites were tarred and feathered while two others had their beards shaved off. In Oklahoma, county officials rescued a Mennonite preacher from a gang that was stringing him up from a telephone pole. Another Mennonite was mobbed twice, the second incident occurring after he had contributed seventy-five dollars to war relief in lieu of bond purchases. His home was ransacked and daubed with yellow paint inside and out, his watch was stolen, he was stripped of his clothing and struck a dozen times with a leather strap, and finally tarred with a roofing compound containing carbolic acid.[12]

As the persecution of Mennonites intensified, the less orthodox compromised by defining war bond purchases as a form of taxation—Christ, after all, had required his followers "to render unto Caesar the things that are Caesar's." Others bought the hated bonds and then quickly donated them to the Red Cross or some other relief agency. But the communitarian sects remained adamant. The Hutterites of

Life, 4 April 1918

"Our Culture is Largely an Imitation of the French"
—*A German Professor*

Indiscriminate hatred of everything German reached a climax in the spring of 1918.

"MY COUNTRY, 'TIS OF THEE."
(*German-American Version*)

My country over sea,
Deutschland, is sweet to me;
　To thee I cling.
For thee my honor died,
For thee I spied and lied,
So that from every side
　Kultur might ring.

Life, 13 June 1918

South Dakota, for example, offered to make large contributions instead of bond purchases, contingent upon assur-
ances that the money would be used for relief purposes. The
government argued, logically enough, that no substitutions
were possible because loan subscriptions were voluntary.
Nevertheless, the Hutterites donated as much as $30,000.
Still the Yankton County Liberty Loan Committee was not
satisfied. Such charities did not fill quotas. So a squadron of
patriots invaded the Hutterite colony and drove off a herd
of 200 steers and 1,000 sheep, which were sold at auction for
about 40 percent of their actual value. The resulting sum
of $16,000 was used to purchase bonds in the name of
the Hutterites. Of course, the communitarians refused
to accept the bonds and they lay unclaimed in a Yankton
bank.[13]

As the irrational hatred of everything German deepened
in the spring of 1918, well-meaning government officials
sought more positive means of meeting the peril posed by
German immigrants. Secretary of the Interior Franklin K.
Lane encouraged comprehensive programs of education
and cooperation as he organized an Americanization conference held in Washington early in April. In session at the
time of Prager's death, the meeting was attended by many
state governors, representatives of state councils of defense,
educators, and social workers. Several resolutions supporting intensified Americanization programs were adopted,
including one urging that in the nation's elementary
schools all subjects should be taught in English only. Unfortunately, the forum tended to generate, rather than discourage, hatred of German-Americans. When Secretary Lane
called for moderation in the suppression of the German
language, arguing that "you cannot make Americans by
coercion," half the delegates reportedly leaped to their feet
to take issue with him. Much publicity attended the bigotry
and misinformation dispensed by conference participants.
For example, Robert Metcalfe, a prominent Bryanite
Democrat, repeated the canard about the German national
anthem being sung in a hundred schools in his state of

Nebraska. Lafayette Young of Iowa declared, "There are 5,000 persons in Iowa who ought to be in the stockade at this very minute." He also claimed that German preachers were a grave menace to America, a belief to which the governor of Idaho also publicly agreed. Secretary of the Navy Josephus Daniels exclaimed that "we will put the fear of God into the hearts of those who live among us, and fatten upon us, and are not Americans."[14]

News stories of this kind combined with numerous fanciful accounts of enemy activities within the United States to produce an extraordinary public frenzy. German submarines allegedly deposited spies on American shores; they in turn flashed secret signals to off-shore submarines at night; mysterious enemy aircraft were observed violating American skies; and German agents spread influenza germs in major cities. Hundreds of rumors swept the land, yet not a single genuine German spy had been arrested, tried, and executed. The fact was that federal authorities rarely considered such reports worthy of investigation.[15] An agitated public, however, was of a different mind. The government was bombarded with thousands of complaints that it was derelict in its duty to apprehend German plotters. Fear-filled citizens charged that the courts were unduly lenient with disloyalists. If the Espionage Act was inadequate, they claimed, the law ought to be amended to put a stop to seditious talk. Unless drastic steps were taken soon, superpatriots warned, the people would take the law into their own hands. They frequently cited the Prager lynching as evidence.

Attorney General Gregory concurred. "Most of the disorder throughout the country," he declared, "is caused by a lack of laws relating to disloyal utterances." The Espionage Act did not in fact cover casual disloyal utterances by individuals, so Gregory asked for modest changes in the 1917 law. Thus stimulated, Congress responded to the popular mood by enacting major abridgments of free speech and press. These amendments, frequently called the Sedition Act, were patterned directly on Montana legislation. On 16

May the new restrictions became law. Forbidden were any words or deeds intended to obstruct the sale of United States war bonds; any disloyal utterance or writing intended to induce contempt for the form of the United States Government, its Constitution, flag, or uniforms; any deed intended to curtail the production of war materiel; or, indeed, any word or act favoring any country at war with the United States. Convictions carried maximum penalties of $10,000 fines or twenty years imprisonment or both.[16]

As usual, Mennonites were especially vulnerable. Soon two of their clergy were charged with obstructing the sale of Liberty bonds. The United States District Court of Martinsburg, West Virginia, which heard the case, recognized the technical character of the charges. But instead of dismissing the case, it charged the defendants $1,000 each plus costs. Even more drastic measures were advanced by the United States district attorney in Cleveland, who, late in 1918, proposed grand jury indictments against 181 Mennonite bishops and ministers for having conspired to violate the Sedition Act. Fortunately, the Justice Department would have none of it.[17]

Acts of violence against German-Americans increased dramatically during the winter months and reached a climax in April 1918. It is neither possible nor necessary to catalogue them all. The well-publicized murder of Robert Prager in Collinsville, Illinois, was merely the most tragic. Although violence was most common in midwestern states, incidents occurred with alarming frequency in all parts of the country, according to newspaper reports. In Pensacola, Florida, for example, an American-born man of German origin was severely flogged by a citizens' vigilance committee. After being forced to shout "To hell with the Kaiser; hurrah for Wilson," he was ordered to leave the state. In Avoca, Pennsylvania, an Austrian-American accused of criticizing the Red Cross was tied up by a group of superpatriots, hoisted thirty feet into the air, and subjected to the force of water from a fire hose. After an hour he was released, still alive. In California, an Oakland tailor of German origin was hanged for a moment by members of an organization known as the Knights of Liberty. Before he strangled, the victim was cut down and tied to a tree. In San Jose, one George Koetzer was tarred, feathered, and chained to a cannon in a park for his alleged pro-Germanism. In Tulsa, Oklahoma, Knights of Liberty tarred and feathered a young German-American, administered fifty lashes, and released him after he promised to leave the city. In Corpus Christi, Texas, a German Lutheran pastor was whipped on the grounds that he had preached in German after the county council of defense had forbidden it. In Bishop, Texas, another was publicly flogged for his comments on local war committees.[18]

Major midwestern newspapers reported anti-German acts almost daily. In Ashland, Wisconsin, there were two tar-and-feather incidents within a two-week period. In Jeffersonville, Indiana, a fifty-year old German-American farmer who had resisted a Liberty Loan sales committee sought the refuge of the state penitentiary to escape a vengeance-seeking mob. In Riverdale, Nebraska, a crowd of patriots hanged an effigy before the parsonage of the local German Lutheran church and in Papillion, Nebraska, the Reverend H. F. Schmidt was attacked and beaten. In Excelsior Springs, Missouri, a German hotel keeper who protested the arrest of a German orchestra leader for disloyalty was rewarded with a coat of yellow paint. In Jefferson City, Missouri, German-born Fritz Monat reportedly declared his hopes for a German victory. On the same night that Prager was lynched, Monat was seized by a vigilance committee, stripped, and beaten. He was then taken to a local theater where a show of some kind was in progress. At the end of the scheduled entertainment an impromptu ceremony was staged. The leader of the mob made a rousing speech against disloyalists. Then, as the orchestra played the national anthem, Monat was forced to kneel and kiss the flag.[19]

Anti-German violence often took the form of property damage. Petty vandalism was common. German church doors were splashed with yellow paint, windows smashed, and sign boards wrecked. In September 1918, a German Luthern parochial school in Herington, Kansas, was destroyed by fire. A month later another in Lincoln, Missouri, was burned and one in Schumm, Ohio, was dynamited. In Inola, Oklahoma, two Mennonite meeting houses were burned to the ground. Commercial establishments were also sometimes vandalized, as in Charleston, South Carolina, where several United States sailors, armed with hammer and chisel, mutilated the stone-carved name of the Germania Bank.[20]

In dozens of communities mobs disguised as volunteer patriotic organizations terrorized allegedly disloyal German-Americans. Placing themselves above the law, the gangs dragged suspects from their homes to be interrogated, threatened, beaten, or deported. Frequently municipal authorities were unable to control the misguided fervor and stood helplessly by as self-appointed courts acted. Sometimes city officials were in the vanguard, supplying patriotic oratory and by their presence granting moral sanction to the illegal proceedings.

Individual German-American reactions to the terror varied with its intensity. In many communities where calm leadership prevailed German-American lives were hardly touched. Elsewhere responses ranged from those who viciously joined the superpatriots to those who huddled in fear and complied with all humiliating demands. Hermann Hagedorn, for example, regaled his fellow ethnics with undiluted propaganda as he accused them of not putting their hearts into their patriotic activities, donations, and bond purchases. Others sought to support the war effort by participating in the activities of the National Patriotic Council of Americans of German Origin or of the CPI-sponsored Friends of German Democracy. Some German-Americans of social pretensions attempted to camouflage their ethnic origins by attacking German music and art. In George Sylvester Viereck's sardonic words, "They would deny the Holy Ghost if He were to approach them in German garb or with a Teutonic accent."[21] In Peshtigo, Wisconsin, members of a German Lutheran church joined a mob that forced one of their fellows to buy a prescribed amount of bonds and to kiss the American flag. In Perry County, Missouri, a bastion of rural German Lutheranism, congregations panicked. Parishioners destroyed German-language textbooks in their parochial schools, and fearing searches, they hid their German-language Bibles and devotional books. Many German-American parents decided that from then on they would speak only English in their family circles.

Name-changing became a common phenomenon, as thousands sought to remove the most conspicuous mark of their ethnicity. Schmidt easily translated to Smith, Koch to Cook, Schwartz to Black; Strauss was transformed to Stratford; Rosenstein was shortened to Rose and Morgenwerk to Morgan. In Milwaukee, court records show more than two hundred such cases during the first four months of the war.[22] George Washington Ochs of Philadelphia asked the court to change his name to Oakes. "Your petitioner," he wrote, "has no purpose or reason in changing the spelling of his father's name, except the desire to relieve his sons of a Teutonic appellation which he believes will arouse hostility and prove an unnecessary burden in their future social, personal, commercial, and professional relations."[23]

Thousands of German aliens sought the protection of citizenship. In May 1918, Congress eased the process by which certain classes of enemy aliens could be naturalized. During the months that followed, 75,000 persons applied for citizenship, and were then investigated by the American Protective League.[24]

As the war entered its second year in April, it became apparent that law enforcement agencies and courts were not likely to protect victims of superpatriotic justice, and vulnerable people prepared to defend themselves. For example, in Steeleville, Illinois, worshippers in a German Lutheran church armed themselves with guns to discourage an

Life, 8 August 1918

MORE CAMOUFLAGE: "PLEASE, YOUR HONOR, I WOULD LIKE
TO CHANGE MY NAME FROM TECKELHEIM VON LIMBURGER
TO SILAS SALTONSTALL"

impending assault by a mob from a nearby community. A
hundred miles north near Havana, Illinois, fifteen German-
American farmers barricaded themselves in the home of a
young man to protect him from a mob intent upon a tar-
and-feather ceremony.[25]

As early as December 1917, many leaders of the German-
American population realized that they had to fight back if
their identity and institutions were to be preserved. They
had already observed the demise of many alliances and
vereins, the drastic contraction of the German-language
press, the virtual elimination of German-language instruction in public schools, and the distressing attacks on German churches and schools. It seemed that mere assertions
of patriotism or appeals to history meant little. Countless
loyalty pledges had been approved, publicized, and sent to

civil authorities. They seemed as ineffective as the declarations of German-American loyalty issued by the President, state governors, and other men of influence. Only the most obvious acts of loyalty, it appeared, could divert suspicion away from German-Americans.

Many editors of the German-language press and spokesmen for German ethnic institutions exhorted their constituents to buy all the bonds they could possibly afford, to contribute generously to the Red Cross and other relief agencies, to display the flag, to extend hospitality to servicemen, to participate as workers in patriotic drives, to be Four Minute speakers for the CPI, to join in patriotic rallies, and to serve on state and local councils of defense. In short, Germans were to venture forth from their ethnic shells and accommodate themselves fully to the new norms of patriotic behavior.

A host of German societies and churches responded positively to this advice. While they continued to adopt loyalty resolutions in their formal meetings, they put new emphasis on active participation in the war effort. Among the churches a special program was launched to assist young men in the army and navy. Hundreds of pastors served as part-time chaplains for nearby army camps and their congretations developed recreational opportunities for soldiers and sailors. Lutherans alone collected nearly a million dollars to support this kind of work. Even many conservatives who had earlier disapproved of such "entanglements" as being outside the church's proper sphere of activity reluctantly agreed by the summer of 1918 that they were necessary.

Armed with impressive records of loyalist activity, some leaders of the German-American community believed they could counterattack. Thus Edward Steiner, a well-known author of Austrian birth, denounced anti-German hysteria in *Outlook* in January 1918. He condemned patriotic excesses he had observed in his home state of Iowa. Flag-kissing ceremonies he found especially offensive, calling them desecrations of the flag itself. Steiner asserted that the bigots, some of whom he implied were chairmen of state and county councils of defense, were alienating good Americans of German origin instead of making patriots of them. A Prussian state of mind, he declared, was taking over. The same issue of *Outlook* carried an article by the Reverend Paul Froehlke who claimed that the strong ethnic identity of German-Americans could be traced to Americans who "continually harped and accentuated our being of *German* extraction, and thus, in the course of time, perpetuated in our minds the idea that we were an incongruity in the American make-up."[26]

Other journals carried similar protestations. One German-American writing in *New Republic* intimated that when the government counseled German-Americans to vilify their origins and traditions it implanted a rancour that does not heal. "Prussianism at its worst," he suggested, never required them "to shout down all their intimate [cultural] values and to demand vociferous lies against themselves."[27] Here and there local newspapers also became more aggressive in defending German-Americans from unwarranted charges.

Church leaders also took courage. In Nebraska, a delegation of German Lutheran church officials conferred with the State Council of Defense to clarify the use of German in their churches and schools. Subsequently one of their number was appointed to the council's Americanization Committee. Samuel Hopkins Adams's attack on the German-Americans in *Everybody's Magazine* also evoked a prompt reply. Theodore Graebner of the *Lutheran Witness* dashed off a scathing open letter in which he thrashed the journalist for the inaccuracy of his facts and the superficiality of his understanding of language and culture in immigrant life. Graebner also hastily authored a pamphlet, *Testimony and Proof Bearing on the Relation of the American Lutheran Church to the German Emperor,* which was given wide distribution. The tract gathered historical evidence and contemporary documentation to establish the Missouri Synod's loyalty to the United States and its long-standing antipathy for the policies of the German Imperial Government. Similarly, other leaders denounced Pan-Germanism; one declared it to be an unchristian and impious abomination to the church. They emphasized that thousands of German Lutherans emigrated to America to escape the ecclesiastical tyranny of Germany.[28]

Wisconsin Synod Lutherans denounced Charles Edward Russell, a prominent prowar Socialist, who had asserted that Lutherans were pro-German because, if the Kaiser were defeated, it would mean the end of their church. This was silly slander, the *Northwestern Lutheran* asserted, based on ignorance of the principles of the separation of church and state. In March 1918, when the popular Scottish comedian Harry Lauder charged in a patriotic address that every German Lutheran congregation in Saint Louis was singing a German hymn of hate each Sunday morning, church officials again responded vigorously. A month later the president of the Missouri Synod appointed a war-time bureau to prepare publicity materials to combat such slanderous reports as Lauder's, and to represent individual congregations before government officials.[29]

These defensive measures made a difference. By summer, 1918, many congregations reported marked improvements in their community relations. Some were even exempted from local language restrictions. The overt display of patriotism and energetic involvement in war activities had worked a subtle change, even though a degree of hostility lasted to the end of the war and beyond.[30] But the mere fact of being German was less a source of offense than it had been before. Instead of being denounced as disseminators of kaiserite propaganda, the churches were now more frequently criticized as inhibitors of the Americanization process. For this reason there was no decrease in the pressure to speed the transition from German-language usage to English, and the war against the German language continued unabated. A Saint Louis spokesman for the National Security League expressed the 1918 attitude in common speech:

We can't engage in hairsplitting between the good and the bad in German. Everything German is being put in the bad column. We acknowledge freely and gladly that most of the people of German descent who are living in America are real Americans. A lot of them rank at the top for Americanism, but there is another lot of dirty, treacherous ones, too, and when they talk in German the rest of us get the loyal and the disloyal all mixed up. We don't understand German and we don't feel called upon to learn it in order to play the hairsplitting game between the good and the bad.[31]

The extent of the switch to English depended upon the conservatism of the denomination, the size of the ethnic community, and the intensity of the superpatriotic sentiment. Among the Mennonite groups, the movement toward English was only slightly accelerated, though it was more noticeable in the more liberal conferences. In Kansas, for example, over half of the General Conference Mennonite congregations introduced English services during the war. Among the Lutheran synods, the transition was painfully abrupt in some quarters, but almost imperceptible in others. Before the declaration of war, approximately one-sixth of the congregations in the Lutheran Church—Missouri Synod held at least one English-language service per month. By the end of the war this figure spiraled to nearly three-fourths of the congregations. In southern states, where the German population was small, English usage predominated; in areas of heavy concentration, as in Minnesota, not much more than 20 percent were using English in 1919. However, many congregations of all denominations individually responded to local pressure and ruled out German services for the duration. In Montana, where the State Council of Defense forbade the use of German in pulpits, a few congregations fearfully stopped all public worship. By contrast, there were individual clergymen in other states who defiantly asserted that orders from state councils lacked the force of law. Risking the wrath of their local communities, they continued to preach in German, apparently without further serious trouble.[32]

The transition to English among the church Germans is also evident in the discontinuance of many German-language periodicals and in the decline in circulation of others. For example, *Der Friedensbote,* the organ of the German Evangelical church, decreased by 20 percent. The privately published *Abendschule* of Saint Louis, which had been vociferously pro-German during the neutrality period, lost 40 percent of its 50,000 prewar subscribers. But the circulation of some held up surprisingly well, especially in the more conservative bodies. At the same time, English-language church journals grew rapidly. The *Lutheran Witness* jumped from 12,000 to 19,000 copies in one year. Meanwhile, advocates of Americanization had organized the American Lutheran Publicity Bureau in 1917 and launched a new periodical at the end of the year, the *American Lutheran,* which was designed in part to help correct misunderstandings concerning the church's stand on the war. German-church publishing houses also reflected the transition. In one instance, the proportion of English titles increased from 49 percent before the war to 70 percent in 1917 and 1918. And hundreds of local congregations, like so many other ethnic organizations, translated their legal names into English.[33]

The impact of anti-German hatred on parochial schools is difficult to measure because of inept record-keeping. In many cases, church records do not make distinctions between full-time parochial schools and part-time educational agencies. Because they stressed German-language study in preparation for participation in the adult church, the part-time schools (conducted on Saturdays, in summer, and other vacation periods) were especially vulnerable, and hundreds were terminated during the war period. But the regular parochial schools survived surprisingly well. In most instances, English-language instruction was standard in nonreligious subjects by 1917. Suspicion usually could be countered by reducing or eliminating German entirely from the curriculum and by introducing patriotic rituals— singing the national anthem and pledging allegiance to the flag. This was done in hundreds of schools, even though some conservatives continued to oppose the abandonment of German. In the Lutheran Church—Missouri Synod, where parochial schools were the strongest and most numerous, perhaps fifty of approximately 1,500 institutions were closed because of anti-German hysteria, according to one estimate. However, in other German Lutheran synods that were less strongly committed to the idea of full-time schools, they practically ceased to exist. But German Catholic schools weathered the storm with comparative ease. Among the Mennonite groups, whose exclusive rural colonies usually made parochial schools superfluous, a few were terminated. But in at least one instance, Mennonites opened a school during the war in order to free their children from what they considered to be the idolatrous practice of saluting the flag of the United States.[34]

Military conscription continued to plague the Mennonites throughout 1918. Church officials lobbied diligently in Washington in behalf of their point of view. President Wilson's clarification of noncombatant service in March solved the problem for many; nearly half of all the Mennonite draftees from Kansas, for example, accepted such service. But most of the rest retained conscientious objector status and endured the concomitant indignities and abuse.

By the summer of 1918 many of the most conservative Mennonites decided that their status within the United States had become intolerable, and for conscience's sake, they considered emigration. Canada was the most logical destination because of its proximity, its extensive land resources, and the fact that it was already the home of many coreligionists and relatives who were willing to help. Most importantly, Canada granted total exemption from military service to all religious objectors. Clandestine movement across the border began intermittently in the fall of 1917, and in the following year the stream of fugitives increased to well over 1,500 persons. The emigration consisted not only of draft-age males, but of families as well. Indeed, in the case of the Hutterites of South Dakota, entire colonies sold their lands and possessions, often at staggering losses, to relocate on the Canadian plains, chiefly in Saskatchewan. Oklahoma and South Dakota provided large numbers of emigrés, although others fled from Kansas, Nebraska, and Minnesota. Very few members of the older Mennonite churches, such as those found in Pennsylvania, Ohio, and Indiana, participated in the movement. Most fugitives came from German families that had fled Russia since the 1870s.[35]

Government officials were aware of the migration. Secretary of War Baker had been informed explicitly by Mennonite delegations of their determination to leave if satisfactory conscientious objector status could not be arranged. The Wilson Administration, however, wisely decided to ignore the flight, thereby shielding it from publicity. And when many of the emigrés drifted back after the war, the federal government made no effort to prosecute them for draft evasion.

By comparison to Lutherans and Mennonites, other German-speaking Protestant churches suffered less persecution. This is not to say that they escaped entirely, for each group had its own problems. The German Evangelical Synod, for example, was especially sensitive about its origins, which were tied to the creation of the Prussian state church in 1817. Synodical officials were therefore anxious to point out that the American church had never had any institutional links with the German government. Unlike the German Lutherans, Evangelicals maintained few parochial schools which could serve as objects of superpatriotic suspicion. Nevertheless, they were hit sharply by the language controversy. According to one report, thirty Evangelical pastors were forced to resign because they were unable to preach in English.[36]

German Methodist conferences, like their Baptist and Congregational counterparts, felt pressures originating in the larger denominations of which they were parts. Strong sentiment developed within the Methodist church to disband its ten German conferences and to merge the congregations with the regular conferences. All German

Methodist publications except one were suspended during the war. Severe personal problems developed. One midwestern bishop, for example, arranged for a Secret Service agent to be assigned to watch a young German-born minister under his jurisdiction whom he suspected of espionage. After winning the clergyman's confidence, the agent provoked him to make an allegedly unpatriotic remark, which led to prompt ecclesiastical discipline. Circumstances forced German Methodist conferences to make special efforts to establish their loyalty. For example, the Saint Louis conference, which included about one hundred midwestern congregations, conducted an energetic war bond drive which netted nearly $750,000. At Baldwin-Wallace College, a German Methodist institution in Ohio, students displayed their patriotic sentiments by demonstrating against the president of the school for his failure to denounce "German crimes and atrocities." A subsequent investigation by several Methodist bishops led to his resignation.[37]

Anti-German hysteria had a devastating impact on the membership and growth of the German Methodist conferences. By contrast to the German churches that were theologically distinctive (e.g. Lutheran and Mennonite bodies), the German Methodist congregations differed from their parent organization in language only. Hence, when language came under attack, they were bound to lose ground. If they switched to English, they abandoned their basic reason for existence. Thus, the high point of German Methodism came just before the American declaration of war, when there were 740 congregations in ten conferences. That number declined rapidly to 688 in 1919. The number of clergymen also dropped, as individual preachers, especially the young, sought transfer to English-speaking conferences.[38]

The wartime experiences of German Catholics were rather different from those of German Protestants. While nativistic superpatriots perceived the Catholic church as foreign, they saw it as Roman, not German. The Pope was

Italian and Italy was our ally. Catholic theology and history were not rooted in Germany, as was the case with Protestantism. The use of Latin in Catholic worship was not offensive; it was strange, but not a threat to patriotism. The schools of distinctively German parishes were rarely identified as nurseries of kaiserism. Indeed, the tendency of Catholic schools to serve as media for German propaganda had been crushed years earlier in the famed Cahensly controversy.

Roman Catholic bishops greatly strengthened the patriotic image of the church by their positive statements on loyalty and war and by their willingness to act decisively when the interests of the church demanded it. Several prelates requested all priests under their jurisdictions to cease preaching in German in 1918 when the frenzy was it its worst.

Yet the war was not without effect on German Catholicism. Individual priests and parishes experienced the same kind of hostility as the German Protestants; and such incidents strengthened the influence of Americanizers within the church. The use of English was accelerated in both sermons and auxiliary organizations such as the Central-Verein. Catholic journals published in the German language also declined. Perhaps as many as one-third were casualties of the war, but those that survived generally managed to sustain prewar circulation figures.[39]

Among German Jews there was little institutional change that could be attributed to the war fever. The Jewish component of their identity was much stronger than the German. Besides, several prominent leaders of the group were outspoken advocates of a patriotism capable of satisfying the most avid chauvinists. Otto Kahn, a well-known New York financier, was one who frequently made eloquent appeals for German-American loyalty. But occasionally German-Jewish rabbis were trapped in superpatriotic muck. Dr. Emil G. Hirsch of Chicago's Sinai Temple, for example, faced a congregational upheaval because of his alleged pro-Germanism. The trouble began in April 1918, when Hirsch publicly criticized the local council of defense for its distribution of a thoughtless letter to Jewish institutions urging "all loyal citizens and organizations to celebrate the anniversary of the entry of the United States into the war for the continuance of *Christian* civilization."[40]

The image of the Socialist party in the United States as pro-German and traitorous was strengthened greatly during the war period. Many prominent Socialists of English antecedents (chiefly journalists and intellectuals with negligible popular following) abandoned the antiwar doctrines of the party and supported the Wilson Administration. Their defection left the Socialist party more than ever in the hands of foreign-born leaders, such as Morris Hillquit and Victor Berger, who continued to fight conscription, to denounce the war as capitalist exploitation, and to plead for immediate peace without forced annexations or punitive indemnities. This fixed their pro-German reputation, even though they had always despised the Kaiser and the ruling classes of Germany.[41]

The Socialist party regularly tried to unite politically all opponents of war. Many immigrant groups lacked enthusiasm for it and there is no doubt that they provided the core of Socialist voter support. Yet in many communities Socialist candidates were able to go beyond the ethnic base and attract general working-class support. In 1917, new Socialist mayors were elected in a dozen cities, and in some industrial centers, such as Chicago, Toledo, and Buffalo, the party attracted up to one-third or more of the votes cast.[42]

Popular support for the Socialist antiwar position was especially apparent in New York's mayoral election of 1917. The incumbent, John P. Mitchel, running on a fusion ticket, based his chances on a superpatriotic, prowar line, while Morris Hillquit, as the Socialist candidate, ran on a peace platform, declaring his refusal to buy Liberty bonds. The Democratic candidate was Judge John F. Hylan, a less-than-distinguished Tammany Hall politician. Mitchel was joined by Theodore Roosevelt and several major newspapers in vicious attacks on both Hylan and Hillquit as disloyal persons with access to the German spy and propaganda network. But the outcome was a sweeping victory for Hylan. Hillquit placed third, only seven thousand votes short of Mitchel's total; he attracted more than four times the normal Socialist vote in New York City.[43]

Following the Communist revolution in Russia in November 1917, the stereotype of the Socialist party as dangerously radical was strengthened. Patriotic Americans were swayed by conservative charges that there were no meaningful distinctions among leftists—all were extremists plotting to destroy the American way of life. Doubly damned as pro-German and radical, Socialists were subjected to much harassment by the government, the press, and private vigilance groups.

The government's standard method of obstruction was to deny Socialist newspapers second-class mailing privileges under the censorship powers granted the postmaster general by the Trading-with-the Enemy Act. Before the war ended in November, the circulation of most radical sheets was drastically reduced. In the case of Victor Berger's *Milwaukee Leader,* the Post Office even refused to deliver first-class mail.[44]

Berger, along with scores of other radicals of all stripes, also ran afoul of zealous functionaries within the Department of Justice. Under the sweeping provisions of the Espionage Act and its 1918 amendments, the mildest criticisms of the draft, of the sale of Liberty bonds, or of the government itself could lead to indictments. The most famous case involved Eugene V. Debs, the perennial Socialist candidate for the presidency. Although Department of Justice officials in Washington discouraged prosecution, doubting that Debs had violated the law, the local United States district attorney went ahead and secured an indictment. He sensed that in those hysterical times no jury would fail to convict a radical, no matter how flimsy the charges. Debs was found guilty and sentenced to ten years imprisonment.

Victor Berger's indictment was closely tied to Wisconsin politics. Following the tragic death of Senator Paul O. Husting in a hunting accident, a special election was held in spring, 1918, to fill the vacancy. Berger had offered himself as the candidate who favored a general, immediate, and democratic peace, in contrast to both his Republican and Democratic rivals. Then, in the heat of campaign, on 9 March, the United States district attorney announced that Berger and four other Socialists had been indicted a month earlier for having conspired to violate the Espionage Act by writing and circulating seditious literature. Despite this blow, Berger continued to campaign, calling for the return of the American troops from Europe and for heavy taxes on war profits. Building on a solid base in Milwaukee, where a Socialist had been mayor since 1910, Berger emerged as a symbol of rebellion against the absurdity of damning everything that happened to be German. Thousands of voters who ordinarily rejected Socialist doctrines, especially persons of German birth or descent, were attracted by his candidacy. They had been humiliated in countless little ways and had been denied, on threat of severe reprisals, any opportunity to express their resentments; but in the privacy of a voting booth they could register disgust without fear.[45]

The main battle in Wisconsin was between the major party candidates. Republican Irvine Lenroot narrowly edged Democrat Joseph E. Davies, who had the backing of President Wilson and the superpatriotic Loyalty Legion. But special significance lay in the remarkable showing of Victor Berger, who polled 26.6% of the total, double the usual Socialist harvest in Wisconsin. Although he ran strongest in the cities, he also attracted unprecedented support among the German voters in the small towns and rural areas, as is suggested by a Pearsonian correlation coefficient of +.56 between Socialist percentages and the German-born at the county level. He won a plurality in Milwaukee, where his 42% more than doubled the Lenroot vote. At the same time Milwaukee's Socialist Mayor Daniel Hoan was reelected over Percy Braman, who had been nominated by both the Republicans and Democrats as the loyalty candidate. In this case percentages of German-born persons correlated with Socialist votes by wards produce a coefficient of +.80, indicating a remarkable cohesion in German-American voting.[46]

Superpatriots were frustrated by the results of the Wisconsin election. Eager to erase the state's reputation for pro-Germanism, they had worked themselves into a frenzy of intolerance, demanding conformity in thoughts, words, and deeds. The *Milwaukee Journal* in particular had seen the campaign as a means of vindicating the city in the eyes of the nation. Although the one-hundred percenters had campaigned for Davies, they were happy enough with Lenroot. But they were appalled by the size of Berger's "disloyal, anti-American, pro-German vote." They shared the sentiments of the *Washington Post,* which abandoned all democratic principles in its espousal of uniformity. Wisconsin's next step, the *Post* screamed, "should be to rid [itself] of the archconspirator of the pro-German ring, Victor Berger—and rid not only the state, but the country of his unwelcome presence." Clean out Berger and his ilk, it commanded, "silence their poisoned tongues, halt their unpatriotic activities, and make them behave like American citizens or forfeit their rights as citizens."[47]

Such attitudes, common as they were, precluded the possibility of organized German ethnic politics in 1918. Any effort to promote a "German vote," as had been customary in previous elections, was unthinkable. On the other hand, some politicians deemed it clever to accuse one's opponents of catering to German-American sentiments. Wisconsin's Republican Governor Emanuel Philipp, for example, was frequently criticized for not pushing programs of coercive patriotism. His enemies suggested darkly that his ties to German-American interests were rather too intimate for the times.[48]

Surviving German-language newspapers were discreet in their comments on the election. Usually they limited themselves to straight reporting of candidates' activities and party platforms. Sometimes they urged the election of tolerant men or they counseled crossing party lines when it suited their unexpressed purposes. Only Socialist newspapers continued to be outspoken. From their point of view, loyalty platforms and patriotic rhetoric were merely fronts to hide candidates' bondage to the plutocracy. Wisconsin's Philipp was no more acceptable to them than his superpatriotic challenger in the primary, Roy Wilcox. Both were tools of Big Business and enemies of the common people, in Socialist eyes.

As the two major parties emerged from the gauntlet of primary elections in 1918, neither was identified clearly as the party of intolerance and superpatriotism. Since 1918 was not a presidential election year, perceptions of parties, candidates, and issues were more deeply influenced by state and local circumstances. Of course, most German voters held Wilson and his Democratic administration responsible for much of their tribulation. But when Republicans were in power locally, they could be blamed for the repression and violence as readily as the national administration. In many areas the Republican party was dominated by a nativistic, superpatriotic wing whose strength lay among small-town Protestants. It was not unusual for them to surpass local Democrats in demanding conformity to the new standards of loyalty.

The election records of 1918 reveal that it was easy for German-Americans to identify candidates of either major party who were hostile to their interests, even though there were neither politicians foolhardy enough to campaign openly for their votes nor German-language journals willing to risk popular displeasure by defining issues in ethnic terms. If, in a given city or state, a Republican candidate had earned a reputation for superpatriotism, German-Americans tended to vote disproportionately for his Democratic opponent; if the shoe fit the Democrat's foot, the Republican benefited from German-American votes. Sometimes, however, both parties were perceived negatively. German-Americans then tended to favor third-party candidates. In some cases, they distributed their votes among the parties much as they had in the past, though the turnout was then usually reduced, presumably because of cross-pressures. In any case, the election of 1918 did not spark great general interest. Despite President Wilson's earnest plea for a Democratic Congress shortly before election day, the public was distracted by the impending armistice and, even more immediately, by a devastating flu epidemic.

The tendency of German-Americans to vote for Republican candidates, which had been noted in the 1916 election, continued in many areas. In Texas, for example, the likelihood of a German voting Republican was three times as strong as it was for the average voter. In Saint Louis, German-born residents correlated by wards with votes for the Republican senatorial candidate produce a coefficient of +.52, a figure almost identical to the one for Hughes in 1916. On the Atlantic coast, the Germans of Hoboken, New Jersey, also continued their strong identification with the Republican party. But in many other places historic attachments with the Democratic party were sustained. In Fort Wayne, Indiana, for example, German-Americans displayed a noticeable preference (+.49) for a Democratic candidate for Congress. Voting data from the very German cities of Saginaw, Michigan, and Lancaster, Pennsylvania, also show continued Democratic voting by German-Americans, even though Republicans made gains over the previous election.[49]

In several states, however, sharp changes occurred which reflected altered perceptions of the several parties and their candidates. In Iowa, for example, Republican Governor William L. Harding had earned the reproach of many traditionally Republican voters among the German-Americans for his attacks on their language. Although German-Americans had supported him strongly in 1916, they now favored his Democratic rival. In counties with more than 8% German-born residents, Harding's percentages were reduced by one-third from 1916. He won another term, but without German-American help, as a coefficient of −.43 at the county level indicates.

Neighboring Nebraska illustrates the reverse partisan relationship. Democratic Governor Keith Neville, who had enjoyed extensive German-American support in 1916, linked his administration with loyalty to the President and with the war effort, even though his political career was originally sponsored by the wet, pluralistic faction headed by Senator Gilbert M. Hitchcock, one of Wilson's severest critics. Neville approved of the coercive Americanization programs of the Nebraska State Council of Defense and personally led an attack on German-language instruction in the public schools of the state. The result was a decisive German vote against Neville. His percentages correlated with German-born residents at the county level dropped dramatically from +.31 in 1916 to –.42 in 1918. Not only was his opponent, Samuel McKelvie, elected, but other Republicans seemed to profit as well. Senator George Norris, a progressive Republican who had opposed American entry into the war, enjoyed increased strength in German-American communities. Coefficients of correlation between Norris votes and Germans jumped from –.40 in his first election to the Senate in 1912 to +.32 in 1918.[50]

Wisconsin illustrates a third relationship. In this instance, the incumbent governor, Emanuel Philipp, was a Republican who had resisted the seduction of superpatriotism. His party, however, had often tried to outdo the Democrats in compensating for Wisconsin's reputation as the most German state in the union. Consequently neither was as attractive to German-Americans as the Socialist party, which had been relentless in its opposition to the war and forced loyalty programs and which virtually became a German ethnic party in Milwaukee in 1918. Victor Berger, still under indictment, defeated Joseph Carney, who had the endorsement of the Republican and Democratic parties, for a seat in the House of Representatives. In the gubernatorial election, Milwaukee Germans moved en masse to support Socialist Emil Seidel, as Table II indicates. Statewide, his support followed a curious pattern in some but not all

TABLE II

Percentage of Votes Cast for Gubernatorial Candidates in Milwaukee by
Wards Grouped According to Percentage of German-Born Residents in
the Election of 1918

% German- Born	N	Moehlenpah Democratic	Philipp Republican	Seidel Socialist
14 and above	2	12.6	29.1	58.2
11–13.9	4	20.2	30.6	48.8
8–10.9	6	22.3	34.2	41.5
5– 7.9	8	30.3	39.2	29.6
0– 4.9	5	48.7	37.5	12.2
City				
(8.7%)		27.1	34.9	36.8

SOURCE: U.S., Bureau of the Census, *Fourteenth Census of the United
States: 1920. Population* (1922), 3: 1137–38; *Wisconsin Blue
Book, 1919* (Madison: State Printing Board, 1919), p. 129f.

strongly German counties stretching north and northwest
of Milwaukee to Wausau and Superior. The association of
German-American inhabitants by counties with Socialist
percentages produces a coefficient of +.50, a figure match-
ing that reached by Berger in April, but much higher than
the +.11 associated with Benson's vote in the 1916 presidential race. At the same time, Wisconsin Germans repudiated
both the Republican and Democratic gubernational candidates at –.40 and –.16, respectively.[51]

In Minnesota, the German-American quest for retribu-
tion at the polls led not to the Socialist party but to a gubernatorial candidate sponsored by farmer and labor organizations. Minnesota Germans were no more attracted to
radical principles than their Wisconsin cousins, and their
alienation from the Republican party was equally keen.

The temptation to associate political conservatism with patriotism, and radical reform with pro-Germanism, was seldom resisted by Minnesota Republicans. Moreover, many German-Americans held Governor Joseph A. A. Burnquist responsible for the excesses of the Minnesota Safety Commission. When the Democrats nominated a candidate unable to lead an anti-Burnquist coalition, Non-Partisan Leaguers joined with the Minnesota Federation of Labor to endorse David H. Evans as an independent candidate. Even though Evans had supported Wilson's war policies, many German-American voters saw his candidacy as being in opposition to forced Americanism.[52] Evans won a plurality in many of the most German counties, attracting roughly 5% more votes there than in the state as a whole.

When the Minnesota data are analyzed according to church membership (categories that include second- and third-generation German-Americans), the preference for the Farmer-Labor candidate becomes more apparent. Strongly German counties having a Catholic population of more than 20% voted 39% for Evans, while those with less than 20% gave him only 28%. Similarly, counties with the highest concentrations of German Lutherans were twice as likely to vote Farmer-Labor as the counties with few or no German Lutherans. Thus it appears that church Germans were associated with the heaviest voting for the Farmer-Labor candidate and, inferentially, with the keenest displeasure with Burnquist's superloyalist administration.

Wisconsin's German Lutherans and Catholics voted in much the same way. Although the German Lutheran counties registered larger Republican percentages than the Catholic counties, both groups tended to favor the Socialist candidate more than did the voting population as a whole. Analysis of township level data shows that Socialist percentages in both groups were gained chiefly at the expense of the Democratic party. For example, in twenty-two German Catholic townships, the Democratic gubernatorial candidate won only 21% compared to 36% for the ten counties of which they formed parts, and to 38% which these same townships registered for Wilson in 1916. Their 1918 Socialist percentage (30%) doubled the county figure (15%). Yet there were striking regional or local differences. For example, four strongly German Lutheran townships in Marathon County (located in north central Wisconsin) went 79% Socialist, recording 533 Socialist votes where there had been only 15 in 1916. By contrast, in strongly German Lutheran townships in Jefferson County (located west of Milwaukee), Republican voting reached 64%, a much higher proportion than the 45% these units give Hughes in 1916.

Smaller religious groups also show reduced Democratic percentages in 1918. For example, in Warren and Gasconade counties, Missouri, where there were large numbers of German Methodists and German Evangelicals, Democratic voting decreased from 21% in 1916 to a mere 13% in 1918. Monroe County, Illinois, which had the highest proportion of German Evangelicals in the United States, showed a similar drop from 42% in 1916 to 30% in 1918. Kansas Mennonite townships displayed the same anti-Democratic reaction. In these units, however, the Socialist candidate for governor made a remarkable showing, due, perhaps, to the keen hatred of war shared by both Socialists and Mennonites.[53]

Notes

1. *Everybody's Magazine,* 37 (December 1917): 9–16; 38 (January 1918): 28–33, 82–84; 38 (February 1918): 30–32, 74; 38 (March 1918): 55–64; *Atlantic Monthly,* 120 (November 1917): 663–85; 120 (December 1917): 819–33; 121 (March 1918): 387–401; 121 (April 1918): 529–41; 121 (June 1918): 844–54; *New Republic,* 14 (6 April 1918): 282–84. See also the five-part series by French Strother, "Fighting Germany's Spies," in *World's Work* beginning 35 (March 1918): 513–28.
2. Carl Chrislock, *The Progressive Era in Minnesota, 1899–1918* (Saint Paul: Minnesota Historical Society, 1971), pp. 166, 169; Joan M. Jensen, *The Price of Vigilance* (Chicago: Rand McNally, 1968), p. 108.
3. *Washington Post,* 12 April 1918.
4. U.S., Congress, Senate, Committee on the Judiciary, *Hearings on the National German-American Alliance,* 65th Cong., 2d sess., 1918; Clifton J. Child, *The German-Americans in Politics, 1914–1917* (Madison: University of Wisconsin Press, 1939), pp. 169–73; *Literary Digest,* 56 (9 March 1918): 16; Phyllis Keller, "German-America and the First World War" (Ph.D. diss., University of Pennsylvania, 1969), pp. 167–68; *New Republic,* 14 (9 March 1918): 154.
5. Child, *German-Americans in Politics,* p. 168.
6. Ibid., p. 173; *Saint Louis Post-Dispatch* (18 April 1918): *New York Times,* 25 January 1918; Guido Andre Dobbert, "The Disintegration of an Immigrant Community: The Cincinnati Germans, 1870–1920" (Ph.D. diss., University of Chicago, 1965), p. 344.
7. H. Wentworth Eldredge, "Enemy Aliens: New Haven Germans during the World War," *Studies in the Science of Society,* ed.

304 Bonds of Loyalty

George P. Murdock (New Haven: Yale University Press, 1937), pp. 213, 216; Bayrd Still, *Milwaukee, the History of a City* (Madison: State Historical Society of Wisconsin, 1948), p. 461; *Chicago Tribune,* 2 April 1918; Andrew J. Townsend, "The Germans of Chicago" (Ph.D. diss., University of Chicago, 1927), pp. 177, 179; *Saint Louis Post-Dispatch,* 1 May 1918.

8. Still, *Milwaukee,* p. 461; Dobbert, "Germans of Cincinnati," pp. 334, 352; Audrey L. Olson, "St. Louis Germans, 1850–1920: The Nature of an Immigrant Community and Its Relation to the Assimilation Process," (Ph.D. diss., University of Kansas, 1970), p. 327 n.; Mary E. Spanheimer, *Heinrich Armin Rattermann: German-American Author, Poet, and Historian,* 1832–1923 (Washington: Catholic University of America, 1937), p. 19.

9. Carl Wittke, *German-Americans and the World War* (Columbus: Ohio State Archaeological and Historical Society, 1936), pp. 175–79; Townsend, "Germans of Chicago," p. 178; *N. W. Ayer and Son's American Newspaper Annual and Directory,* 1917 and 1920 (Philadelphia: N. W. Ayer & Son).

10. Wittke, *German-Americans and the World War,* pp. 151–54.

11. Ibid., pp. 154–60; Nathaniel R. Whitney, *The Sale of War Bonds in Iowa* (Iowa City: State Historical Society of Iowa, 1923), pp. 128–40; Marcus L. Hansen, *Welfare Campaigns in Iowa* (Iowa City: State Historical Society of Iowa, 1920), pp. 232f., 247; Charles D. Stewart, "Prussianizing Wisconsin," *Atlantic Monthly,* 123 (January 1919): 99–105.

12. J. S. Hartzler, *Mennonites in the World War: Nonresistance under Test,* 2d ed. (Scottdale, Pa.: Mennonite Publishing House, 1922), pp. 150–66; Wittke, *German-Americans and the World War,* p. 159; Arlyn J. Parish, *Kansas Mennonites during World War I* (Fort Hays [Kansas State College] Studies, History Series, no. 4, May 1968), pp. 47, 51; C. Henry Smith, *The Coming of the Russian Mennonites* (Berne, Ind.: Mennonite Book Concern, 1927), p. 291.

13. James C. Juhnke, "The Political Acculturation of the Kansas Mennonites, 1870–1940" (Ph.D. diss., Indiana University, 1966), p. 165; Gertrude S. Young, "The Mennonites in South Dakota," *South Dakota Historical Collections,* 10 (1920): 498; Parish, *Kansas Mennonites during World War I,* p. 50; Norman Thomas, "The Hutterian Brethren," *South Dakota Historical Collections,* 25 (1951): 277–78.

14. *Washington Post,* 4, 5 April 1918; *New York Times,* 4, 5 April 1918; *Chicago Tribune,* 4, 5 April 1918.

15. Zechariah Chafee, Jr., *Free Speech in the United States* (Cambridge: Harvard University Press, 1954), pp. 64–66, 70; Wittke, *German-Americans and the World War,* p. 44; Robert

Lansing, *War Memoirs of Robert Lansing* (Indianapolis: Bobbs-Merrill, 1935), pp. 83–84.

16. Chafee, *Free Speech,* pp. 39–41, 286; Walter Nelles, ed., *Espionage Act Cases* (New York: National Civil Liberties Bureau, 1918), pp. 1–3; Horace C. Peterson and Gilbert C. Fite, *Opponents of War, 1917–1918* (Madison: University of Wisconsin Press, 1957), pp. 208–21.

17. Hartzler, *Mennonites in the World War,* pp. 159–63; Juhnke, "Kansas Mennonites," p. 163.

18. Wittke, *German-Americans and the World War,* lists dozens of incidents in addition to these. *Washington Post,* 12 April 1918, 7 May 1918; *Saint Louis Post-Dispatch,* 16 April 1918, 2 May 1918; *Lutheran Witness,* 37 (16 April 1918): 158.

19. *Washington Post,* 12 April 1918; Robert N. Manley, "Language, Loyalty, and Liberty: The Nebraska State Council of Defense and the Lutheran Churches, 1917–1918," *Concordia Historical Institute Quarterly,* 37 (April 1964): 7; *Saint Louis Post-Dispatch,* 29 April 1918; *Edwardsville* [Illinois] *Intelligencer,* 6 April 1918.

20. Alan N. Graebner, "The Acculturation of an Immigrant Lutheran Church: The Lutheran Church—Missouri Synod, 1917–1929" (Ph.D. diss., Columbia University, 1965), p. 30; *Lutheran Witness,* 37 (29 October 1918): 349; Smith, *Russian Mennonites,* p. 291; *Washington Post,* 9 April 1918.

21. Hermann Hagedorn, *Where Do You Stand? An Appeal to Americans of German Origin* (New York: Macmillan, 1918); Keller, "German-America in the First World War," pp. 418–20; James R. Mock and Cedric Larson, *Words that Won the War* (Princeton: Princeton University Press, 1939), pp. 216–18; George Sylvester Viereck, *Roosevelt: A Study in Ambivalence* (New York: Jackson Press, 1920), p. 39.

22. Wittke, *German-Americans and the World War,* p. 184; Still, *Milwaukee,* p. 461.

23. Quoted in Michael Singer, "Kämpft Amerika gegen Deutschamerika?" *Jahrbuch der Deutschamerikaner für das Jahr 1918* (Chicago: German Yearbook Publishing Co., 1917), p. 13.

24. Jensen, *Price of Vigilance,* p. 167.

25. August C. Stellhorn, *Schools of the Lutheran Church—Missouri Synod* (Saint Louis: Concordia Publishing House, 1963), p. 314; *Chicago Tribune,* 7 April 1918.

26. *Outlook,* 118 (2 January 1918): 13–15. See also the example of Samuel Untermeyer, *New York Times,* 9 April 1918.

27. *New Republic,* 14 (20 April 1918): 356.

28. Manley, "Language, Loyalty, and Liberty," pp. 10–12; *Lutheran Witness,* 37 (8 January 1918): 5; Graebner, "Acculturation of an

Immigrant Church," pp. 70–72; *Saint Louis Post-Dispatch,* 1
May 1918; Niel M. Johnson, "The Patriotism and Anti-Prussianism of the Lutheran Church—Missouri Synod 1914–1918,"
Concordia Historical Institute Quarterly, 39 (October 1966):
112.

29. *Lutheran Witness,* 37 (5 February 1918): 39; 37 (9 July 1918):
219; Graebner, "Acculturation of an Immigrant Church," pp.
23–24, 77–81.

30. Johnson, "Patriotism and Anti-Prussianism," p. 112; *Lutheran
Witness,* 37 (5 February 1918): 45. This is not to say that all
congregations cooperated in the effort to display patriotism or
that all experienced improvements in their community relations. See Graebner, "Acculturation of an Immigrant Church,"
pp. 56–83.

31. *Saint Louis Post-Dispatch,* 30 April 1918.

32. Parish, *Kansas Mennonites during World War I,* p. 52; Paul T.
Dietz, "The Transition from German to English in the Missouri
Synod from 1910 to 1947," *Concordia Historical Institute Quar-
terly,* 22 (October 1949): 106; Graebner, "Acculturation of an
Immigrant Church," pp. 149–53; *Proceedings of the Thirteenth
Convention of the Montana District of the Lutheran Church—
Missouri Synod* (Glendive, Montana, August 24–26, 1964), p. 69;
Manley, "Language, Loyalty, and Liberty," p. 12; Wilhelm
Mueller, *Die Deutschamerikaner und der Krieg* (Wiesbaden:
Hofbuchhandlung Heinrich Staadt, 1921), p. 37.

33. *N. W. Ayer Newspaper Directory,* 1917 and 1920; Graebner,
"Acculturation of an Immigrant Church," pp. 145–48.

34. Stellhorn, *Schools,* p. 301; Parish, *Kansas Mennonites during
World War I,* pp. 52–53; Melvin Gingerich, *The Mennonites of
Iowa* (Iowa City: State Historical Society of Iowa, 1939), p. 287;
Grant M. Stolzfus, *Mennonites of the Ohio and Eastern Confer-
ence* (Scottdale, Pa.: Herald Press, 1969), p. 182.

35. Allan Teichroew, "World War I and the Mennonite Migration to Canada to Avoid the Draft," *Mennonite Quarterly Review,* 45 (July 1971): 219–49; Thomas, "Hutterian Brethren,"
p. 278.

36. Mueller, *Deutschamerikaner und der Krieg,* p. 37.

37. Wittke, *German-Americans and the World War,* p. 187; Paul F.
Douglas, *The Story of German Methodism* (New York and Cincinnati: Methodist Book Concern, 1939), pp. 189–91.

38. Louis A. Haselmayer, "German Methodist Colleges in the
West," *Methodist History,* 2:40; Douglas, *German Methodism,*
p. 210.

39. Philip Gleason, *The Conservative Reformers: German-American Catholics and the Social Order* (Notre Dame: University of

Notre Dame Press, 1968), pp. 172–76; *N. W. Ayer Newspaper Directory,* 1917 and 1920.

40. *Chicago Tribune,* 13 April 1918. Italics added.
41. *Outlook,* 118 (17 April 1918); Wittke, *German-Americans and the World War,* p. 150.
42. *Current Opinion,* 63 (December 1917): 361; James Weinstein, *The Decline of Socialism in America, 1912–1925* (New York: Vintage Books, 1969), pp. 145–59.
43. Ibid., pp. 149–154.
44. Oscar Ameringer, *If You Don't Weaken* (New York: Henry Holt, 1940), p. 318.
45. Edward J. Muzik, "Victor Berger: Congress and the Red Scare," *Wisconsin Magazine of History,* 47 (Summer 1964): 310; Chafee, *Free Speech,* pp. 247–50; David Shannon, "The World, the War, and Wisconsin: 1914–1918," *Historical Messenger of the Milwaukee County Historical Society,* 22 (March 1966): 50f.
46. Clifford L. Nelson, *German-American Political Behavior in Nebraska and Wisconsin, 1916–1920,* University of Nebraska-Lincoln Publication no. 217 (Lincoln, 1972), pp. 37–40; Lorin L. Cary, "Wisconsin Patriots Combat Disloyalty: The Wisconsin Loyalty Legion and Politics, 1917–1918" (M.A. thesis, University of Wisconsin, 1965), pp. 110–19.
47. *Washington Post,* 4 April 1918.
48. Robert S. Maxwell, *Emanuel L. Philipp: Wisconsin Stalwart* (Madison: State Historical Society of Wisconsin, 1959), pp. 169–80.
49. Unless otherwise noted, these data and those which follow are based on U.S., Bureau of the Census, *Fourteenth Census of the United States: 1920. Population* (1919), 3; Edgar E. Robinson, *The Presidential Vote, 1896–1932* (Stanford: Stanford University Press, 1947); and a variety of state blue books, legislative manuals, and local newspapers containing election data for wards and townships.
50. Nelson, *German-American Political Behavior in Nebraska and Wisconsin,* pp. 42–49.
51. Ibid., pp. 49–50.
52. Chrislock, *Progressive Era in Minnesota,* pp. 164–81.
53. Juhnke, "Kansas Mennonites," pp. 184–85, 289.

CHAPTER TEN

Beyond the Armistice

NOVEMBER 1918–NOVEMBER 1920

The warring nations signed an armistice agreement nine days after the election, on 11 November 1918. Germany had been beaten in the field; the Kaiser had abdicated and fled to the Netherlands. Although the fighting was over, a technical state of war continued for many months and there was no letup in the vigilance of the superloyalists. Indeed, Armistice Day itself provided the occasion for a special effort by a gang of Kansas patriots to force their version of Americanism upon a defenseless citizen.

Their victim was John Schrag, a Mennonite farmer whose religious principles would not permit him to support the war in any way. Remembering Schrag's earlier refusal to purchase Liberty bonds, they crowded into five automobiles and drove to his farm eleven miles from Burrton, Kansas. Schrag was dragged off to town, where he became the central figure in an impromptu celebration. A crowd gathered around the captive and demanded that he buy bonds, salute the American flag, and march at the head of a parade, "Old Glory" in hand. Schrag offered to contribute $200 to the Red Cross and the Salvation Army, but he adamantly refused to perform those acts that were against his conscience. Then someone thrust a flag into his hand. It fell to the ground and unavoidably was stepped upon. Enraged by this dishonor to the national emblem, the mob attacked

Schrag, doused him with yellow paint, and threw him into the city jail. Plans to hang him were frustrated as the sheriff carried him off to Newton, the county seat, where he was charged under the Espionage Act for having desecrated the flag of the United States.[1]

The John Schrag case epitomizes the irony of the treatment German-Americans received during the era of World War I. During the long neutrality period German-American advocates of language and culture maintenance had brazenly trumpeted their partiality for the Kaiser's cause, as was their right as citizens of a neutral nation. In essence, their activity had not been much different from the behavior of those who championed the Allies; it was to be expected of a numerous, prosperous, and respected ethnic group. Pro-Germanism had been a by-product of the cultural chauvinism sponsored by hundreds of ethnic associations, newspapers, and the like, of which the National German-American Alliance was the best known. Not all German-Americans, however, had shared this enthusiasm for Imperial Germany. Many had been eager to divest themselves of the marks of German ethnicity and to become indistinguishable from Americans of Anglo-Saxon heritage. Others, whose lives were organized around religious values, had sought to maintain German language and culture as a means to achieve religious goals. Such persons had seen no close relationship between their own retention of German cultural forms and the political goals of the Kaiser.

As the neutrality period wore on, however, German-American cultural chauvinists became increasingly shrill in their partisanship and ever more offensive to persons whose emotional bonds were with England. Many prominent Americans, with President Wilson in the vanguard, responded by impugning the loyalty of German-Americans whose understanding of the American interest differed from their own. Other Germans in America, much less concerned with international affairs than the chauvinists, sensed a resultant loss of status in the American social structure and were angered and frightened by the change.

The declaration of war against Germany in 1917 altered the German-American position radically. Because of the intemperate partisanship of the cultural chauvinists, all persons of German origin or descent were suspected of harboring some measure of loyalty for the Fatherland. Self-appointed guardians of the democracy demanded that all citizens conform to narrowed standards of patriotic behavior, including the abandonment of German language and culture.

Compliance was relatively easy for the club Germans. They were able without great psychological loss to give up the fight for what was essentially a lost cause. With each succeeding year the assimilation process rendered the maintenance of German culture for its own sake more unnatural. Thus, as pressures to conform built up, the majority of German-Americans complied, though not without resentment. Hundreds of vereins and scores of German-language newspapers disappeared and organized German ethnic politics ceased.

But the times were more difficult for persons whose religious values were touched by the crisis of loyalty. Each German-speaking denomination had erected its own complex of schools, colleges, seminaries, publishing houses, insurance companies, hospitals, orphanages, homes for the aged, and a multitude of social organizations, designed in part to preserve the religious identity of the group. Unlike that pyramid of artificiality, the National German-American Alliance, the German churches and their institutions refused to fade away. Thus, when war came, the church Germans were the most likely to persist in behavior deemed offensive or disloyal by the superpatriots. They continued to use the German language; they were reluctant to permit their institutions to serve secular goals. Inevitably, they suffered most. There was an inverse relationship, it seemed, between the degree of persecution endured by a German-American group and the threat it posed to American security. Erstwhile champions of German imperialism, such as George Sylvester Viereck and the leaders of the German-American Alliance, escaped unscathed, while at the opposite extreme harmless German-speaking Mennonites and Hutterites from the Plains states—rural, separatistic, pacifistic, nonresisting, apolitical, most of them immigrants from Russia rather than Germany—were ridiculed, harassed, beaten, painted, tarred, robbed, and betrayed in the name of American democratic ideals.

Gradually, after November 1918, the anti-German hysteria began to subside. But even before the fighting ended, the German menace was replaced by a wave of antiradicalism, the so-called Red Scare. The later aberration was more anticommunist than anti-German in its emphasis, although some superpatriots continued to imagine that the exiled Kaiser was the mastermind of an international Pan-German conspiracy well into the Twenties. Moreover, the war on the German language raged on as certain journalists and politicians exploited popular fears. Gustavus Ohlinger, for example, in a tract published in 1919, railed against German instruction in American schools, calling it the keystone of subversion. He identified the German-language press as the arch enemy of Americanization.[2]

Legislators succumbed to these pressures and enacted new laws restricting instruction in the German language. The Smith-Towner Act, passed by Congress in 1918 at the behest of the National Education Association, provided that no state could share in federal funds unless it enacted and enforced laws requiring that the chief language of instruction in all schools, public and private, be English. Early in 1919 fifteen states responded with appropriate measures. Indeed, seven (Colorado, Indiana, Iowa, Nebraska, Ohio, Oklahoma, and South Dakota) went beyond the requirements to prohibit entirely all instruction in German up to and including the eighth grade.[3]

Much litigation resulted from these laws. Cases developed in Ohio, Iowa, and Nebraska. Usually they were initiated by German Lutheran denominations and had strong support from the Roman Catholic Church. The central case

concerned Robert T. Meyer, a teacher in a Lutheran parochial school in Hampton, Nebraska, who had deliberately
violated Nebraska's Siman Act by teaching a Bible story in
the German language during regular school hours. Fined
twenty-five dollars and costs, Meyer began a series of appeals which reached the United States Supreme Court in
1923. The Court ruled in Meyer's favor and declared the
language laws to be unconstitutional restrictions upon
individual rights guaranteed by the Fourteenth Amendment.[4]

Advocates of Anglo-conformity also struck at the very
existence of parochial and private schools. In several states,
including Michigan and Nebraska, laws to wipe them out
were bitterly contested and ultimately defeated. But in Oregon a public referendum in 1922 approved a measure,
backed by Masonic orders and the Ku Klux Klan, compel-
ling children to attend public schools. According to its sponsors, the law was intended, ironically enough, to preserve
the public school system as the means to prevent racial,
religious, and social antagonism. In this instance, the Roman Catholic Church took the lead in challenging the law
and in June 1925, the Supreme Court, acting on the prece-
dent established by the Meyer case, decided against Oregon.[5]

The continuing efforts to force Americanization by restricting parochial schools in their use of foreign languages
was only one manifestation of the nationalistic mood of the
Twenties. The Red Scare, the repudiation of the League of
Nations, immigration restriction, prohibition, and woman
suffrage were interwoven with strands of anti-Semitism,
anti-Catholicism, antiforeignism, and the lingering Germanophobia. More time was needed to blur the stereotype
of the German as a malevolent creature capable of committing any atrocity. The patriotism of all who had been pro-
German in the neutrality period or who had opposed
American entry into the war remained suspect. Persons
with German names or German accents in their speech
continued to feel subtle forms of discrimination (some of
which were more imagined than real). Given the climate of

intolerance and suspicion, it is remarkable how quickly many Germans in America recovered from the trauma of World War I.

This was particularly true of the churches. The Mennonite sects, for example, were not significantly affected in terms of memberships, institutions, and language usage, even though individual members had suffered grievously during the war. As exclusive, separatistic groups, they had never recruited members outside their subsociety, nor did their institutions depend on outside approval or support. Once wartime restrictions were removed, Mennonites continued to use the German language much as before; for them eventual transition to English was more closely related to the slow process of assimilation.

The Americanization of the Mennonite churches was stimulated to some extent by the war experiences of its members. Hundreds of young Mennonite men had been wrenched from their closed communities to serve in the army as noncombatants, agricultural workers, or as conscientious objectors, and a few participated in relief activities in France; their horizons were broadened accordingly. But many Mennonite contacts with the larger society had been abrasive and produced deep feelings of alienation. Political acculturation, it seems clear, was slowed. In Kansas, for example, the succession of Mennonites elected as county officials virtually ceased after the war, as did editorial comment on political affairs in Mennonite newspapers. At the same time, however, some sought positive ways to demonstrate their worth as American citizens. Unable by reason of their religious convictions to fight for their country, they turned to volunteer relief work as a substitute and developed extraordinary benevolence programs, especially in the postwar years. Millions of dollars were collected and thousands of hours were devoted to serving needy persons outside the Mennonite community.[6]

Other Mennonites were spurred by their wartime experiences to try to reform their churches along more progressive lines. Their aims included greater use of the English language and an increased emphasis on education, especially for the clergy. But for the most part, the progressives were unsuccessful in their attempts to win leadership posts in the church and its institutions. In general, it appears that the Mennonite churches gained inner strength through the misfortunes of World War I. The persecutions they endured reminded them of their own long tradition of martyrdom for conscience's sake.[7]

While the crisis of loyalty had caused some Mennonites to withdraw further into their ethnoreligious shells, it tended to flush out the less separatistic and more numerous German Lutherans into the main currents of American life. Common adversities and common problems had brought about much intersynodical cooperation, especially in their work with young men in the armed forces. The National Lutheran Council was a permanent agency created in 1918 to coordinate joint endeavors. Indeed, the merger of several Lutheran bodies to form the large and influential United Lutheran Church, long in the making, was hastened by bruising wartime experiences. Many Lutherans discovered that aloofness from other Protestant denominations was damaging to their institutional goals; in order to be effective they had to break down ethnic barriers.[8]

Despite appearances, this trend was less evident in the Lutheran Church—Missouri Synod, the single most severely criticized body during the war. No longer replenished by immigrant infusions, the Missouri Synod was forced to face the realities of assimilation. In the past, German language and culture had been retained by the church fathers to promote group cohesion and loyalty. But the intolerance of a nation at war had demonstrated that this policy was no longer possible. Besides, a rapid transition to English was mandatory if the loyalty of the younger generation was to be retained. Thousands of returning servicemen who had discovered that being German Lutheran could be a source of embarrassment in an army barracks were determined to erase unnecessary ethnocultural marks from their church. They wanted a church that was American rather than German, one that was known and respected by the communities in which they lived. Thus, both external and internal pressures combined to effect a remarkably swift language transition during the decade following the war. Although public worship in German continued in many congregations, English was the more common language by 1925 and the exclusive use of German was rare by 1929. Soon 90 percent of all titles published by the synodical press were in English, and by the end of the Twenties religious instruction in German had all but vanished in the church's 1,300 parochial schools.[9]

The advocates of language change in the Missouri Synod were nonetheless theological conservatives, determined to retain their church's traditional orthodoxy. They believed that the use of German had prevented doctrinal erosion in the past and that as linguistic barriers fell, the breach had to be filled with English publications to sustain the creed. A sweeping program was therefore inaugurated to produce sermons, instructional materials, religious literature of all kinds, and a suitable hymnody in English. Many articles and editorials of a polemical character were produced to tell the typical parishioner what he was to believe and how he differed theologically from other Christians. A number of Missouri Synod pastors believed that dropping the German language exposed their people to a host of new temptations and evils—jazz music, dancing, movies, drama, godless novels and poetry, birth control, universities infected with the God-denying evolutionary theories of Charles Darwin. Thus the postwar literature of the synod is filled with blanket proscriptions and strong exhortations against these allegedly Satanic devices in order to equip the faithful for life in an English-speaking world. Paradoxically, denominational self-consciousness and separatism were encouraged in this way at the very time that the synod was emerging from its immigrant cocoon.[10]

The Evangelical Synod and other specifically German church bodies were affected by the war in ways similar to the Lutheran experience. The language transition was greatly accelerated but the institutions themselves weathered the storm. The Evangelical Synod, however, suffered a 7.5 percent loss in membership between 1916 and 1926. True to its ecumenical instincts, this church sought others with which it could merge—first the German Reformed, later non-German denominations. Small losses were also registered over the decade in the German conferences of the Presbyterian and Baptist churches. Once the use of English prevailed in these congregations, they lost their ethnic identity and merged with their parent bodies. This trend was especially dramatic in the Methodist church, which initiated the liquidation process as a general policy in 1924. By 1926 only five German Methodist conferences remained, their membership down to less than half the prewar figure.[11]

Among the German Catholics the impact of the anti-German hysteria may be assessed by studying a specifically ethnoreligious organization, the Central-Verein. Some leaders tried to keep the verein alive in the postwar era by retaining its distinctiveness as a German organization in spite of the shift to the use of English. The official minutes of the annual conventions were published in German until 1928, even though English was often spoken in its meetings after the war. The trauma of war, followed by revolution in Russia, unrest in Germany, and the Red Scare at home, worked a profound change in the social philosophy of the Central-Verein. In contrast to its earlier socialism, the organization now embraced a rigid conservatism, according to historian Philip Gleason. Reform proposals that it had formerly promoted were now opposed as paternalistic measures that would lead to a prodigious expansion of federal power. A flood of memories—the draft, manipulation of public opinion by the Creel Committee, adoption of nationwide prohibition, and government control of food production, transportation, and prices—all prompted fears of centralization.[12]

By the end of the Twenties most German Catholics agreed that the goals of the church could not be served by the preservation of German language and culture. The number of German Catholic publications continued to decline and the membership of the Central-Verein itself dropped by a third. Though these trends were the normal concomitants of assimilation, it seems clear that they were stimulated by the experiences of the war period.[13]

Each of the German churches participated extensively in the postwar relief work for Germany, where many thousands of persons faced malnutrition and starvation. Other German ethnic organizations also sprang into action in 1919, risking further nationalistic hostility. Attempts to help relatives and friends in Germany began immediately after the fighting ended. The armistice had not terminated the technical state of war, and the Allies, unreasonably fearful of Germany's recuperative powers, maintained their blockade of German ports until July 1919, when Germany ratified the Treaty of Versailles. Shortly after the ban on food shipments was lifted, ethnic leaders staged a massive rally in Philadelphia to mobilize German-American support for relief efforts. Volunteer *Hilfswerk* committees, as they were called, were hastily established in cities wherever there were large numbers of Germans. Seventeen were created in Connecticut alone. They collected and dispatched packages of food and clothing, organized festivals and bazaars, staged concerts, and solicited gifts of money to support the program. Such activities were continued for five or six years until Germany regained a semblance of internal stability. Rarely, however, was the work coordinated. The vereins and the churches preferred to work independently in developing methods and goals of relief work and in deciding who in Germany would receive their aid.[14]

Besides relieving much suffering in Europe, these humanitarian efforts temporarily restored a spark of life to many German ethnic associations, giving them a purpose that transcended the maintenance of language and culture. Singing societies were often the first to revive, along with mutual aid societies. Turnvereins began to reappear, sometimes with English names. Surviving social clubs, however, were often transformed. Some that had been elitist or exclusive broadened to appeal to all classes and occupations of German-Americans, while others abandoned ethnicity entirely and welcomed anyone who wished to join. Examples of revived German organizational life may be discovered in most of the nation's major cities, yet only a remnant of the prewar societies survived or were reconstituted. As a group, Germans in America were badly demoralized and few were willing to engage again in the same activities that had evoked so much hostility during the war. Those who drifted back rarely displayed the old chauvinism, which had called for the infusion of German ideals into American culture. Mostly they were American-born persons interested only in conserving the folk traditions of their fathers.[15]

Like the vereins, the German-language press never regained its prewar power and influence. Surviving papers welcomed the armistice with a great sense of relief, and gradually, as the weeks and months passed, the editors began to discuss war aims and the kind of peace they wanted. They had approved Wilson's Fourteen Points as the basis for the settlement ever since he had offered them to the world in January 1918; they supported the President in his decision to go to Paris to negotiate with the Allies, confident that he could win the peace as he had won the war. In marked contrast to their behavior during the neutrality period, they called for no resolutions, no petitions, no delegations—no organized activity to influence the administrations's foreign policy decisions.[16]

German-American journalists cautiously tested the public temper in 1919. An occasional article appeared attacking the accepted doctrine that Germany was solely responsible for having plunged the world into war; others showed the spurious character of wartime German atrocity tales. Many newspapers opposed the campaign to further restrict instruction in the German language. Writers grew bolder in unmasking superpatriotism as bigotry. They reemphasized the loyalty of German-Americans and backed the Victory Loan campaign of 1919. Some journalists tried to dispel the hatred and suspicion of all things German by reprinting letters from American soldiers in the army of occupation that described in glowing terms the cordiality of the German people and how clean and orderly their homes were. But in spite of these moves to reestablish the place of Germans in American society and to rejuvenate German ways of life, the German-language press languished in the postwar era. Subtle pressures and rough treatment had pushed most German-Americans out of their cultural ghettos. They could not go back.[17]

This fact was apparently lost on some of the old cultural chauvinists. The more intransigent among them hoped to play at ethnic politics as they had before the war, but there were moderates who believed that altered circumstances demanded new approaches. In May 1919, they founded the Steuben Society in New York, which, despite certain similarities, was not a revival of the discredited National German-American Alliance. The society used the English language in its meetings and publications and pursued explicitly political goals. Moreover, it accepted memberships of persons only, rather than of organizations, thereby avoiding the deception that had characterized alliance statistics. Headed by former Congressman Richard Bartholdt and by Carl Schmidt of the defunct American Independence Conference, it sought to defend German-Americans and their institutions from nativist attacks, to recoup the respect they had once held, and to pursue their interests in electoral politics. Though its founders were motivated by ethnic pride, cultural maintenance was a matter of secondary importance to them.[18]

The Steuben Society never achieved much popularity. German-speaking Americans were not comfortable in the organization and many other potential constituents were alienated by its explicitly political orientation. Clearly the product of the *Vereinsdeutschen* mentality, it inherited the mistrust the church Germans had held for the National Alliance. Moreover, it was plagued by internal dissension and indecisive leadership. It held national conferences throughout the Twenties, endorsing candidates and issues, but its membership never exceeded 20,000 persons, if that many.[19]

The German-American Citizens League, more consciously patterned on the National Alliance, fared no better. Guided by ethnic militants such as George Sylvester Viereck, Edmund Von Mach, and a corps of erstwhile alliance officers, the league had its informal beginnings in Chicago in June 1918, several months before the fighting ended. At first it was a local affair, but in 1920 it sponsored a national conference of German-Americans to support the candidacy of Republican Warren G. Harding for the presidency. This was followed in February 1921, by the formal founding of the Deutschamerikanische Bürgerbund der Vereinigten Staaten, as it was called in German. Viereck sparked the organization and structured it closely on the National Alliance pattern, with state and city branches organized wherever sufficient interest could be generated.[20]

Like the National Alliance, the Citizens League was dedicated to the revival of German language and culture, in addition to its political objectives. But German diversity was much too great for it to attract much support. One German Catholic commentator described the problem several months before the 1924 election. The Bürgerbund, he wrote,

will no more be able to swing that [German] vote than its predecessor, the *Nationalbund*. The great majority of Catholics of German descent are holding aloof from the former organization just as they did from the latter. It is the so-called "liberal" element that is chiefly represented in the *Bürgerbund*, and these freethinkers have had and have little use for the *Kirchendeutschen*, except possibly as *Stimmvieh* [voting cattle] to help them attain their particular aims.[21]

Viereck and his followers apparently had learned nothing from the war. As self-appointed leaders of the German ethnic group, they were chiefs without Indians, persisting in the alluring fiction that they could manipulate opinions and deliver votes as a bloc on election day to the candidates or to the party that would do their bidding.

While united political action was scarcely possible for Germans in the postwar years, it does not follow that they were apathetic. Interest was keen, for example, in the results of the peace conference at Versailles. Not surprisingly, most German-Americans were appalled by the harsh terms the Allied powers imposed upon Germany. Already disillusioned with Wilson's domestic wartime policies, they deplored his failure to negotiate a peace based on his Fourteen Points. German-language newspapers criticized the treaty as an imperialist document devoid of justice and humanity, though they admitted that Germany had no alternative to signing it. Only German Jews seemed pleased. In their view, Zionism (the proposal to establish a Jewish state in Palestine) was intimately linked with the Allied cause, and they believed that Jewish rights in Europe would be promoted by the League of Nations that was to be created by the signatory nations.[22]

Despite much cynicism and bitterness, the response of the German-American journalists to the Treaty of Versailles and the League of Nations was mild, compared to their typical prewar style. In Viereck's words, the German-language press was "still too intimidated to call its soul its own."[23] Instead, a mood of resignation and helplessness prevailed among the Germans as they awaited the opportunity to settle the score in the election of 1920.

As in every national election, there were many issues impinging upon individual voting decisions in 1920, and each voter saw them in his own way. Both political parties, however, were willing enough to consider the election "a great and solemn referendum," as Wilson wanted it, on the treaty and American participation in the League of Nations. It was hardly that, of course, but this issue tended to obscure other important domestic problems at home. While farmer discontent, labor disturbances, and the rising costs of living plagued large segments of the population, these problems were frequently more important in state than national politics. Most Americans, it seemed, were determined to return to normalcy, to use Republican candidate Warren Harding's expression. They wanted to solve the problems of everyday life and to forget the nation's frustrating venture into international affairs. Large numbers of Americans were fed up with Wilson and his league. They were turned off by his moralistic idealism, rhetorical style, and refusal to compromise. Wilson and the Democratic party had come to symbolize all that had gone wrong during the war years. It was a time for a change.

For the Germans it was a time for revenge as well. Republicans, of course, had contributed their share to the anti-German hysteria, but the Democrats got the blame. It was a Democratic president who had asked for war, who had set the tone for superloyalist propaganda, and who was responsible ultimately for the Committee on Public Information, the Department of Justice and its American Protective League, the Post Office Department and its censorship, the Department of War and its failure to define noncombatant service, and later for Attorney General A. Mitchell Palmer and his Red Scare. It was a Democratic Congress that had declared war; that had enacted the draft law, the Espionage Act, the Trading-with-the-Enemy Act, and the Sedition Act; that had conducted discriminatory investigations of the German-American Alliance and of the brewing industry. Moreover, the coincidence of Mr. Wilson's War had made prohibition possible. A Democratic Congress had identified prohibition with patriotism when, in December 1917, it had submitted to the states for their approval a constitutional amendment to forbid the manufacture, sale, and transportation of alcoholic beverages. And in the fight over the Treaty of Versailles, Democratic members of Congress had obediently voted as they had been instructed by the unyielding schoolmaster in the White House, who was so debilitated after October 1919 by the effects of a stroke that he was probably incompetent to perform the duties of his office.

As Wilson's successor the Democrats nominated Governor James M. Cox of Ohio. A worse choice could not have been made as far as German-American voters were concerned. Though he was not a major political figure before his nomination, Cox was known to the German-Americans as the sponsor of the 1919 Ohio law banning instruction in the German language. He had thoughtlessly repeated the threadbare propaganda that the German Government, now prostrate, was continuing to push the teaching of German in order to make American school children loyal to the Fatherland. Cox also had scuttled an alternate bill sponsored by Republican legislators that would have permitted instruction in German in private and parochial schools while forbidding it in public schools. Such a measure, Cox asserted, would create "preserves of treason" in the state. "If any person in Ohio wants his child indoctrinated with Prussian creeds," he cried, "let our safeguards be such that he must go elsewhere for it."[24]

Although the German-Americans were happy enough with Senator Warren G. Harding of Ohio as the Republican candidate, they would have preferred Hiram Johnson of California, whose vociferous attacks on the League of Nations were widely applauded. Harding equivocated shamelessly on the league issue, but he was identified by the German-Americans as its opponent, partly because Cox backed it fully. Moreover, Republican party efforts to court ethnic voters dispelled any lingering doubts. Full-page advertisements in foreign-language papers were purchased by the national committee linking Cox with Wilson and quoting Harding testimonials that had appeared in the ethnic press. A *Literary Digest* survey of German-language newspapers revealed unanimous sentiment for Harding. This was in addition, of course, to the active support of the Steuben Society and of the German-American Citizens League. "Between Harding and Cox we are for Harding," wrote George Sylvester Viereck. "We do not hate Cox. We do not love Harding. But we mean to repudiate in no uncertain terms the party tainted with Wilsonism." Still, there were local German organizations that refrained from endorsements, believing that anti-German hostility remained too strong.[25]

Throughout his campaign, Cox tied himself to Wilson's apron strings, consistently taking the President's position on everything from the League of Nations to Germanophobia. During his defense of the Versailles Treaty in 1919, Wilson had lapsed into unreserved denunciation of "hyphenates" as traitors. In Pueblo, Colorado, just before his physical collapse, Wilson again lashed the Germans with stinging words:

I want to say—I cannot say too often—any man who carries a hyphen about him carries a dagger which he is ready to plunge into the vitals of the Republic. If I can catch a man with a hyphen in this great contest, I know I will have got an enemy of the Republic.[26]

At the urging of Joseph Tumulty, Cox likewise attacked the patriotism of his ethnic enemies. Resentful of German-American opposition, he hoped to capitalize on what remained of superpatriotic sentiment. Tumulty supplied him with ammunition from his file on German-American organizations, and as the campaign drew to a close, the Ohioan fired round after round at allegedly traitorous "pro-Germans," using George Sylvester Viereck as a prime target. In a ploy deliberately patterned on Wilson's 1916 telegram to Jeremiah O'Leary, Cox repudiated the support of Viereck and other German-American political activists. His final accusation was as broad as Wilson's: "Every traitor in America will vote tomorrow for Warren G. Harding." "Cox is Wilson," grumbled the *Cleveland Wächter und Anzeiger;* no German-American could vote for him.[27]

Not very many did. Examination of voting data shows that there were dramatic shifts away from Democratic voting in most places where German-American population was concentrated, especially in midwestern states. These shifts, however, were not limited to voters of German stock. Various ethnic groups repudiated Wilson's heir with equal emphasis, as did other collectivities of voters defined in economic, social, or religious terms, thereby obscuring statistical measurement of the trend. In any case, few Democrats expected Cox to win the election of 1920, but they were appalled by the magnitude of the Harding landslide. Cox received a mere 34% of the total national vote and was unable to win a majority in any state outside the South. His share dwindled to less than 20% in Wisconsin, Minnesota, North Dakota, and South Dakota. In Cox's home state of Ohio, where a large part of the German population had traditionally voted Democratic, the swing was especially strong. In states such as Missouri where Republican voting was standard among German-Americans, the change was necessarily small.[28]

That German-Americans continued their politics of revenge in 1920 is especially apparent when data from wards and townships are examined. Scores of rural precincts and small towns with heavy concentrations of German Protestants registered minuscule totals for Cox. In Lebanon township, Dodge County, Wisconsin, Harding outpolled Cox 478 to 4; in Berlin, Stettin, and Hamburg townships, Marathon County, Wisconsin, Cox got 9 of 843 votes. In Concordia, Missouri, the vote was Cox 39; Harding 1178; downriver at Hermann, Missouri, it was 69 to 1008. In Frankenmuth, Michigan, Cox scored 34 to Harding's 892. Measured in terms of percentages, however, the swing from 1916 was actually greater in German Catholic communities, where traditions of Democratic voting were stronger. Ellis County, Kansas, recorded 27% for Cox, compared to 65% for Wilson in 1916; in Stark County, North Dakota, the Democratic percentage plummeted from 39% in 1916 to 23% in 1920; Stearns County, Minnesota, recorded 10% for Cox, only a fourth of Wilson's 42% in 1916. Sixteen German Catholic townships in Wisconsin, taken collectively, gave only 6% of their votes to Cox, compared to 21% for the counties of which they are parts. In 1918 these townships had cast 21% for the Democratic gubernatorial candidate and 38% for Wilson in 1916.

German-American antipathy for Cox may also be measured by analyzing ward data of large cities. As in rural areas, Cox's percentages were usually lowest in wards with the largest proportions of German-born voters. Harding was commonly the beneficiary of the German-American disaffection for the Democratic party, although this varied according to local traditions and circumstances. In Milwaukee and Davenport, for example, German-American voters continued their predilection, so clear in 1918, to vote for the Socialist party candidate, who in 1920 was Eugene V. Debs, still in federal prison, a victim of the Espionage Act. (See Table III.) Milwaukee was not typical, of course, because it had the largest proportion of German-born inhabitants of any major city in the nation and, on that account, experienced the sharpest ethnopolitical clash.

German-stock voters in the United States continued to display distinctive patterns of political behavior throughout the Twenties and Thirties. Indeed, the influence of German ethnicity in voting can be traced well past World War II, through the McCarthy era of the 1950's and beyond. But there is no way to determine exactly the extent to which their voting may be attributed to memories of the loyalty crisis of World War I. There is no question, however, about the 1920s. Robert M. LaFollette, for example, enjoyed much German-American support in 1924 because of his wartime intransigence. Richard Bartholdt believed that "every American of German blood owed the Wisconsin leader a lasting debt of gratitude, not only for his manly courage in stubbornly resisting a pernicious war propaganda, but also for defending almost singlehandedly the honor of the German name against a pogrom as conscienceless as it was unworthy of America." Having been victimized by the Leviathan state in wartime, German-American voters feared any candidate, party, or issue that promised to augment the power of the central government to regulate their lives or restrict their freedoms. Circumstances varied greatly from state to state. In Minnesota, for example, the Farm-Labor party achieved major-party status partly because the Democrats continued to be identified with Wilson-

TABLE III

Percentages of Votes Cast for Presidential Candidates in Milwaukee by Wards Grouped According to Percentages of German-Born Residents in the Election of 1920

% German- Born	N	Cox Democratic	Harding Republican	Debs Socialist
14 and over	2	6.0	45.4	48.4
11–13.9	4	10.7	49.1	39.9
8–10.9	6	14.6	49.2	35.9
5– 7.9	8	20.3	53.6	25.7
0– 4.9	5	33.8	53.8	12.0
City				
(8.7%)		18.0	50.9	30.7

SOURCE: U.S., Bureau of the Census, *Fourteenth Census of the United States: 1920. Population* (1922), 3: 1137–38; *Wisconsin Blue Book, 1921* (Madison: State Printing Board, 1921), pp. 144–45.

ism and the war. Furthermore, "McGeeism" as a synonym for Republican superpatriotism remained in the political vocabulary of Minnesotans at least until 1930.[29]

In any case, however, generalizations about the impact of World War I on the Germans in the United States have little value unless they take into account the amazing diversity of the group. Club Germans often saw things differently from church Germans; the experiences and behavior of German Catholics were not always identical to those of German Protestants; the respective problems of Mennonites and German Methodists, for example, were strikingly different. Moreover, the anti-German hysteria was more intense in some places than others and therefore could not be expected to have uniformly enduring consequences.

Yet one simple conclusion seems warranted. World War I had the effect of accelerating the assimilation of most German-American groups. The conditions that had promoted ethnic consciousness—large numbers, economic success, public esteem—had been more than offset by the intolerance of the war years, leaving the people for the most part demoralized, lacking in self-confidence, no longer proud of being German. Their ethnic associational structures were dismantled, despite the efforts at reconstruction by a small minority. Church Germans tended to stress their religious identity and to deemphasize the ethnic component as they pursued distinctive goals.

Mostly the German-Americans wanted to forget what had happened. Families gave up speaking German in their homes. Programs for the maintenance of language and culture withered and died. Unlike certain smaller ethnic groups, the Germans never established a long-lived national association for the preservation of sources and the publication of scholarly historical studies. The Carl Schurz Memorial Foundation tried to fill the void with its attractive publication, *The American-German Review,* but it never won much support. A few state and local German-American historical societies struggled for existence, but almost none survived the 1930s. To this day the body of literature treating the history of Germans in America remains small in relation to the size and importance of the group and in comparison to that which exists for Norwegians, Irish, Jews, and certainly the Blacks.

A sort of cultural amnesia characterized the new generation of persons of German antecedents who grew up between the first and second world wars. They were thoroughly Americanized; they spoke almost no German and knew little of German culture. Few participated in ethnic associational activities of any kind. Their ethnic heritage had almost no importance for their daily lives; rarely did it impinge upon ordinary personal decisions. Yet being of German descent still seemed to be a source of social deprivation for some. Based on few acts of discrimination, this perception betrayed persistent group memories of hostility and consequent feelings of insecurity.

Students of ethnic assimilation have pointed out that the third generation of an ethnic group tends to display a revived interest in its ancestral heritage. As one sociolinguist has described it, grandchildren often "embrace the intangible ideals and values attributable to the distant past of the respective ethnic group."[30] Virtual strangers to their heritage, they want to know more about it, but in an abstract and impersonal way. It is another irony of the history of Germans in America that the Nazi era coincided with the very time when they could have been expected to revive the study of their past and, incidentally, to regain the self-confidence lost during World War I.

The stormy appearance of Adolf Hitler on the world stage during the Thirties intensified the tendency of German-Americans to bury their ethnicity. Hitler and Naziism—strutting arrogance, maniacal speeches, chilling pageantry, racism of the most outrageous kind, flagrant offenses in international affairs—all evoked negative responses in most Americans. Hitler was in fact doing the kind of things Allied propagandists had accused the Kaiser of two decades earlier. It was no time to take pride in German heritage.

The rise of Naziism and a revitalized Germany had the opposite effect on a small part of the German-American population, chiefly persons who immigrated during the 1920s and who had not personally experienced the superpatriotic hysteria of World War I. A few, perhaps not more than one percent, were drawn to Fritz Kuhn's stridently pro-Nazi German-American Bund. Kuhn, who had immigrated in 1927, contended unsuccessfully with the leaders of the older, gentler, established German ethnic organizations—moderate men whose memories of 1918 remained vivid. Even though the latter were sympathetic to Germany, they were determined to remain within the American consensus. By 1938 Naziism had become an embarrassment and a disgrace to the overwhelming majority of Germans in America; by 1939 Kuhn was in a New York prison for having stolen Bund funds.[31]

After World War II, communism and the Soviet Union quickly replaced Nazi Germany as symbols of international evil. Americans learned to sympathize with West Germany as it regained political and economic stability during the 1950s and 1960s. Gradually the negative elements of the German stereotype eroded. At the same time, only the faintest traces of German ethnic life remained. The Germans as a group had disappeared, completely assimilated into mainstream America. Here and there a few belated efforts have been made, chiefly by academics, to revive the study of German culture in America. But few persons of German descent have been interested. Instead, German ethnicity has been exploited by entrepreneurs of all kinds—entertainers, restauranteurs, and specialists in trapping tourist dollars. While this phenomenon should not be mistaken for a genuine revival of interest, its importance lies in the way it demonstrates that it is respectable once again to be German in America, as it was before the madness of World War I.

Notes

1. James C. Juhnke, "John Schrag Espionage Case," *Mennonite Life,* 22 (July 1967): 121–22.
2. Gustavus Ohlinger, *The German Conspiracy in American Education* (New York: George H. Doran, 1919).
3. Wallace H. Moore, "The Conflict Concerning the German Language and German Propaganda in the Public Secondary Schools of the United States" (Ph.D. diss., Stanford University, 1937), p. 91.
4. Jack W. Rodgers, "The Foreign Language Issue in Nebraska, 1918–1923," *Nebraska History,* 39 (March 1958): 1–22.
5. Lloyd P. Jorgenson, "The Oregon School Law of 1922: Passage and Sequel," *Catholic Historical Review,* 54 (October 1968): 455–66.
6. James C. Juhnke, "The Political Acculturation of the Kansas Mennonites, 1870–1940" (Ph.D. diss., Indiana University, 1966), pp. 175–82; Grant M. Stolzfus, *Mennonites of the Ohio and Eastern Conference* (Scottdale, Pa.: Herald Press, 1969), pp. 184, 188.
7. Ibid.
8. David L. Scheidt, "Some Effects of World War I on the General Synod and General Council," *Concordia Historical Institute Quarterly,* 42 (May 1970): 83–92.
9. Alan N. Graebner, "The Acculturation of an Immigrant Lutheran Church: The Lutheran Church—Missouri Synod, 1917–1929" (Ph.D. diss., Columbia University, 1965), pp. 83–161.
10. Ibid.
11. U.S., Bureau of the Census, *Religious Bodies, 1916* and *1926* (1919 and 1929); Wilhelm Mueller, *Die Deutschamerikaner in*

der Krieg (Wiesbaden: Hofbuchhandlung Heinrich Staadt, 1921), pp. 38–39; Paul F. Douglas, *The Story of German Methodism* (New York and Cincinnati: Methodist Book Concern, 1939), pp. 191–92, 199, 213; Ray H. Abrams, *Preachers Present Arms* (New York: Round Table Press, 1933), p. 212; *Deutscher Kalender*, 1917 to 1920 (Cincinnati: Methodist Book Concern Press, 1916–1919).

12. Philip Gleason, *The Conservative Reformers: German-American Catholics and the Social Order* (Notre Dame: University of Notre Dame Press, 1968), pp. 172–203.

13. Ibid.

14. H. Wentworth Eldredge, "Enemy Aliens: New Haven Germans during the World War," in *Studies in the Science of Society*, ed. George P. Murdock (New Haven: Yale University Press, 1937), pp. 216–18; Austin App, "The Germans," in *The Immigrants' Influence on Wilson's Peace Policies*, ed. Joseph P. O'Grady (Lexington: University of Kentucky Press, 1967), pp. 47–48; John B. Duff, "German-Americans and the Peace, 1918–1920," *American Jewish Historical Quarterly*, 59 (June 1970): 433.

15. Phyllis Keller, "German-America and the First World War" (Ph.D. diss., University of Pennsylvania, 1969), p. 439; Guido A. Dobbert, "The Disintegration of an Immigrant Community: The Cincinnati Germans, 1870–1920" (Ph.D. diss., University of Chicago, 1965), p. 410; Dieter Cunz, *The Maryland Germans: A History* (Princeton: Princeton University Press, 1948), p. 403.

16. App, "The Germans," p. 37; Duff, "German-Americans and the Peace," pp. 424–34; Carl Wittke, *The German-language Press in America* (Lexington: University of Kentucky Press, 1957), pp. 275–76.

17. Ibid.

18. Heinz Kloss, *Um die Einigung des Deutschamerikanertums: Die Geschichte einer unvollendeten Volksgruppe* (Berlin: Volk und Reich Verlag, 1937), pp. 286–95; Duff, "German-Americans and the Peace," p. 433; Richard O'Connor, *The German-Americans* (Boston: Little, Brown, 1968), p. 431; Keller, "German-America," p. 440.

19. Kloss, *Um die Einigung*, p. 287.

20. Ibid., pp. 295–300.

21. "A Questionable Undertaking," *Centralblatt* (June 1924), quoted in Kloss, *Um die Einigung*, p. 299.

22. App, "The Germans," p. 42; Morton Tenzer, "The Jews," in *Immigrant's Influence*, p. 317.

23. *Viereck's American Monthly*, June 1919, quoted in Duff, "German-Americans and the Peace," p. 432.

24. Quoted in *Lutheran Witness,* 38 (18 March 1919): 86–87.
25. *Literary Digest,* 60 (18 September 1920); Viereck is quoted in Keller, "German-America," p. 365; Dobbert, "Cincinnati Germans." p. 426 n.
26. Woodrow Wilson, *The Public Papers of Woodrow Wilson,* ed. Ray Stannard Baker and William E. Dodd (New York: Harper & Brothers, 1925–1927): 6.
27. Duff, "German-Americans and the Peace," pp. 439–40; Wittke, *German-language Press,* pp. 277–78.
28. These data and those that follow are based on U.S., Bureau of the Census, *Fourteenth Census of the United States: 1920. Population* (1922), 3; U.S., Bureau of the Census, *Religious Bodies, 1916* (1919); Richard M. Scammon, *America at the Polls: A Handbook of American Presidential Statistics, 1920–1964* (Pittsburgh: University of Pittsburgh Press, 1965); and a variety of state blue books, legislative manuals, and local newspapers containing election data for wards and townships.
29. Richard Bartholdt, *From Steerage to Congress* (Philadelphia: Dorrance & Co., 1930), p. 400; Carl Chrislock, *The Progressive Era in Minnesota, 1899–1918* (Saint Paul: Minnesota Historical Society, 1971), pp. 184, 189, 190; Samuel Lubell, *The Future of American Politics,* 2d ed., rev. (Garden City, N.Y.: Doubleday, 1955), pp. 140–55.
30. Joshua Fishman, ed., *Language Loyalty in the United States* (The Hague: Mouton & Co., 1966), p. 350.
31. O'Connor, *German-Americans,* pp. 429–52.

A Bibliographical Note

An extraordinary wealth of materials exists upon which to base a history of the Germans in America. These sources, scattered in depositories of all kinds across the country, have only begun to be tapped by scholars, and few published studies treat the ordeal of the German-Americans in World War I. My interpretation of that unhappy time rests on a multitude of events, most of which were individually unimportant but were powerful in their cumulative impact. I have gathered them from a wide variety of sources —newspapers, magazines, tracts, congressional hearings, autobiographies, published papers, and in a few cases personal interviews and correspondence.

Of the major newspapers, none proved to be more valuable than the *New York Times,* but I have also depended on the *Washington Post, Saint Louis Post-Dispatch,* and *Chicago Tribune.* A variety of other newspapers in the English and German languages were consulted as the need demanded. The *Literary Digest* and to a lesser extent *Current Opinion* provided samples and summaries of journalistic opinion. Dozens of articles treating the problem of German-Americans in the era of World War I appeared in *Atlantic Monthly, Century, Dial, Everybody's Magazine, Forum, Nation, New Republic, North American Review, Outlook,* and *World's Work.*

Tracts of the times by Andre Cheradame, Newell Dwight Hillis, Gustavus Ohlinger, Earl Sperry, and others also proved to be useful. The National Security League publication edited by Albert Bushnell Hart, *America at War: A Handbook of Patriotic Education* (New York, 1918) contains a variety of materials relating to the problem. German-Americans produced materials of their own of varying points of view, such as Rudolf Cronau's *German Achievements in America* (New York, 1916); Frederick F. Schrader's *Handbook, Political, Statistical, and Sociological for German-Americans* (New York, 1916); Otto Kahn, *Right Above Race* (New York, 1918); and Hermann Hagedorn, *Where Do You Stand? An Appeal to Americans of German Origin* (New York, 1918).

Two congressional hearings constitute invaluable sources for organized German ethnic activities, especially during the neutrality period. These are U.S. Congress, Senate Committee on the Judiciary, 65th Congress, 2d Session, 1918, *Hearings on the National German-American Alliance* and *Hearings on the Brewing and Liquor Interests and German Propaganda* (2 vols.).

Autobiographies provide insights into individual values and attitudes. Among the most useful are Ernest L. Meyer, *"Hey, Yellowbacks!": The War Diary of a Conscientious Objector* (New York, 1930); Oscar Ameringer, *If You Don't Weaken* (New York, 1940); Theodore Laer [pseud.] *Forty Years of the Most Phenomenal Progress....* (New York, 1936); Richard Bartholdt, *From Steerage to Congress* (Philadelphia, 1930); and Louis P. Lochner, *Always the Unexpected* (New York, 1956). George Sylvester Viereck's personal account of his activity during the neutrality period, *Spreading Germs of Hate* (New York, 1930), must be used with care. Viereck's *Roosevelt: A Study in Ambivalence* (New York, 1920) contains some useful documents. *My Three Years in America* (New York, 1920), by Count Johann Bernstorff, is often illuminating.

The published papers of major political figures, such as Woodrow Wilson, Theodore Roosevelt, and Edward M.

House are another basic source. A valuable account of Dr. Karl Muck's troubles with the Boston Symphony Orchestra is contained in the *Life and Letters of Henry Lee Higginson* (Boston, 1921), edited by Bliss Perry.

I have drawn demographical data from several volumes on population produced by the U.S. Bureau of the Census. Much important census data is restructured in *Immigrants and Their Children, 1850–1950* (New York, 1956), by Edward P. Hutchinson. Statistics of churches have been taken from U.S. Bureau of the Census, *Religious Bodies, 1916* (2 vols., Washington, 1919) and its 1926 counterpart. Various synods and conferences published statistical reports of their own in yearbooks and calendars. Data of newspaper and periodical circulation have been drawn from *N. W. Ayer and Son's American Newspaper Annual and Directory* (Philadelphia, 1915–1920).

Election data on the county level are from Edgar E. Robinson, *The Presidential Vote: 1896–1932* (Stanford, 1947) and Richard M. Scammon, *America at the Polls: A Handbook of Presidential Statistics, 1920–1964* (Pittsburgh, 1965). Ward and precinct level data are taken from the variously titled manuals, registers, and blue books published for state legislatures, usually biennially. I have used volumes for Wisconsin, Iowa, Michigan, Minnesota, Missouri, Pennsylvania, and New Jersey. These have been supplemented by newspaper sources when necessary, as in Indiana and Nebraska.

Valuable nonstatistical data is available in *Compilation of War Laws of the Various States and Insular Possessions* (Washington, 1919), gathered by the Office of the Judge Advocate General. Judicial opinions are excerpted in *Espionage Act Cases with Certain Others on Related Points* (New York, 1918), edited by Walter Nelles. Several states issued reports of their councils of defense. Few, however, are sufficiently forthright or detailed to be of much value.

Although few general studies of the German-Americans during the World War I era exist, scores of books, articles, and dissertations treat limited aspects of the problem. The most valuable published study is Carl F. Wittke's *German-Americans and the World War* (Columbus, 1936). Rich in detail, it is based on German-language newspaper sources. Wittke's *German-language Press in America* (Lexington, 1957) is a useful supplement. The National German-American Alliance is the subject of Clifton J. Child's *The German-Americans in Politics, 1914–1917* (Madison, 1939). A recent study of great merit is Phyllis Keller's "German-America and the First World War" (Ph.D. dissertation, University of Pennsylvania, 1969), which concentrates on German ethnic intellectuals, notably Hugo Muensterberg, George Sylvester Viereck, and Hermann Hagedorn. Two briefer studies of high quality are monographs by Clifford L. Nelson, *German-American Political Behavior in Nebraska and Wisconsin, 1916–1920* (Lincoln, 1972) and John B. Duff, "German-Americans and the Peace, 1918–1920," *American Jewish Historical Quarterly*, 59 (January 1970): 424–44.

Secondary materials in the German language, such as Wilhelm Mueller, *Die Deutschamerikaner und der Krieg* (Wiesbaden, 1921), add little to what is available in English. Michael Singer, "Deutschamerikaner in den Kriegsjahren," *Jahrbuch der Deutschamerikaner für das Jahr 1918* (Chicago, 1917), pp. 159–204, is an impassioned contemporary analysis, a primary document in itself. Heinz Kloss, *Um die Einigung des Deutschamerikantums: Die Geschichte einer unvollendeten Volksgruppe* (Berlin, 1937) includes some material on the postwar period, though the chief emphasis is on the nineteenth century. Kloss was the first scholar to distinguish systematically the group differences between the *Kirchendeutschen* and the *Vereinsdeutschen* and their subdivisions.

General treatments of the Germans in America are inadequate for the World War I period. John A. Hawgood's *The Tragedy of German-America* (New York, 1940) emphasizes the mid-nineteenth century and offers an unconvincing interpretation that German slowness to assimilate was a response to nativism. Richard O'Connor's popular book, *The German-Americans: An Informal History* (Boston, 1968), is uneven in quality and superficial in its treatment of World War I.

German-American experiences during World War I are significant parts to two important Ph.D. dissertations: Guido A. Dobbert, "The Disintegration of an Immigrant Community: The Cincinnati Germans, 1820–1920" (University of Chicago, 1965) and Audrey L. Olson, "Saint Louis Germans, 1850–1920: The Nature of an Immigrant Community and Its Relation to the Assimilation Process" (University of Kansas, 1970). *The Maryland Germans* (Princeton, 1948), by Dieter Cunz and *The Virginia Germans* (Charlottesville, 1969), by Klaus Wust, contain material on World War I. Andrew J. Townsend, "The Germans of Chicago" (Ph.D. dissertation, University of Chicago, 1927) is informative but superficial. H. Wentworth Eldredge, "Enemy Aliens: New Haven Germans during the World War," in George Peter Murdock, ed., *Studies in the Science of Society* (New Haven, 1937), pp. 201–24, is brief but valuable. The Collinsville lynching has been treated by Donald R. Hickey, "The Prager Affair: A Study in Wartime Hysteria," *Journal of the Illinois State Historical Society,* 62 (Summer 1969): 117–34.

Among the best studies for the background of German stereotypes and perceptions are Mildred S. Wertheimer, *The Pan-German League, 1890–1914* (New York, 1924); Clara E. Schieber, *The Transformation of American Sentiment toward Germany, 1870–1914* (Boston, 1923); and Edward N. Saveth, *American Historians and European Immigrants, 1875–1925* (New York, 1948). Patrician attitudes are brilliantly assessed by Barbara Miller Solomon in *Ancestors and Immigrants: A Changing New England Tradition* (New York, 1956). The German influence on American universities is treated admirably in Walter P. Metzger's *Academic Freedom in the Age of the University* (New York, 1955). Guido A. Dobbert discounts the importance of ideology and stresses sociological variables in "German-Americans between the New and Old Fatherland, 1870–1914," *American Quarterly,* 19 (Winter 1967): 663–80.

Biographies constitute another genre of useful secondary sources. Rarely critical of their subjects, such works nevertheless offer insights into German ethnic experience. For examples, see Margaret Münsterberg, *Hugo Münsterberg: His Life and Work* (New York, 1922); Mary E. Spanheimer, *Heinrich Armin Rattermann* (Washington, 1937); Josephine Bente, *Biography of Dr. Friedrich Bente* (Saint Louis, 1936). By contrast, Niel M. Johnson's *George Sylvester Viereck* (Urbana, 1972) is a first-rate biographical study.

The Mennonite experience in World War I has received extensive and judicious study. An old but still useful work is J. S. Hartzler's *Mennonites in the World War: Nonresistance Under Test* (Scottsdale, 1922). C. Henry Smith, *The Coming of the Russian Mennonites* (Berne, Indiana, 1927) is a general treatment that includes some material on World War I. James C. Juhnke has produced an excellent Ph.D. dissertation, "The Political Acculturation of the Kansas Mennonites" (Indiana University, 1966). *Kansas Mennonites During World War I* (Hays, Kansas, 1968), by Arlyn J. Parish, is an M.A. thesis published in the Fort Hays State College Studies. Allen Teichroew's "World War I and the Mennonite Migration to Canada to Avoid the Draft," *Mennonite Quarterly Review,* 45 (July 1971): 219–49, is an exceptionally fine essay.

The Hutterites, often confused with their religious cousins, the Mennonites, are treated broadly in John A. Hostetler and Gertrude Enders Huntington, *The Hutterites in North America* (New York, 1967). Their experiences in World War I have been summarized by John Unruh in "The Hutterites During World War I," *Mennonite Life,* 24 (July 1969): 130–37. The *South Dakota Historical Collections* contain two useful studies: Gertrude S. Young, "The Mennonites in South Dakota," 10 (1920): 470–506 and Norman Thomas, "The Hutterian Brethren," 25 (1951): 265–99.

Of the several Lutheran groups, none has been studied more thoroughly than the Missouri Synod. The best analysis is to be found in Alan N. Graebner's "The Acculturation of an Immigrant Lutheran Church: The Lutheran Church

—Missouri Synod, 1917–1929" (Ph.D. dissertation, Columbia University, 1965). A spate of articles of varying quality have appeared in *Concordia Historical Institute Quarterly.* See especially Niel M. Johnson, "The Patriotism and Anti-Prussianism of the Lutheran Church—Missouri Synod, 1914–1918," 39 (October 1966): 99–118; David L. Scheidt, "Some Effects of World War I on the General Synod and General Council," 42 (May 1970): 83–92; and Frederick C. Luebke, "Superpatriotism in World War I: The Experience of a Lutheran Pastor," 41 (February 1968): 3–11.

Other German-American Protestant churches have received very little scholarly attention. The best of the denominational histories containing material on World War I is *The Story of German Methodism* (New York, 1939), by Paul F. Douglas.

German-American Catholicism has been treated most perceptively by Philip Gleason in *The Conservative Reformers: German-American Catholics and the Social Order* (Notre Dame, 1968). *Catholic Historical Review* has published two fine studies relating to World War I: Dean R. Esslinger, "American German and Irish Attitudes toward Neutrality, 1914–1917," 53 (July 1967): 194–216 and Edward Cuddy, "Pro-Germanism and American Catholicism, 1914–1917," 54 (October 1968): 427–54. Colman Barry's *The Catholic Church and German Americans* (Milwaukee, 1953) is useful for understanding the ethnoreligious background.

Most historical literature on the German Jews is embedded in studies treating Jews generally. Guido A. Dobbert has recounted "The Ordeal of Gotthard Deutsch," in *American Jewish Archives,* 20 (November 1968): 129–55. See also Morton Tenzer's essay on "The Jews," in *The Immigrants' Influence on Wilson's Peace Policies* (Lexington, 1967), edited by Joseph P. O'Grady. Much valuable background information may be found in Oscar Handlin's *Adventure in Freedom* (New York, 1954); Moses Rischin's *The Promised City: New York's Jews, 1870–1914* (Cambridge, 1962); and Lawrence H. Fuchs's *The Political Behavior of American Jews* (Glencoe, 1956).

Although historians have long recognized the importance of the German ethnic dimension of socialism in America, none have analyzed the movement from an ethnic point of view. I have found James Weinstein, *The Decline of Socialism in America, 1912–1925* (New York, 1967) to be especially helpful.

The context of American social and political history is treated admirably by Frederic Logan Paxson in his three-volume study, *American Democracy and the World War* (1936–1948). Arthur S. Link provides invaluable details of the national administration in his massive biography of *Wilson* (Princeton, 1947–1965). Volumes III to V treat the neutrality period and carry the story to the American declaration of war. Ernest R. May, *The World War and American Isolation, 1914–1917* (Cambridge, 1959) is a broad treatment of foreign policy formation during the neutrality period. John Milton Cooper, Jr., *The Vanity of Power: American Isolationism and the First World War, 1914–1917* (Westport, 1969) concentrates on congressional opposition to war. Seward W. Livermore, *Woodrow Wilson and the War Congress, 1916–1918* (Seattle, 1968) treats national politics during the war.

Popular perceptions of the war issues during the neutrality period have been examined in several state studies. The best of these are Cedric C. Cummins's *Indiana Public Opinion and World War, 1914–1917* (Indianapolis, 1945) and John C. Crighton's *Missouri and the World War, 1914–1917* (Columbia, 1947). David W. Hirst has produced a balanced and judicious study of "German Propaganda in the United States, 1914–1917" (Ph.D. dissertation, Northwestern University, 1962). James M. Read, *Atrocity Propaganda, 1914–1917* (New Haven, 1941) and Horace C. Peterson, *Propaganda for War: The Campaign against American Neutrality* (Norman, 1939) are both useful though they are influenced by attitudes of the pre-World War II period. Felice A. Bonadio, "The Failure of German Propaganda in the United States," *Mid-America,* 41 (January 1959): 40–57, relies heavily on George Sylvester Viereck's propaganda sheet, the *Fatherland.* The war period itself is treated by Karen Falk in "Public Opinion in Wisconsin during World War I," *Wisconsin Magazine of History,* 25 (June 1942): 389–407 and by Joel A. Watne, "Public Opinion Toward Non-Conformists and Aliens during 1917," *North Dakota History,* 34 (1967): 5–29.

The most useful general study of dissent during World War I is by Horace C. Peterson and Gilbert C. Fite, *Opponents of War, 1917–1918* (Madison, 2957). The broader context of nativism is treated in John Higham's splendid book, *Strangers in the Land: Patterns of American Nativism, 1860–1925* (New York, 1965). Robert K. Murray effectively analyzes the hysteria of the postwar period in *Red Scare* (Minneapolis, 1955).

Several agencies of superpatriotism have been studied carefully. The Committee on Public Information is examined in *Words that Won the War* (Princeton, 1939), by James R. Mock and Cedric Larson. Joan Jensen is sharply critical of the American Protective League in her detailed study, *The Price of Vigilance* (Chicago, 1968). George T. Blakey analyzes academic propagandists in *Historians on the Homefront* (Lexington, 1970). Ray H. Abrams's *Preachers Present Arms* (rev. ed., Scottsdale, 1969) is an angry book filled with anecdotes of clerical intolerance. Coercive Americanization programs are included in Gerd Korman's *Industrialization, Immigrants, and Americanizers: The View from Milwaukee, 1866–1921* (Madison, 1967). Robert D. Ward has probed "The Origin and Activities of the National Security League, 1914–1919" in *Mississippi Valley Historical Review,* 47 (June 1960): 51–65. Few state councils of defense have been scrutinized, but see Robert N. Manley, "The Nebraska State Council of Defense: Loyalty Programs and Policies During World War I" (M.A. thesis, University of Nebraska, 1959) and Lorin Lee Cary, "Wisconsin Patriots Combat Disloyalty: The Wisconsin Loyalty Legion and Politics, 1917–1918" (M.A. thesis, University of Wisconsin, 1965). The fullest treatment of the language controversy is by Wallace H. Moore, "The Conflict Concerning the German Language and German Propaganda in the Public Secondary Schools of the United States" (Ph.D. dissertation, Stanford University, 1937).

In addition to the Nelson study noted above, the most useful examinations of German ethnic voting behavior are to be found in Meyer J. Nathan's "The Presidential Election of 1916 in the Middle West" (Ph.D. dissertation, Princeton University, 1966); Seth S. McKay, *Texas Politics, 1906–1944, with Special Reference to the German Counties* (Lubbock, 1952); and an early effort at social analysis by John T. Schou, "The Decline of the Democratic Party in Iowa, 1916–1920" (M.A. thesis, University of Iowa, 1960). Thomas J. Kerr, "German-Americans and Neutrality in the 1916 Election," *Mid-America,* 43 (April 1961): 95–105 examines the impact of German propaganda. Carl Chrislock has studied the context of ethnopolitical clash in his excellent book, *The Progressive Era in Minnesota, 1899–1918* (Saint Paul, 1971). David Burner's analysis of the Democratic party during the Twenties, *The Politics of Provincialism* (New York, 1968), begins in the war period and offers useful data. See also Burner's "Breakup of the Wilson Coalition of 1916," *Mid-America,* 45 (January 1963): 18–35 and R. A. Burchell's "Did Irish and German Voters Desert the Democrats in 1920?" *Journal of American Studies,* 6 (August 1972): 153–64. Herbert F. Margulies, "The Election of 1920 in Wisconsin," *Wisconsin Magazine of History,* 41 (Autumn 1957): 15–22, is brief but perceptive. Louis L. Gerson, *The Hyphenate in Recent American Politics and Diplomacy* (Lawrence, 1964) is reluctant to grant the legitimacy of ethnic politics.

Several states produced accounts of their participation in the effort to win World War I. Nathaniel R. Whitney's *Sale of War Bonds in Iowa* (Iowa City, 1923) and *Minnesota in the War with Germany* (2 vols., Saint Paul, 1928–1932), by Franklin F. Holbrook and Livia Appel, are especially useful.

Few books on World War I treat adequately the conflict it generated between liberty and loyalty. Harry N. Scheiber,

The Wilson Administration and Civil Liberties, 1917–1921 (Ithaca, 1960) is highly critical of Wilson. William Preston, *Aliens and Dissenters* (New York, 1963), places the wartime suppression of radicalism in a larger context. Zechariah Chafee, *Free Speech in the United States* (Cambridge, 1954) is helpful on wartime and postwar prosecutions. Donald Johnson, *The Challenge to American Freedoms* (Lexington, 1963) treats the origin of the American Civil Liberties Union. Paul L. Murphy's penetrating article, "Source and Nature of Intolerance in the 1920's," *Journal of American History,* 51 (June 1964): 60–76, is an important contribution. The problem of democratic patriotism in crisis is treated with wisdom and warmth in *The Loyal and the Disloyal* (Chicago, 1956), by Morton Grodzins.

Index